Discovering
MEDIA
LITERACY

Discovering MEDIA LITERACY

Teaching Digital Media and Popular Culture in Elementary School

RENEE HOBBS
DAVID COOPER MOORE

CORWIN
A SAGE Company

CORWIN
A SAGE Company

FOR INFORMATION:

Corwin
A SAGE Company
2455 Teller Road
Thousand Oaks, California 91320
(800) 233–9936
www.corwin.com

SAGE Publications Ltd.
1 Oliver's Yard
55 City Road
London EC1Y 1SP
United Kingdom

SAGE Publications India Pvt. Ltd.
B 1/I 1 Mohan Cooperative Industrial Area
Mathura Road, New Delhi 110 044
India

SAGE Publications Asia-Pacific Pte. Ltd.
3 Church Street
#10–04 Samsung Hub
Singapore 049483

Acquisitions Editor: Carol Chambers Collins
Associate Editor: Julie Nemer
Editorial Assistant: Francesca Dutra Africano
Production Editor: Melanie Birdsall
Copy Editor: Sarah J. Duffy
Typesetter: Hurix Systems Private Ltd.
Proofreader: Caryne Brown
Indexer: Wendy Allex
Cover Designer: Gail Buschman

Analyze image: Copyright Betsy Streeter, used by permission, www.betsystreeter.com.

Reflection image: All rights reserved by Stefano Libertini Protopapa.

Taking Action image: Some rights reserved by Hamed Saber.

Printed in the United States of America

Library of Congress Cataloging-in-Publication Data

Hobbs, Renee. Discovering media literacy : teaching digital media and popular culture in elementary school / Renee Hobbs, David Cooper Moore.

pages cm
Includes index.

ISBN 978-1-4522-0563-2

1. Media literacy—Study and teaching (Elementary)
2. Digital media—Study and teaching (Elementary)
3. Popular culture—Study and teaching (Elementary)
I. Moore, David Cooper. II. Title.

P96.M4H63 2013

371.33'4—dc23

2013011069

This book is printed on acid-free paper.

13 14 15 16 17 10 9 8 7 6 5 4 3 2 1

Contents

Preface

We created this book to share our learning experiences with elementary students and their teachers in a project called Powerful Voices for Kids. You might be wondering: What does it mean, actually, for someone to have a powerful voice? Is this a book about public speaking? How might the world be better off if children—and by extension, all people—were able to use language and other symbol systems to express themselves effectively to address family, peers, neighbors, and members of the global society?

Actually, this book *will* help you craft activities to enable students to become better public speakers. But more important, it is a book about literacy in the broadest and most inclusive sense of the term: literacy as the sharing of meaning through symbols. Today people use a wide variety of symbols to communicate, including images, language, sound, and multimedia. So the phrase "powerful voices for children" is a metaphor for inspiring children and young people to use these symbols effectively to become engaged and active learners, listeners, leaders, and citizens.

Learning to share meaning is the art of being human. Growing up in a culture rich with symbols, children and young people face enormous challenges in sorting through the many complex messages that they receive each day. Children have so many choices available to them—books, TV, video games, music, movies, the Internet, and social media. In everyday life, with our friends and family, we all struggle sometimes with expressing ourselves appropriately. Being a responsible communicator means coming to terms with our relationships with others and with the role of popular culture, digital technologies, and mass media in our lives.

You may be a classroom teacher, a principal, a parent, a school library media specialist, a concerned professional, a researcher, an independent media artist, or a student. You may be interested in making a difference in urban education, as we are. You may value creative projects that bring children together with civic leaders, artists, writers, media makers, and community activists. If you're like us, you're attracted to collaborations that connect people with different types of skills across different types of institutions.

You may simply love children and want to support their development by providing immersive, hands-on experiences that help them build critical thinking skills that connect the classroom with contemporary culture. You may be curious about how to use children's interest in digital technologies, mass media, and popular culture to support learning through creative and collaborative play in either formal contexts (like K–6 schools) or informal settings (like summer camps or afterschool programs). You may have broader questions about the consequences of linking the worlds of mass media and popular culture with the practice of learning and teaching.

We don't have all the answers, of course. But in this book, we'll share our process of discovery, revealing what we have learned from working with young children and their teachers. We have helped hundreds of elementary educators "teach the media" to their students. Read on to learn a variety of practical strategies for strengthening children's abilities to think for themselves, communicate effectively using language and technology tools, and use their powerful voices to contribute to the quality of life in their families, their schools, their communities, and the world.

Acknowledgments

This book relies on knowledge and ideas that come from so many people whom we have learned from during the trajectory of the Powerful Voices for Kids project. We want to acknowledge the talents and contributions of Laurada Byers, Anna Hadgis, Akosowa Watts, Salome El-Thomas, Drew Smith, and John Landis, who are all associated with the Russell Byers Charter School. We are also grateful for the creative energies of the many educators, artists, and media professionals who participated in the program. They have been influential in shaping our thinking about the work we present in this book.

PUBLISHER'S ACKNOWLEDGMENTS

Corwin gratefully acknowledges the contributions of the following reviewers:

Troy Hicks
Associate Professor of English
Central Michigan University
Mt. Pleasant, MI

Kristin Ziemke Fastabend
First-Grade Teacher
Chicago Public Schools
Chicago, IL

About the Authors

Renee Hobbs is one of the nation's leading authorities on digital and media literacy education. She spearheaded the development of an online journal and national organization to support the work of media literacy educators and scholars. At the Media Education Lab (www.mediaeducationlab.com), she creates videos, websites, digital games, and multimedia curriculum materials for K–12 educators. She offers professional development programs to educators in school districts across the United States and around the world, and her research has been published in more than 50 scholarly and professional books and journals. She is the founding director of the Harrington School of Communication and Media at the University of Rhode Island. Renee enjoys sharing ideas and learning via Twitter—you can follow her online @reneehobbs.

David Cooper Moore is the program director for Powerful Voices for Kids. He teaches courses in media production at Temple University's School of Media and Communication and has also developed media literacy projects and productions with PBS Teachers, the Center for Social Media, Drug Free PA, and the Girl Scouts of America on topics including digital citizenship and civic responsibility, public health, and fair use in K–12 education. David worked with Media Education Lab on videos and curricula for the PBS Elections 2008 curriculum, Access, Analyze, Act: A Blueprint for 21st Century Civic Engagement. He blogs on education, media, and technology issues at DavidCooperMoore.com. and is on Twitter @dcoopermoore.

Introduction

We wrote this book because we have discovered that children of all ages can learn vital competencies when it comes to literacy, media, and technology. By sharing our experiences, we hope you'll be inspired to bring these ideas to the children and teachers in your community.

HOW WE CREATED THIS BOOK

This book is part of the Powerful Voices for Kids initiative developed by Renee Hobbs and Laurada Byers, who collaborated in a university-school partnership involving the Russell Byers Charter School in Philadelphia and Temple University's Media Education Lab. Co-author David Cooper Moore began as a teacher in the program, then took on increasingly significant roles as a program manager, teacher educator, curriculum developer, and researcher. The program developed with support from grants from the Wyncote Foundation, the Otto and Phoebe Haas Charitable Trusts, and the Verizon Foundation. We're especially grateful for support from David Haas, whose generous support made this project possible. A partnership with the National Writing Project (NWP) helped us expand the reach of the program regionally and nationally, and we learned along with NWP teachers and leaders, including Elyse Eidman-Aadahl, Paul Oh, Sam Reed III, Troy Hicks, Danielle Nicole DeVoss, and Christina Cantrill.

Components of the program included the following:

1. *Summer Learning Program.* Children ages 5–13 participated in a monthlong summer program that combined play and learning about media, popular culture, and digital technologies. More than 150 children participated in the program in the summers of 2009 and 2010. They learned about the different purposes of media messages—to inform, to entertain, and to persuade. They critically analyzed a wide variety of media genres, including news, advertising, drama, music video, documentary, reality TV, and online media. Children used Flip brand video cameras (which we

refer to in the book as FlipCams) to create hundreds of videos and used simple wiki software to create web pages. Children increased their confidence in using digital technology as tools for learning, and felt increased comfort in expressing their ideas and working in a team.

2. *Staff Development.* Over a period of 5 years, we offered a variety of professional development programs to teachers. More than 150 school leaders, elementary educators, school library specialists, technology educators, artists, community activists, media professionals, and parents participated in a wide range of programs through which they learned how to use digital media, mass media, and popular culture to build connections between the classroom and the child's daily life as a media user.

3. *In-School Mentoring.* In pioneering an approach to staff development that we call *elbow-to-elbow* support, we engaged someone with expertise in media literacy and technology integration to work directly in the classroom with a teacher or a small group of faculty to support a particular unit of instruction or media production project.

4. *Parent Outreach.* When parents have the opportunity to learn from other parents, they deepen their sensitivity to the explicit and implicit choices that occur each and every day when it comes to music, TV shows, news and current events, movies, video games, the Internet, and social media. In these workshops and discussion groups, families explored the uses of media and technology in the home.

5. *Multimedia Curriculum Development.* In collaboration with classroom educators and summer learning instructors, we created a variety of lesson plans that activate numerous learning outcomes. These lessons are effective with a variety of young learners in both "low-tech" and "high-tech" classrooms. You will find these lessons at the end of each chapter and on our website at www.powerfulvoicesforkids.com.

6. *Research and Assessment.* Using observation, data collection, and interviews to understand children's media and technology uses in the home and at school, we explored teachers' motivations for digital and media literacy and examined how children's conceptions of author, audience, and purpose shape their reading comprehension and academic achievement.

In this book, we share stories from all of these experiences. We identify what we learned from helping instructors and classroom teachers discover how to develop children's critical thinking, creativity, collaboration, and communication skills in response to the complex messages offered to them through news and current events, advertising, popular music and music videos, celebrity culture, movies and TV shows, video games, the Internet, and social media. But first, you should learn more about us, the authors.

Here's a brief description of our stories, our backgrounds, and how we came to collaborate to write this book.

RENEE'S STORY: WHY I CREATE EDUCATIONAL PROGRAMS IN DIGITAL AND MEDIA LITERACY

I learn best by doing and making things. My research lab, called the Media Education Lab, helps fulfill my interest in improving the quality of digital and media literacy education through research and community service. Most of my work has focused on children and teachers in Grades 7–12. But back in the 1990s, I worked with the Norrback Elementary School in Worcester, Massachusetts, to explore what media literacy might look like in urban elementary education. Then the Discovery Channel and the Maryland State Department of Education invited me to create *Assignment: Media Literacy*, a comprehensive K–12 curriculum for media literacy. In 2006, thanks to support from the U.S. Office on Women's Health, I got to create MyPopStudio (www.mypopstudio.com), a creative online play environment to introduce media literacy concepts to girls ages 9–13. And in 2007, the Powerful Voices for Kids program enabled me to craft a long-term university-school partnership, one that could truly be a "win-win" for researchers, teachers, and students.

Looking back, much of my career can be viewed as developing a series of informal experiments: I like to create new programs and projects as a form of learning. The process of initiating, implementing, and assessing media education programs in K–12 schools helps develop new knowledge to advance the field. With this particular project, I was looking for opportunities to work with younger children and involve graduate students in the process of teacher education and curriculum development.

There's no substitute for hands-on experience as a way to generate new ideas for writing and research. While living in Philadelphia, I was deeply aware of the real need to provide direct service to poor and minority children. So when I met Laurada Byers, the inspiring leader who created the Russell Byers Charter School, we decided that a summer learning program for young children might be perfect as the cornerstone for launching the Powerful Voices for Kids program. During the spring of 2009, we reached out to parents to encourage them to enroll their children in the program. We emphasized the hands-on nature of the program with a list of activities, including making movies, producing music, creating video games, and going on field trips. We emphasized academic skills, including language arts, writing composition, research and technology skills, public speaking and citizenship, collaboration and teamwork, and health and nutrition.

All the members of the Powerful Voices for Kids program were invited to keep an online journal of reflective writing about the learning experience. In the first week of the program in the summer of 2009, I wrote:

> I think that each team member is a gem—what a great group we have! However, I am worried about both the scope and the quality of the work—will there be the right balance of analysis and composition? Will we meet the requirements of the funder, who thinks we're exploring the topic of advertising and persuasion? Are my expectations too high? Is this too much to ask from this group of young people, most of whom have never had any formal exposure to media literacy education as a subject of study? What about the first week, when I am juggling 25 elementary teachers in a professional development program—I will really need to be able to depend on my team to manage the mentoring process. Will it be controlled chaos or just chaos?

As you can see from my reflections on the process at the very beginning of the journey, I was struggling with some real challenges. The management practices to keep the whole enterprise running were substantial. It took many meetings to develop a shared understanding of what might be possible. I needed to spend time in the Russell Byers Charter School, meeting with the assistant principal, observing children and their teachers, and sitting in on staff meetings. My school partners needed to better understand our capacities and our limitations as faculty and students at a university; they also needed to appreciate and respect the core concepts and instructional values that underpin digital and media literacy education. My graduate students needed to understand that *learning-in-action* calls for demanding levels of creativity and intense focus combined with a robust spirit of self-reflection, courage, and openness to inquiry.

For years, communication scholars and education theorists of all stripes have called for innovative educational programs to support children's "critical viewing" or media analysis or Internet evaluation skills, urging teachers to offer creative media production opportunities for children to write a school newspaper, create videos, and build web pages. It sounds pretty easy. But education scholars have long recognized that one of the primary reasons for the failure of school reform initiatives is the unwillingness of the partners to commit to collaboration over an extended period of time.[1] One scholar notes, "It takes so long just to develop trusting relationships based on respect that to think improvements in school or useful research can be produced quickly is at best naive."[2]

My experience working in long-term relationships with school districts in Massachusetts had taught me that such programs didn't magically happen overnight. It takes time for teachers to develop the knowledge and skills they need to open up meaningful conversations about mass media and popular culture, to learn how to organize a simple media production project from start to finish, and to navigate the complicated terrain involved in building connections between media culture and school culture.

First, could we establish long-term relationships with the school by engaging an ever-changing cadre of graduate students to "get their feet wet" through experiential learning as teachers and researchers? Second, would this process also simultaneously support the creation of new knowledge in the field? Finally, could the fruits of our labor result in the development of the social, intellectual, and emotional needs of young children? Juggling these three priorities seemed a near-impossible task. That's why it was just the right project for me.

DAVID'S STORY: FROM TECHIE TO TEACHER

I came to media literacy as a self-professed film geek and professional filmmaker. I was often enamored of gear—lenses, high-definition cameras, and trucks full of tripods, Steadicams, sandbags, dollies, gobos, and snoots. (I was a sucker for the ones with silly names.) But it was not until I worked with younger children that I began to realize and clarify my own interest in media production and analysis as a broader component of more fundamental literacy skills. I knew—or thought I knew—that children brought a wealth of unique knowledge and insight to subjects that adults often take for granted. I also knew that their media worlds were even more complex than my own at the dawn of the digital age.

I had my "aha" moment about why digital and media literacy mattered in elementary classrooms in the summer of 2009. As a new instructor in the Powerful Voices for Kids program, I was thrilled to work with Renee, with new peers who went on to find roles of their own in PK–6 education, and with an amazing co-teacher, Angela Carter. We worked with sixth-grade students for 4 hours a day, 5 days a week for a whole month, and it was one of the most memorable teaching and learning experiences I've ever had. I noted in my teaching journal—a sprawling document that was part observational and part confessional—what "clicked" on Week 1, Day 3:

> Worked on our websites. Angela had half of the students in the computer lab to work on research, and I had half the kids in

the room to work on web design on the website Glogster. The researchers were far more productive, learning a lot about online sources and how to use multiple strands of information to make a single argument. I would call this a more explicitly media literacy lesson—we were asking students to synthesize print, visual, and audio information into an argument that they would express first in print (on oversized note paper) and then visually on their websites. They had to understand complex messages and then turn them into their own unique message to communicate to the rest of the world online.

In Chapter 4, you will see that "going online on paper" by making "paper websites" with younger students is, in fact, a great strategy for helping students focus on the learning process as they explore design and aesthetics.

How could I continue to help good teachers figure out how to connect elementary students' media worlds, as messy and complicated as any classroom, to meaningful learning experiences? It was only later, as the program director of Powerful Voices for Kids, that I also learned how crucial the respect of teachers is to changing the way kids learn. I am not a classroom teacher, although I know that it is classroom teachers, not technologies, school design, or funding alone, that will change learning in the most profound ways. I'm glad to see that some research has started to bear this observation out by suggesting that feedback, high expectations, mentorship, and more time for instruction—all of which involve the effort and skill of educators—are indispensable characteristics of effective classrooms.[3]

Having too often blamed institutions, social contexts, and parents for the "state of education" myself as an armchair education pundit, I discovered in working directly with younger students and, just as important, working beside classroom teachers how messy, complicated, and powerful classrooms really are. I only hope that by sharing some of our experiences with Powerful Voices for Kids, we can help others continue to learn and relearn what it means to be a powerful *teacher*.

HOW THIS BOOK IS ORGANIZED

This book is divided into four parts:

In Part I, we offer an introduction to the context and background of our work and share what we have learned about the many different kinds of teachers who have participated in the Powerful Voices for Kids initiative.

We learned that teachers' approach to digital and media literacy depends on their existing attitudes and beliefs about media, popular culture, technology, and their big-picture goals of teaching and learning. You'll get a chance to reflect on your own values and priorities as a teacher and consider how these values shape the choices you make in bringing digital and media literacy to young learners.

In Part II, we share our experiences working with children ages 9–11 by offering stories about how teachers and students explored a variety of topics. We learn about the ways that young children can become powerful communicators by using their creativity and collaboration skills to address real issues in an urban community—homelessness and littering. Teachers show us how they helped students experience the power of authorship by using a range of technology tools, from simple to more complex, that included PowerPoint, screencasting, and video production with young children. We also examine the impact of students asking questions about celebrity culture and social media, finding that teachers' ability to manage the unpredictability of classroom conversation is a key factor in creating a robust learning environment. Finally, we look at the development of children's critical thinking skills about popular culture and advertising and learn about what we observed in the development of children's active reasoning skills in responding to popular media like television, music, and video games.

In Part III, we share our experiences working with the youngest children in the primary grades. We take a close look at teachers who are working to develop children's understanding of language and other symbol systems, like photographs, animation, and drama. We explore the primary theory behind our work: learning about concepts like author, audience, and purpose in conjunction with familiar texts like TV shows and advertising supports children's comprehension skills and academic achievement by increasing motivation and engagement, and activating critical thinking skills that transfer from one symbolic form to another.

In Part IV, we reflect on the staff development models we used and outline the learning that resulted from field-testing. Powerful Voices for Kids program strategies aimed at developing and implementing a comprehensive approach to digital and media literacy education for K–6 teachers. You'll learn more about the variety of programs we offered: one-on-one tutorials, weeklong summer institutes, and intensive programs where small groups of teachers in a single school gathered monthly over the course of an entire school year. At the back of the book, in Resource A, you'll find a list of learning targets for each of the five competencies—Access, Analysis, Composition, Reflection, and Taking Action—framed up specifically to align with the developmental needs of primary and elementary children. In Resource B you will find a glossary with digital and media literacy vocabulary words for children ages 5–12. And for teacher educators and scholars, in Resource C we've listed many of the concepts and ideas that are unique to this book as we advance theoretical ideas through describing and reflecting upon our practice.

On our website (www.powerfulvoicesforkids.com), we are creating an online community with educators who are teaching and learning media literacy. You'll find a wide variety of video excerpts that document the instructional practices described in the book. We also offer additional lesson plans and resource materials, and showcase samples of student creative work. On the website, educators share their own ideas about how to bring digital and media literacy to young learners.

If you're a teacher in a formal or informal learning environment, after reading this book and viewing our website, you'll be able to experiment with some of the lesson plans at the end of each chapter and explore these activities with your own students. If you're a teacher educator or curriculum specialist, this book and companion website give you the tools you need to lead a staff development program to share ideas from the Powerful Voices for Kids program with your colleagues. If you're a researcher, activist, artist, media professional, or student, you can use what you learn in this book and on the website to implement a Powerful Voices for Kids program in your community.

Our fundamental challenge in writing this book was the sharing of the complex results of an inquiry that we still only partially understand ourselves, a process we have called *messy engagement*. Indeed, we are rather limited by our perspective, as stakeholders and change agents in initiating the Powerful Voices for Kids program. Like other scholars and practitioners with interests in media education for young learners, including people like Anne Haas Dyson, Lisa Guernsey, Faith Rogow, Cyndy Scheibe, Rebecca Hains, Jeff Share, Amy Jussell, Petra Hesse, Janis Kupersmidt, Erica Scharrer, Jordi Torrent, Rhys Daunic, Jesse Gainer, Donna Alvermann, Margaret Hagood, Glynda Hull, Wendy Ewald, Damiano Felini, Carol Craggs, Cary Bazalgette, and many others, we have been learning through engaging in practical work with elementary learners. For this reason, we may not see the value of our ideas as clearly as our readers do. With your critical thinking and active reading strategies, you will examine the importance of this work—and its many limitations— adding your insight on what we've tried to accomplish here. For you, we are grateful.

NOTES

1. Sarason, S. (1971). *The culture of school and the problem of change.* Boston, MA: Allyn & Bacon.
2. Noguera, P. (1998). Toward the development of school and university partnerships based upon mutual benefit and respect. *In Motion Magazine.* Retrieved from http://www.inmotionmagazine.com/pnsup1.html
3. Dobbie, W., & Fryer, R. G. (2011). *Getting beneath the veil of effective schools: Evidence from New York City* (National Bureau of Economic Research Working Paper No. 17632). Retrieved from http://nber.org/papers/w17632

Part I

Why Digital and Media Literacy Matters

1 Digital and Media Literacy

In this chapter, you'll learn about

Digital and Media Literacy

- What is digital and media literacy?
- Why should we expand the concept of literacy to acknowledge the worlds of print, visual, audio, and interactive media in the elementary grades?

Technology Integration

- Why does technology integration support learning?
- How may it distract from meaningful learning practices in the classroom?

Bridging Classroom and Culture

- How can teachers use digital and media literacy to engage students' interests and passions, and develop knowledge, competencies, and skills?

It was lunchtime, and Ms. Dominguez's second-grade students had just finished eating. A few minutes remained for table talk before recess. Three girls had opened up their black-and-white composition notebooks and were pretending to use a laptop, tapping their fingers on the pages.

One little girl, Natalia, had propped up her composition notebook against her milk carton so that the top half of the page displayed a "screen" of sorts. Here, she had written the word "Facebook" and had sketched a close-up picture of herself. On the lower page of the notebook, she had drawn a keyboard, complete with small square boxes to represent keys, including the alphabet, space bar, return, shift, and enter keys.

Giving each other knowing glances around the lunch table, Natalia and the other girls were "typing" on their composition notebooks, pretending to be working on their laptops. As Ms. Dominguez surveyed her classroom, she took note of this activity, smiling to herself because, unbeknownst to the children, she also had briefly checked her own Facebook page using her cell phone at the teacher's desk while eating her lunch that day.

GROWING UP WITH MEDIA AND TECHNOLOGY

All of us, children and adults alike, are growing up with more access to media and technology than at any point in human history. Well before they enter kindergarten, young children spend many hours with screen media. About half of all babies and toddlers under the age of two watch 2 hours of television per day. In 2011, a national survey showed that nearly one in three babies and toddlers has a TV in his or her bedroom, up from 19% just 6 years earlier.[1]

Although TV viewing is the most frequent screen activity of childhood, one fourth of young children's screen time now includes the use of computers, handheld and console video game players, and other interactive mobile devices such as cell phones, iPods, and iPad-style tablet devices.[2] Natalia, her mom, and her sister Sara like playing Angry Birds on the family cell phone or checking out what their other family members are posting on Facebook and Twitter.

More than half of all 5- to 8-year-olds have used an app (an application) on a mobile device of some sort, researchers tell us. And for Natalia, as with many young children, video game and computer use is a part of daily life, with one in five using a video game or a computer every day. Most children who use video games or computers begin when they are just 3½ years old.[3]

In her home in West Philadelphia, Natalia is among the 75% of children under the age of 8 who don't often watch educational television programs like *Sesame Street* or *Between the Lions* on PBS. Instead, she enjoys the Toonzai block on Channel 57, the CW network in Philadelphia, which airs imported Japanese anime shows like *Yu-Gi-Oh!* and *Dragon Ball Z Kai*. Natalia's family is among the 50% of low-income families who do not have access to cable or satellite television programming. In her house, the TV is on most of the time, even when no one is watching.

Because Natalia's mom works a lot, she doesn't get much opportunity for what is sometimes called *co-viewing* or *joint media engagement*, where parents or caregivers help support the use of TV shows, movies, video games, or the Internet explicitly as a tool for children's learning.[4] Natalia and her mom, Joyce, do watch "regular" television together, including *Good Morning America, Entertainment Tonight*, and *American Idol*, but generally this time together is a place of relaxation and escape. Neither Natalia nor her mom perceive it as a time for learning.

We still know relatively little about how digital technology and entertainment media make a positive contribution to children's understanding of the political and social world.[5] By watching TV and movies, Natalia has learned much about the world around her: She's familiar with different types of family structures, recognizes the president, and knows about the types of jobs done by people in hospitals and in law enforcement. The many stories Natalia watches also shape her understanding of social relationships, including both *prosocial* behaviors like kindness, generosity, and helping others and *antisocial* behaviors like aggression, lying, and being mean to others.

Today, Natalia's mom and her teachers aren't thinking much about children's TV time; they're far more concerned about children's use of the Internet and social media. Right now, we're in a paradigm shift where all of us—young and old—are learning to adapt to rapid changes in media and communication technology.

When teachers like Ms. Dominguez notice the ways in which social media, popular culture, and digital media enter the lives of their students, they may have a sense of both the promise and the possibility but also the profound ways that these things may complicate classroom life. How could Ms. Dominguez use her own knowledge of social networks—and her students' developing knowledge of how computers, laptops, and mobile devices work—in a way that somehow connects a rich digital media culture to the everyday business of teaching her students how to better understand and communicate in the world around them?

LEARNING, LITERACY, AND LIFE

Education supports the development of the whole human being: the head, the heart, and the spirit. As children grow and develop, they transform basic sensory experiences into thoughts, feelings, and ideas, gradually moving from simple reactions toward more complex and nuanced responses, translating experience into "a model of the world" through actions, images, and, finally, symbolic representation.[6] Through active engagement with the process of meaning-making, children develop their identities as literate, social, emotional, and moral individuals.

What does it mean to be literate? For most of human history, to be literate meant to be effective as a speaker and a listener. The concept of *rhetoric* emerged more than 2,500 years ago as people discovered that certain ways of talking were more effective and powerful in achieving social power and influence. When the Gutenberg revolution brought printed books to a mass audience, the concept of literacy expanded to include the skills of reading and writing, which required many years of practice to master fully.

Today, people need to be able to "read" and "write" messages using symbols in a variety of forms. Each genre and medium of expression and communication demands certain learned competencies. For example, reading on screen, reading from a page, writing with a keyboard, and writing with a pencil are all practices that require particular skills. In this book, we'll show how mass media, social media, popular culture, and digital media texts can be used to support the development of children's reading, writing, speaking, listening, and communication skill development.

Talking About Popular Culture Builds Listening Comprehension

Children's talk about popular culture and mass media is deeply tied to language development, comprehension, and expressive skills. For example, in hands-on work with media literacy in over 60 elementary schools in England, scholars found that film viewing and discussion activities promote high levels of talking and sharing in extended discourse. While watching, young children listen closely and are able to comprehend narratives and notice details about dialogue and music, plot, setting, and character.[7]

When children learn how to apply concepts like audience, message, purpose, and point of view to both familiar media (like TV shows and music) and unfamiliar media (like nonfiction textbooks and news articles), they strengthen their critical reading strategies.

Many children who are just learning to decode and comprehend print texts can demonstrate complex reasoning and sophisticated thinking skills using familiar visual or digital materials. Especially for those children who have become disengaged and alienated from school, getting a chance to display one's funds of knowledge and reasoning skills with mass media, popular culture, and digital media activities enables children to bring their at-home media and technology experiences into the classroom. Not only are such practices engaging and motivating to young learners, but such connections are also at the heart of what real learning is all about.

Today, many communication competencies are needed to be effective in society. Digital and media literacy includes the ability to access, analyze, compose, reflect, and take action in the world. It's a broad and expansive array of life skills. We think it's absolutely essential for elementary educators to help strengthen children's self-expression and advocacy, reasoning, critical thinking, and communication skills. Social development, self-confidence, conflict-resolution skills, and sensitivity to the social responsibilities of using 21st century technologies are habits of mind that enable children to thrive. The following list outlines the kind of competencies that are increasingly valued both inside and outside the classroom.

POWERFUL VOICES FOR KIDS: DIGITAL AND MEDIA LITERACY COMPETENCIES

Access

✓ Listening skills
✓ Reading comprehension
✓ Using appropriate technology tools
✓ Asking questions
✓ Gathering information using multiple sources
✓ Applying information to solve a problem

Analysis

✓ Understanding how symbols work and how they are used
✓ Recognizing particular types (genres) of messages
✓ Identifying authorship, message purpose, and target audience with a variety of texts
✓ Recognizing evidence of quality and credibility in different types of messages

Composition

✓ Speaking to an individual and demonstrating listening skills

✓ Speaking to a large group and responding to feedback

✓ Communicating a personal reaction and expressing a point of view

✓ Selecting messages and texts to use, respond to, remix, and combine in a creative way

✓ Composing, writing, and creating images to inform, persuade, and entertain

✓ Composing in a variety of formats, including emails, reviews, reports, film scripts, music lyrics, web pages, nonfiction, fiction, and other literary genres

✓ Composing for a variety of audiences, including peers, family members, educators, special interest groups, government leaders, and members of the general public

Reflection

✓ Recognizing and valuing relationships and engaging in socially appropriate behavior

✓ Brainstorming and contributing ideas

✓ Staying on task and following directions

✓ Using good judgment and social responsibility when communicating with others

✓ Exercising leadership, integrity, and accountability

✓ Offering feedback to, helping, and teaching others

Taking Action

✓ Participating in a creative community

✓ Sharing and expressing ideas with others

✓ Being aware of and sensitive to differences among people

✓ Making connections between current events, the community, and the self

✓ Generating ideas in order to improve a thing or an event

✓ Collaborating on solving a meaningful real-world problem

These are precisely the competencies and skills that make people effective in both classroom and society. These are also the skills that employers seek out in the workforce. Young children between the ages of 5 to 11 can also demonstrate these competencies and skills. How?

First, children need the chance to ask questions about what they watch, listen to, see, and read. Second, children need opportunities to develop creative and collaborative skills using a variety of symbol systems to communicate, including language, images, sound, and multimedia. In an increasingly complex global environment, people need habits of mind that "involve new levels of communication, shared vision, collective intelligence, and direct coherent action."[8]

How Has Literacy Changed?

The concept of literacy is not fixed and static. It's based on the changing needs of people in a society. Today we recognize that literacy is not just reading and writing. In this book, you'll find teachers who are strengthening both the "old literacies" and the "new literacies" nearly simultaneously.

Rhetoric	Speaking and listening
Print Literacy	Reading and writing
Visual Literacy	Image design, interpretation, and creative composition
Information Literacy	Information access, retrieval, evaluation, and usage
Media Literacy	Analyzing messages from media and popular culture and composing with technology tools
Critical Literacy	Recognizing and resisting power relationships in messages and information
Computer Literacy	Understanding and using computer technologies effectively
News Literacy	Understanding and evaluating news and current events
Digital Literacy	Being a socially responsible user of the Internet and social media

TECHNOLOGY INTEGRATION IN THE ELEMENTARY GRADES

As we write this book, we are concerned about the possibility that the current approach to the use of digital media and technology in education may inadvertently widen the inequality gap in our society. In some American elementary schools, there are well-stocked school libraries, gleaming interactive whiteboards, video monitors, data projectors, classroom computers, and well-maintained computer labs, all supported by capable technology staff and helpful school librarians. In other elementary schools, however, especially in urban and rural schools, technology resources are often outdated, poorly maintained, and underused. In some cases, they are simply unavailable.

Unfortunately, many American elementary schools lack a full-time school librarian or technology specialist. In general, elementary schools have been the lowest priority for technology integration in school districts large and small. High schools get the lion's share of technology resources, followed by middle schools.[9]

But it's not just a matter of differences in mere access to technology. Differences in skill level in using technology are generally influenced by a person's level of education and social class. Some children arrive to kindergarten able to turn on a computer, find programs, use the Internet, and whiz through a variety of applications; other children have not yet used a mouse or a trackpad.

Family influences clearly play a giant role. Sociologist Eszter Hargittai has conducted research with Internet users to understand differences among people in their levels of skill in using technology. As it turns out, people generally feel that their skills are adequate for their needs. Most of us are unaware of the magnitude of differences that exist between more skilled and less skilled users, since we tend to use the Internet independently and have few opportunities to observe others doing routine tasks. But skill differences in the use of the Internet can have real consequences when it comes to careers and jobs.[10]

OUR LOVE-HATE RELATIONSHIP WITH MASS MEDIA, POPULAR CULTURE, AND TECHNOLOGY

Elementary educators have long been ambivalent about the use of media and technology tools for young learners. Screen-based media activities are already such a dominant part of children's lives outside of school; many American children will spend more than 8 hours per day with television, video games, music, and the Internet. Figure 1.1 shows the variety of websites that depend on children's attention for their success.

And while there's plenty of content that supports the needs of young children, there's a lot of content that we wish they didn't see. When little boys imitate aggressive moves from kung-fu cartoons or little girls dance sexy while reciting profane music video lyrics they don't actually understand, many of us get a headache. We sympathize with the many parents and teachers who seek to provide alternatives to television, video games, and mass media that support children's physical, emotional, social, and

Figure 1.1   Popular Websites for Children

intellectual growth and development. Renee herself is a parent who set limits on her own children's media and technology use in order to be sure that her kids spent time outdoors and in artistic, creative, or dramatic play activities. For these reasons, we are sympathetic to the feelings of those educators who *ignore* the role of popular culture in the lives of young children.

But whether we like it or not, media culture is our culture. We can't escape it. That's why we also sympathize with parents who fully participate in media culture and who raise children who make active use of it. Indeed, more than one third of U.S. elementary teachers *embrace* the use of various types of media and technology, including videos, personal computers, interactive projectors and whiteboards, DVD players, and other forms of educational technology, for regular instruction—that is, at least once a week. About another third use them at least once a month, and another third use them hardly ever or not at all.[11]

Computer games in education, similarly, have generally been conceptualized as either a waste of time, harmless fun, or a powerful new resource that will transform education. Since the 1980s, when *The Oregon Trail, Math Blaster*, and other programs first became commercially available, some educators have used computer games as a tool for learning; however, such activities were not always incorporated into the context of whole-classroom learning. Today, school librarians and classroom teachers still assemble links to a variety of generally free online learning games for children to use on the computer without integrating the activities into the routines of classroom practice.

Some elementary educators are discovering how to fully integrate gaming in ways that move beyond drill-and-practice stand-alone use. This generally requires teachers with particular kinds of expertise and skill. For example, one innovative school, Quest to Learn, teaches systems thinking to middle school students using concepts of digital and media literacy. There, children practice "decoding, authoring, manipulating and unlocking meaning" by exploring games as learning environments.[12]

In the chapters that follow, you'll learn about how all different sorts of media composition activities can engage young children in creating content themselves to discover the power of multimedia authorship. But in this book, we steer clear of either a "gee-whiz" approach to technology or a "danger, danger" mentality. Instead, we adopt a middle ground. We respect the differing motives that teachers have in using (or not using) media and technology with young learners.

One thing is certain: This book isn't just about computers, technology, or gaming in education or the use of cool technology tools. To be frank with you, we don't think that media and technology, in and of themselves, can transform education. Instead, we see media analysis and creative media production activities as a dimension of formal and informal *literacy education*. In this book, we will show how a new approach to literacy education can transform teaching and learning. Mass media, popular culture, and technology are resources that, when used well, promote the development of critical thinking, collaboration, communication, and creativity that support academic achievement.

MOTIVATION: CONNECTING CLASSROOM TO CULTURE

It's no surprise that the use of digital media and technology tools engages and motivates young learners. Many educators can remember a time when simply wheeling in the TV cart would yield a squeal of excited happy voices. Today, many children enjoy the opportunity to use interactive whiteboards, clickers, and other new technologies. But some researchers have found that, when it comes to technology use in school, the novelty may wear off over time.[13]

The best educators do not simply use technology for its own sake; instead, they use media and technology to meet the genuine needs of their learners.

One reason technology may motivate and inspire student learning is that digital media, mass media, and popular culture help children make connections between the classroom and their ordinary everyday experiences. Adults and children alike enjoy talking about social media, online games, celebrities, musicians, actors, books and movies, news, and current events. References to television often dominate children's informal social interactions, games, and jokes on the playground and in the lunchroom, as children use program details, celebrities, or other media incidents as points of discussion for informal peer engagement.[14]

High levels of student motivation and engagement are stimulated when children are empowered to bring their own interests, including their emerging tastes and preferences in popular culture and digital media, into rich and complex conversations with their teachers and peers. As we will see in this book, conversations move from trivial and superficial to complex and deep when children and students ask *why* and *how* questions about what we watch, listen to, play, see, and read.

When teachers permit and promote serious conversation about mass media and popular culture in the classroom, often these conversations are more substantive (and more unpredictable) than the relatively simple talk that children are having in responding to the content of basal readers.

For example, researchers in one classroom discovered that when talking about advertising, children developed spontaneous critiques of the representation of race, childhood, and class, even when curriculum materials did not suggest this approach.[15] Researchers have argued that the use of children's popular culture in educational institutions may offer recognition of children's identities and the things they value, thus enhancing self-esteem and motivating children to participate more deeply in learning.[16] For example, Anne Haas Dyson has examined how children blend images of football players, popular songs, plots from movies, and cartoons, using them in both personal narratives and extended pieces of writing.[17] Such instructional practices engage learners and deepen their ability to participate fully in the learning process.

Why Does Digital and Media Literacy Matter? A Theory of Change

Rationale

1. Children are growing up with more access to media and technology than at any point in human history.

2. The rapid rate of change in the development of new communications technologies is likely to continue.

3. People now need to engage actively in lifelong learning in order to use new tools and resources to accomplish ordinary personal, social, cultural, and civic activities.

4. Digital media create *empowering* opportunities for people to connect with others and share ideas, engage in dynamic new forms of formal and informal learning, express their creativity, and use digital media and technology tools to participate as citizens in a democracy.

5. There are also real and potential *risks* associated with the digital age, including exposure to violent, harmful, or offensive content; manipulative advertising; inaccurate information, including sexual/racist/hate material; contact with strangers, privacy, cyberbullying, and cyberstalking; illegal downloading, gambling, hacking; and more.

6. Respect for intellectual property and reputational safety are important in a time when we are experiencing rapidly shifting notions of ownership, authorship, privacy, and social appropriateness.

7. Therefore, to protect against the negative aspects of contemporary media culture and to take advantage of the empowerment potential offered by digital media and technology, a constellation of life skills is needed.

Theory

8. Digital and media literacy includes the ability to

   Access: make responsible choices and access information by finding and locating materials and comprehending information and ideas;

   Analyze: understand messages in a variety of forms through textual and contextual analysis, identifying the author, purpose, and point of view and evaluating the quality and credibility of the content;

   Create: compose content in a variety of forms for authentic purposes, making use of language, images, sound, and new digital tools and technologies;

   Reflect: consider one's own conduct and communication behavior by applying social responsibility and ethical principles; and

   Act: take social action by working individually and collaboratively to share knowledge and solve problems in the family, workplace, community, nation, and world.

9. People share meaning through language (in print and oral forms), images, sounds, music, graphics, and interactivity.

10. Texts come in many forms. Each genre and medium of expression and communication demands certain learned competencies. For example, reading on screen, reading from a page, writing with a keyboard, and writing with a pencil are all practices that require particular skills.

11. Mass media and popular culture texts that connect children's experiences at home with new ideas and information increase the perceived relevance of school.

12. Learning textual and contextual analysis concepts like audience, purpose, and point of view supports the development of reading strategies. Critical analysis of mass media, popular culture, and digital media texts strengthens literacy development, especially with reluctant readers.

13. When learners use technology tools to compose and create messages, they activate multimodal literacy competencies.

14. Young children who are just learning to decode printed symbols can demonstrate comprehension, critical thinking, and textual and contextual analysis skills when using familiar media, including the texts of mass media and popular culture.

15. The practice of critical analysis and composition with digital media texts, tools, and technologies promotes intellectual curiosity and supports lifelong learning.

Lesson   What's Inside and Outside the Frame

Lesson Description

The youngest students can learn about the frame—the special rectangle that goes around the edges of the television. Students learn that when media makers create messages, they make choices, intentionally using the frame to show some things, but leave others out.

Objectives

Students will

- understand that all media messages are constructed by people who make choices
- use imagination and make inferences
- create an informal video that intentionally includes and excludes various events

Vocabulary

Camera

Monitor

Frame

Visible

Attention

Imagination

Resources and Materials

✓ A television or projector large enough for the entire group to view at once

✓ A camera that is capable of displaying a live image on your television or projector

✓ Tripod

✓ Painter's tape

✓ *Mister Rogers' Neighborhood* episode titled "Work: Go Behind the Scenes," which features the making of an episode of the program Cue the video so that the countdown timer reads 28:00.

Activity

Access

✓ Begin with students seated on the floor. Turn on your camera so that the students may see themselves on the screen and allow the students some time to giggle and experience seeing themselves on television.

✓ Turn off the camera and refocus the students' attention. Point out that the television screen is a rectangle. This rectangle is called the frame. The television shows us what is inside the frame, but it can't show us what is outside the frame.

✓ Invite each student to share one person or thing that they saw inside the frame, and then invite each student to point out one person or thing that was *left out*.

Analysis

✓ Invite a few students to share their favorite television shows. Let the students know that you would like to share a television show with them that many older people viewed when they were children.

✓ Play the *Mister Rogers* episode up until the end of the opening song, pausing as Mr. Rogers is finishing tying his shoes.

✓ Looking over the paused image with your students, invite them to share the things that they can see inside the frame. Encourage students to notice the background as well as Mister Rogers himself.

✓ Ask the students to use their imagination: What do you think is left out because it is outside the frame?

✓ Continue the video. After a brief introduction, Mister Rogers will show you that his "television house" is part of a large television studio. Pause the video after Mister Rogers sits down again and takes out the sheet music.

✓ Ask your students: What are some of the things that were outside the frame that we missed before? Did any of them surprise you?

Composition

✓ Have the students stand along the tape lines, and point out that they will be inside the frame on one side of the line, and outside the frame on the other side.

✓ Play a round of Simon Says with the frame: "Simon Says put just your hand in the frame," "Simon says put just your feet in the frame." Alternatively, you may sing/do the "Hokey Pokey" and put your hands, feet, and so on in and out of the frame. Record these activities and review them later as an assessment.

Reflection

✓ Discuss: What did students notice about what was in and out of the frame when we played the game?

Taking Action

✓ Explain that all TV images are made by people who make choices. When students create a message, they make these choices themselves. When they read books or watch TV, they can notice the choices made by other authors.

Source: Created by John Landis.

NOTES

1. Common Sense Media. (2011). *Zero to eight: Children's media use in America.* Retrieved from http://www.commonsensemedia.org/sites/default/files/research/zerotoeightfinal2011.pdf
2. Commonsense Media. (2011).
3. Commonsense Media. (2011).
4. Media and Learning Group at SRI. (2010). *Joint media engagement and learning.* Menlo Park, CA: SRI International.
5. Montgomery, K. (2007). *Generation digital: Politics, commerce and childhood in the age of the Internet.* Cambridge, MA: MIT Press.

6. Bruner, J. (1966). *Toward a theory of instruction.* Cambridge, MA: Belknap Press of Harvard University (p. 11).
7. Marsh, J., & Bearne, E. (2008). *Moving literacy on: Evaluation of the BFI lead practitioner for moving image media literacy.* Sheffield, UK: University of Sheffield.
8. Stephens, R. & Scott, E. V. (n.d.). *Ensuring workforce skills of the future: The birth to work pipeline.* Retrieved from http://www.nsrconline.org/pdf/whitepaper105.pdf (p. 2).
9. Gray, L., Thomas, N., & Lewis, L. (2010). *Educational technology in U.S. public schools: Fall 2008* (NCES 2010–034). Washington, DC: U.S. Government Printing Office.
10. Hargittai, E. (2008). The digital reproduction of inequality. In D. Grusky (Ed.), *Social stratification 2008* (pp. 936–944). Boulder, CO: Westview Press (p. 938).
11. Cuban, L. (2010, January 31). Confessions from a skeptic on computers in school [web log]. Retrieved from http://larrycuban.wordpress.com/2010/01/31/confessions-from-a-skeptic-on-computers-in-school/
12. Quest to Learn. http://q2l.org.
13. Bethel, E. C., Bernard, R. M., Abrami, P. C., & Wade, A. C. (2007, October). *The effects of ubiquitous computing on student learning: A systematic review.* Presentation at E-Learn 2007: World Conference on E-Learning in Corporate, Government, Healthcare, & Higher Education, Chesapeake, VA.
14. de Block, L. (2012). Entertainment education and social change: Evaluating a children's soap opera in Kenya. *International Journal of Educational Development, 32,* 608–614.
15. Banaji, S. (2010). Analysing advertisements in the classroom. In C. Bazalgette (Ed.), *Teaching media in primary schools* (pp. 62–74). London, UK: Sage.
16. Bazalgette, C. (2010). *Teaching media in primary schools.* London, UK: Sage.
17. Dyson, A. H. (2003). *The brothers and sisters learn to write.* New York, NY: Teachers College Press.

2 Motivations for Teaching Digital and Media Literacy

In this chapter, you'll learn about

What Motivates Teachers

- Why do teachers integrate digital media, mass media, and popular culture into the classroom?

Engaging Students With Cool Tools and Media

- How do teachers incorporate digital technologies and children's popular culture into their teaching practices?

Amplifying Student Voice

- How do teachers foster a learning environment in which children can share ideas both in the classroom and with the wider world?

How Media Is Constructed

- How do teachers engage younger students in conversations and activities that reveal how media is funded and created in professional environments?

Participation In and Out of School

- How do teachers incorporate participation and collaboration into learning through civic engagement and digital storytelling?

It's not easy to become a reflective practitioner when it comes to teaching. There is just too much to do, every single day and even on the weekends. A teacher's day is packed. First there are the planning and preparation, the gathering of resources and materials, getting ready for the kids. Then there's the whirlwind of the day, with its intense social interaction, moments of spontaneous improvisation, and bodies-in-motion activity. For many professionals, the drive home is decompression time, pure and simple, followed by a new round of activity: addressing the needs of family and friends, with thoughts about tomorrow's school day running in the mind. Tomorrow the cycle starts all over again.

But in spite of the busy schedule, some of us squeeze in time to reflect on our work and learn new things. We may do this by reading books (such as this one), taking online courses, or surfing the web to find lesson plans. Although resources that offer new ideas, instructional techniques, and research are plentiful, our time and attention is limited.

One of the reasons why teachers enjoy social media resources like Amy Mascott's We Teach (www.weteachgroup.com) and Jim Burke's English Companion (www.englishcompanion.com) is that these online communities give educators an opportunity to reduce the isolation they can experience as part of the job. Online communities like these offer a fantastic opportunity for professional development, and we hope that reading this book and using our website are important parts of your professional learning plan.

It's ironic that a teacher's job is simultaneously so highly socially connected and yet so socially isolating. We teach in front of students and yet out of sight of colleagues.

To achieve excellence as teachers, we must engage in the habit of reflective practice—giving ourselves time to inwardly consider the choices we make in the classroom and strive for continuous improvement. But the process of becoming an excellent teacher is not just a matter of reflection and trying out a new tool or a new lesson plan. In a profound way, the quality of our work as teachers is deeply inflected by who we are as human beings. As Parker Palmer has written, "Good teaching cannot be reduced to technique; good teaching comes from the identity and integrity of the teacher."[1]

Teachers are complex human beings who benefit from opportunities to reflect on the choices we make each day. Reflection is highly personal, and the act of sharing reflections requires a climate of trust and respect. In working with dozens of teachers to develop digital and media literacy education programs with young learners, we were able to encourage the kind of reflective thinking that leads to fresh insights.

Teachers inevitably make curriculum choices based on personal values and identity. For example, when one of the Powerful Voices for Kids (PVK) instructors, John, reflected on his teaching, he acknowledged how his own love of computers shaped his ideas and values. He wrote in a journal entry:

For me, my effectiveness as a learner and a thinker (not to mention citizen, artist, and family member) is greatly enhanced by my highly wired lifestyle. One-to-one laptop schools are only now starting to emerge as a simple reality of education. Yet in their school, I can't help but feel bad that I am asking my students to think and learn, mostly deprived of the one tool (or multitude of tools) that I find most valuable.

John's identity as a technology user also shaped the way he thought about various kinds of texts. He knew that literacy practices were bound up with issues of power. In his online journal, he wrote:

Even as a geeky kid, I didn't feel too differently than my students do now. Print media are alienating. Written language is the only medium which is purely symbolic, and which actually requires active education for basic comprehension. By contrast, photography, movies, music, and other visual and auditory media (even speech) can be at least comprehended using skills that are gained simply through viewership and participation. For the young, it can easily feel as if print is a secret language.

Another teacher, LaShon, had an approach to teaching that was less focused on technology tools and more focused on adopting the point of view of the child. Working each day with young children, she saw herself as learning about the world from her 6- and 7-year-old students. In her online journal, she wrote:

I had an "aha" moment on Monday when one of the students said something to me and I responded using the word "similar," or something like that, and he said, "Miss LaShon, what does *similar* mean?" Just that quick I had forgotten that I was not speaking in a vernacular that he could understand. The incident turned into a learning moment to define the word *similar*, and needless to say, *similar* has been added to our Lexicon [a colorful box for vocabulary words written on index cards]. I have definitely discovered a level of patience within myself that I didn't even know existed. If I construct my lessons plans using the students' level of "expertise"—instead of my own—I garner better results.

REFLECTIVE PRACTICE: WHAT'S MOTIVATING YOU?

All teachers want to help students learn, but they have many different motivations for teaching. As Mary Kennedy observed in her study of teaching behavior and motivation, many teachers consider teaching itself to be a kind of a call to duty.[2] Others view it as a vocation, a career with high demands for workplace professionalism. Some teachers are particularly sensitive to their students' social and emotional development, providing a space for sensitive dialogue about touchy subjects. Some teachers put the subject matter first, engaging students in becoming passionate about a subject and challenging them to think critically and ask deep questions about classroom content. Still others see themselves as catalysts for student voice, bringing out the best of their students' innate talents and abilities.

In this chapter, we detail eight core motivations for integrating digital media and technology into the classroom. We've found that we can predict what kinds of activities, lesson plans, and content a teacher will use in the classroom by understanding her or his motivations. When it comes to digital and media literacy, the curriculum choices that teachers make about *what* to teach and *how* to teach reflect one or more of these core motivations.

We've identified these motivations from our experience in professional development workshops in the United States and abroad, from kindergarten through graduate programs in workshops and summer institutes, and from developing other programs designed to help educators learn more about how they can use digital and media literacy in their own teaching practice. In addition, Renee developed a research agenda with German colleague Silke Grafe to develop quantitative measures of teacher motivations for media literacy. She and Silke worked with international samples of teachers using survey research data to identify the relationship between teacher motivations and instructional practices with digital media.[3]

Different motivations have different results in the classroom—but teachers with very different teaching styles can be comparably effective in the classroom. We have found that each core motivation also encompasses both *protectionist* and *empowerment* approaches in relation to the world of digital media, mass media, and popular culture. Renee likes to help teachers reflect on their love/hate relationship with media and technology. She's found that in the heart of every protectionist is a strong desire for students' voices to be valued through thoughtful interactions in the world, while even the staunchest empowerment advocate has considered the limits and boundaries of appropriateness, comfort, and taboo in children's media environments.

In this chapter, we introduce you to some of the instructors and teachers you'll be reading about in this book using eight different categories that reflect their motivations for bringing digital and media literacy to their students. At the Powerful Voices for Kids website, you can take an online quiz to discover which motivators match your distinct attitudes, beliefs, and values. We learned about the motivations of instructors and teachers through classroom observations, conversations about practice, project-based learning activities, lesson plans, and teachers' reflective writing.[4]

In each of the categories, we offer a portrait of teaching motivations by identifying both the strengths and the downsides that may be associated with this type of motivation. We also recognize that no teacher has only one motivation; in fact, the ways in which different motivations come into play in different contexts and with different learners is an important part of the process of reflection. What motivates you? As you read, see if you can recognize yourself, your colleagues, or other teachers you know.

Four Corners on the Media

Children can explain what they like and don't like about media at a young age. When we break media into its most basic components, children begin to understand and share their own love/hate relationships with different kinds of media. In Four Corners, one piece of large chart paper is hung in each of the four corners of the room. Then students form small groups and rotate from station to station to talk about and write a brief summary of what it is they love and hate about the four types of media. The stations are labeled as follows:

Print: What you read

Like: "When my sister reads Harry Potter to me"

Dislike: "When I forget which page I was on"

Visual: What you watch

Like: "Avatar: The Last Airbender—I like the characters."

Dislike: "Shows my parents watch—they're boring."

Audio: What you listen to

Like: "Backyardigans and the Fresh Beat Band—silly and fun!"

Dislike: "The rock music my older brother listens to—too loud."

Interactive: Machine you use or play with

Like: "Playing with my Nintendo DS—racing games are exciting."

Dislike: "When my friend doesn't have an app I like a lot."

When children share their experiences as media consumers, they reveal aspects of their personal identity. Self-disclosure activities like this can promote the development of trust and respect, deepening the quality of classroom dialogue.

ENGAGING STUDENT VOICE: MOTIVATORS AND SPIRIT GUIDES

Some teachers want to use holistic, child-centered approaches to motivating and engaging students by using media to tap into their creative energy and support their unique voices.

Motivators use digital and media literacy activities as a catalyst for their students' creative energy, expression, and student voice.

Spirit guides are sensitively aware of their students as whole human beings—mind, body, and spirit—and want to use every part of their emotional worlds, including their media worlds, to help them become more comfortable in their emerging identities.

Motivators and spirit guides share a strong connection to student-centered approaches to learning. They often capitalize on the emotional power of media to inspire learners. For example, two instructors used poetry and rhyme to explore the process of multimedia composition with their students. Osei worked with children entering Grade 5, while Mona worked with rising third graders. At the center of both instructors' teaching practice was a personal, emotional connection with their students' lives. But the two had different agendas in forming these connections. While Osei wanted his students to direct their voice outward to the world, Mona wanted her students to feel comfortable sharing *within* the classroom with each other, giving intimate feedback and connecting their media experiences to their developing creative spirit.

Osei provided lots of powerful examples of motivating students to express themselves. In one lesson, he was working with two boys to teach them how to construct the more complicated rhymes that the rappers they knew and loved used in their own work. Osei pointed out that when rapper Eminem (a classroom favorite) raps a line, he often has multiple syllables and internal rhymes; that's what gives his flow the patter that it has. (Throughout the lesson, Osei also checked for vocabulary and comprehension, just as LaShon did: "Can you tell me what a syllable is?") For example, in "Not Afraid," a popular 2010 song that inspired Osei's two students, Eminem raps:

> You can try and read my lyrics off of this paper before I lay 'em
> But you won't take the sting out these words before I say 'em
> 'Cause ain't no way I'm-a let you stop me from causing mayhem

Eminem uses parallel structure in the first two lines to strengthen the rhyme at the end, adding "before I" prior to both "lay 'em" and "say 'em." In all three lines, the "ay" sounds at the beginning of a phrase echo the rhyme at the end—"paper," "take," and "ain't"/"way" predict "lay 'em," "say 'em," and "mayhem," respectively. The way Eminem emphasizes these vowel sounds throughout adds to the forcefulness of his rapping style.

As Osei explained concepts like internal rhyming and polysyllables, we couldn't help but observe the look on the boys' faces. They were absolutely mesmerized in this lesson, hanging onto Osei's every word. Osei was physically engaging, making hand gestures to accentuate particular syllables and keeping intense eye contact with both boys. It was as though he was letting them in on a secret that the three of them would share through the songwriting process. When Osei went to work with a different group, the boys began to quickly write new lines into their composition notebooks.

Mona had a different experience with her students that revealed her deep sensitivity to their inner lives. They, too, were studying poetry and lyrics in popular music, but it was in preparation for a poetic public service announcement they would write. When Mona asked children to create rhymes about whatever came to mind, at first many students made uninspired rhymes with common school-sanctioned constructions, like "I had a cat; it was lying on a mat."

Mona invited children to create a powerful theme to unify and extend the value of their work. After the class had brainstormed the theme "Never give up" for a subsequent poem, several boys began to incorporate violent imagery into their poems:

> A guy pushed me
> He had to pay a fee
> I stabbed him
> And jabbed him

And another student wrote:

> I slapped him with a kick.
> He cost me my life
> Then I cut his head off with a knife.

What a dramatic and frightening contrast to the simplistic rhymes of the Grade 2 basal reader! Mona was startled by the writing the children had produced. They were only 7 or 8 years old. What did it mean for them to produce these rhymes? She wasn't sure how to respond.

There are many different ways teachers might handle this poem. She might have explained that talk about violence was "inappropriate." Perhaps classroom rules about content might have prevented such language from being used altogether. There are also deflection strategies that might allow a teacher to sweep such an incident under the rug. But Mona knew that this imagery was a complicated part of her students' everyday lives and media experiences. She was careful to honor their writing as a set of choices that the children themselves had made. Upon reflection, Mona tried to understand why her students were so drawn to violence. In an interview, she observed, "When we think of 'never give up,' sometimes we think of never giving up because life is amazing. But it can also mean, 'Never give up through your hardships.'"

Quick to think not just of violent media her students absorb or tropes they learn from popular music, Mona assumed there were important and genuine feelings underlying her students' reliance on violent imagery. She didn't just dismiss or trivialize the choices that these children had made in their writing.

Her students had other opportunities in class to discuss hardships, feelings, pleasures, and fears, often through responding to popular culture that activated their emotions. The intimate space for sharing that Mona created allowed her students to reveal vulnerable parts of themselves, and to therefore more honestly reflect on their thoughts and feelings.

Student voice is often an uncertain or vague concept in elementary education. Younger students are at the very beginning of exploring who they are. Teachers who are motivated to act as a springboard for student ideas need to also be sensitive to when students have trouble, whether developmentally or otherwise, articulating those ideas. As we will see in the following chapters, students sometimes need structure to be truly creative. Before students can create media about a social issue like homelessness, for example, they first must gather information by reading, listening, looking at online documents, and building their background knowledge on a variety of subjects.

What we call *voice* is, in a sense, the foundation for human communication—and not all forms of communication are equally desirable in a classroom setting. This is where teachers motivated by the social and emotional well-being of their students can have both the biggest strengths and the biggest challenges. Mona was successfully able to redirect her students' immediate connection to violence as a means of problem solving by shifting the focus to learning how to help their community through the creation of a public service announcement. She also had to address communication that surprised and concerned her, but to do so in a way that did not affect her students' self-esteem or sense of self-worth.

Self-disclosure and personal expression may occur in structured environments, but children and young people may also seek freer rein. Teachers must carefully balance order and chaos in the classroom when student voice is highly valued. Mona's experience illustrates how this type of circumstance can offer opportunity for rich and life-impacting teachable moments.

Pop Star Producer

Ages 9+

http://mypopstudio.com/music

In this group of four interactive learning games, children explore the emotional power of music to affect attitudes and behaviors. Children create a musical performer by selecting body type, hair, clothing, and accessories and then identify a values message for her performance. By selecting lyrics and choosing musical instruments, beats, and sound effects, children compose a song and, in the process, discover that the message they intend to send with their song may or may not match the message that audiences receive.

UNDERSTANDING MEDIA SYSTEMS: WATCHDOGS AND DEMYSTIFIERS

Some educators want to help learners understand media systems—the ways in which all forms of media are constructed, targeted to specific groups of people, designed to advance private gain or public good, and how all media represent reality in ways that are partial and incomplete.

Watchdogs are keenly aware of the pervasive influence of economics on media production of all kinds. Coming from the cultural studies and *critical literacy* tradition, these teachers are keen to offer an ideological critique of mass media and culture as well as an examination of the politics of representation, including race, gender, socioeconomic class, social control, resistance, and pleasure.[5] They want their students to recognize and resist stereotypes.

Demystifiers go behind the scenes to identify how and why media is constructed. These teachers may draw on concepts of *semiotics*, the study of how symbols represent the world through language, images, sounds, interactive design, and technology. Elementary teachers reveal to students the ways in which advertisements persuade people to buy products or services, examining the blurring of entertainment, information, and persuasion. Other educators have experienced success in helping students learn the graphic design, computer programming, editing, and production techniques that are used to create photos, movies, video games, and web pages.

Both Watchdogs and Demystifiers are big-picture thinkers and thrive on the "aha" moment in which people gain deeper awareness of some structural or institutional aspect of media and technology. In exploring institutional issues, a Watchdog might ask such questions as "Who made this app?" or "How is this magazine paid for?" Demystifiers, on the other hand, explore media's structure, by asking such questions as "How do special effects work?" or "What choices do authors have to make to develop an online video game?" Many students have never really thought about how it is that their favorite media go from being an idea in someone's head to being real texts and tools that people use in the world. For this reason, creative activities frequently demystify the production process.

Ms. Capaldo, a Grade 5 teacher, displayed her Watchdog sensibilities by designing an activity that required students to ask critical questions about fast food websites. Fast food sites, like many other child-oriented websites, contain a good deal of interactive and gaming activities. These *advergames* feature popular characters from companies like Kraft or Kellogg's and never explicitly advertise a product. Instead, advergames immerse students in the interactive world of a product, so that they associate online fun with a particular brand.

Ms. Capaldo was concerned about the lack of transparency in these websites, particularly given the notoriously unhealthy content of fast foods. But like many other teachers, Ms. Capaldo knew that directly challenging McDonald's, Burger King's, or Taco Bell's motivations for attracting young consumers might backfire in the classroom. When children feel passionately about a brand, restaurant, or celebrity, they may resist any critique of the pleasure they take in popular culture. Some students resist by opting out or denying a teacher's challenge. Others simply pretend by giving a teacher-appropriate response. Some young children have learned to say "McDonald's is bad" when in fact they may eat there three times a week.

Instead, Ms. Capaldo wanted her students to discover the ways that the graphic design of corporate media reflects the motivations of parent companies. To do this, she had her students explore several fast food websites and look for information. Students noticed that a Burger King website was designed for fun, not information. On the website, users can use a sliding bar to customize information and games about "Fun," "Food," and "BK." When students moved the bar toward the "Fun" side, they found lots of games. When they moved the bar to "Food," they found menu options. When they moved the bar toward "BK," they found coupons and promotions. This level of interactivity made it difficult for them to find the nutritional information they were looking for, and the class reflected on many reasons why the company might not want to make nutritional information easily accessible on the website (see Figure 2.1).

Ms. Capaldo found that this kind of spontaneous learning was more effective than a top-down approach in which she simply *told* students that

Figure 2.1   Identifying Media Mystification: Exploring Fast Food Websites

Burger King intentionally makes it difficult to find nutritional information. As they searched on their own, students themselves became Watchdogs, experiencing a sense of frustration that they wanted to share with the class and, later, with younger students in school.

In other instances, teachers are motivated more broadly to pull back the curtain on the constructed nature of media messages and technology tools. By emphasizing the process of moving from ignorance to awareness, demystification can result in profound and unforgettable learning experiences.

For example, working with kindergarten children, instructors Nicole and Raph helped students as young as 5 years old become aware of the construction of advertisements, cartoons, and other media. In one memorable lesson, Nicole took her group of kindergartners on a field trip to the PBS Sprout children's television studios in Philadelphia. There they learned about how puppets "talk." They watched adults handle puppets and record their own voices using a lavalier (wireless) microphone. As one child explained, "They [the puppeteers] make them talk. They have a microphone that runs up their leg to their shirt." For students who sometimes confuse cartoon and live-action reality, understanding the mechanics of media construction helps them understand that stories on TV come from authors, just as stories in books do.

Younger children live in a world where differences between real and fake can be blurry.[6] Raph created a game called *Red Light, Green Light* to help kindergarten students activate their reasoning skills. She showed them different characters from books, news media, TV shows, and movies. Children were asked to hold up a cardboard "red light" for things they thought were fake and a "green light" for things they thought were real and to use words to explain their responses.

Children liked playing the game and explaining their ideas, but Raph often wasn't sure if they understood the underlying concepts. For example, one student who wasn't sure if Robert Downey Jr.'s character in *Iron Man* was real or fake said, "Iron Man isn't really real, but they could make a suit like that with technology." One of Raph's students, whom we will call Sean, seemed to get the *least* out of Raph's lesson plans. He repeatedly seemed to zone out in class, occasionally throwing temper tantrums and causing trouble with other children.

But when David later placed 10 TV Sort Cards in front of Sean and asked him to sort them by identifying the author's purpose, Sean glanced at the cards and within seconds had quickly sorted them into two piles. He pointed to a pile he'd put together that consisted entirely of live-action programs from television. "Real," he said. Then he pointed to a pile of cartoons. "Fake."

David realized Sean didn't appear to understand the concept of *purpose*— he had provided a response outside the scope of our research, which we explore in more detail in Chapter 8. David was about to spread the cards out for the second sort task when Sean happened to pick up one from the "fake" pile, a screen shot from the animated series *Family Guy*. "This one's a cartoon. I watch this one sometimes. They have actors that talk into the microphone that makes them talk. It's not real." He looked at the next card, a screen shot of a commercial for a *Sesame Street* toy. "They make that one talk, too," he said. "It's just a puppet." Sean, it seems, had become a Demystifier. Now that Sean had an understanding of how animated and children's TV shows actually make fuzzy puppets talk, magical explanations were no longer needed.

TV Card Sort Task: SNAPS

http://powerfulvoicesforkids.com

SNAPS is a set of TV screenshot images, reproduced on heavy card stock paper, that depicts various types of current TV shows, including comedy, drama, action adventure, documentary, reality, news, and advertising. The cards can be used for a variety of sorting activities that help children talk and think about television. For example, children can be asked to distinguish between TV shows that are fiction and nonfiction. They can sort cards by considering the message purpose (inform, persuade, or entertain) or by identifying which programs are designed for target audiences (children, teens, or adults). In Chapter 8, you'll learn how we used these cards to measure the media literacy competencies of children.

COOL TOOLS AND COOL TEACHERS: TECHIES AND TRENDSETTERS

Some teachers are interested in the novelty, communicative power, and classroom engagement of mass media, digital media, and technology.

Techies believe that new digital media tools can transform teaching and learning. They are often a school's self-professed technophiles or "geeks"—the teachers who are familiar with new devices, hardware, software, and educational technology in the world of K–12 education.

Trendsetters are drawn to the contemporary popular culture and digital media of students, finding ways to connect learners' academic interests to their at-home use of media like popular music, websites, video games, television, and films; celebrity culture; professional sports; and young people's private and public lives online.

Techies and Trendsetters share a fundamental respect for the ways that media and technology shape culture, often in powerful ways that can be harnessed for classroom learning. They tend to be unafraid of trying things out in the classroom, whether that means finding ways to incorporate new tools into classroom discussion or navigating children's media to find ways to connect home viewing, listening, and surfing with in-school learning.

Many teachers are fascinated with the power of digital tools and educational technology for learning. These days, many teachers are using Twitter as a form of professional development. Teachers like Kristin Hokanson, an educational technology expert, self-identify as someone who enjoys exploring new technology resources. Kristin's up to date with all of the latest technology tools. In one particularly memorable lesson we watched, she demonstrated an infrared notebook device that recorded sound as she wrote her notes. When she played back the recording on her computer, it animated her writing on the monitor while it played back the sounds of people talking as she wrote. Such a tool can help a to remember not only the words, but the way thoughts formed and how conversations spark the writing process.

When we are searching for *cool tools* for the classroom, we go to Kristin first. She knows about all of the latest software, hardware, freeware, and educational technology. She knows which apps are good for students and which are good for teachers. She tests out new programs, fiddles with new gadgets, and has a passionate sense of discovery around new media and technologies.

Techies are sensitive to the way technology shapes students' lives. They teach students how to use technology tools safely and responsibly and how to use technology to make their voices heard in the world.

They engage student interests around the new and emerging platforms, programs, and technologies that they also often use to teach classroom content. Teachers like Kristin frequently serve as both formal and informal mentors to other teachers who are not as adept at using the educational technology they already have in their classrooms. They also understand that the skillful and thoughtful use of technology plays an increasingly important role in the everyday lives of all of us, and they sometimes seek to transform school cultures in order to integrate communications technology.

Sometimes, however, Techies can rely on cool tools and simple engagement strategies to pander to students' interests. In our work with K–6 schools, we have seen educators who use SMART Boards—the brand-name term for interactive whiteboards (touch-screen projector systems)—as a reward for student engagement, allowing students to blast at math problems, pop word bubbles, and, in one particularly vivid example, explode the contents of a sperm cell into its constituent parts—even in 3-D!

However, there is no denying the beneficial impact technologies can have on learning. With the push of a button, students have access to untold amounts of online information through libraries, websites, and other databases. Lecture formats and peer interaction can be approximated through distance education. Cameras, recorders, tablets, and other portable devices make media production activities easier than ever before. The skillful Techie teacher finds inventive ways to harness the power of new technology and to openly question the implications of such power, revealing both the promise and the challenges of a life rich with new technologies.

Trendsetters are particularly keen to better understand the popular culture that their students know and love. Trendsetters have an appreciation for youth popular culture, sometimes because they have children of their own (we know teachers who have their children's favorite music on their personal iPods) or because they are conversant with the world of popular culture that children are discovering.

Trendsetters are particularly adept at engaging students. They may be seen as the cool teachers—and they may scare others who see themselves as "uncool." In one professional development workshop, teachers were invited to identify their anxieties about popular culture, including dislike of students' favorite media, lack of knowledge about the world of popular culture, and fear of inappropriate content. During the discussion, one teacher bristled at the very idea of talking about popular culture in the classroom, explaining, "I don't want to be the teacher that comes in with a boom box on her head gettin' jiggy with it."

This teacher was evocatively describing the phenomenon David calls *Rappin' Grandma*. Rappin' Grandma uses popular culture to appeal to students. Pandering—a type of exploitation—is what happens when teachers use students' favorite popular culture in the classroom *just* to get kids' attention or *just* to present themselves as cool and trendy.

As a young teacher with an interest in popular culture, David is also aware of both positive and negative outcomes that result from his own Trendsetter impulses. He illustrates the complicated relationship between engaging students through their popular culture and focusing on learning goals and a positive classroom environment with a story from his own experiences teaching in the Powerful Voices for Kids program. In 2010, David created an age-appropriate mix of popular music that instructors could play for inspiration, downtime, or song analysis. It included popular pop, hip-hop, and R&B tracks from the previous year. When he played this mix for a group of third graders as students and instructors ate lunch, he noticed that one side of the room was animated, discussing every song, creating impromptu dances, and generally enjoying the music. The other side of the room, however, was silent, and children were subdued. They seemed to have receded from the music-centered activity happening across the room.

David later learned that some children did not identify with popular music at all. For them, it served as an object that increased alienation and feelings of uncoolness. These children were just as anxious and uncertain about the popular culture of their own generation as some of the teachers we worked with. Of course, David prides himself on being careful not to use popular culture in a way that reinforces the role that it plays in students' emerging sense of social hierarchy, the separation of the "haves" and "have nots." But in this instance he failed; his motivation—to engage students in connecting their personal interests to classroom learning—conflicted with a secret motivation to appear receptive to students' pop culture. By wanting to present himself as the cool teacher, he forgot how painful it is *not* to be a cool student.

David also served as an occasional co-facilitator in Tanya's classroom. Tanya taught rising seventh graders, the majority of whom identified with pop, rap, and hip-hop music by artists like Drake and Nicki Minaj, artists that Tanya herself was familiar with. Her connection to contemporary popular culture was helpful in creating general rapport in the classroom. Students who were used to making inside jokes about popular culture knew that they couldn't stump Tanya, and often conversations centered on complex experiences students had with popular music, television, and websites.

One student, however, identified primarily with rock, emo, and metal music, putting her outside of the references that Tanya shared with the rest of her class. Here, David shared some insider knowledge about this genre of music and found some historical precedents and readings to accompany the kind of rock music that this student identified with, in just the same way that Tanya offered vinyl records, films, and other conversations about the lineage of rap and hip-hop.

Still, the most successful class activities were not ones that catered specifically to students' individual interests in popular culture. Instead, students were most engaged when they participated in collaborative discussions and activities that required students to share divergent experiences, tastes, and ideas about popular culture.

In one class, students made personal mixtapes with unique cover art and shared the results with the class. In their final productions, students incorporated their interests in fashion, video games, and popular music into collaborative projects. The Trendsetter motivation at its best can be used to bring students and teachers together in the spirit of inquiry, when both teachers and students are ready to learn from each other's cultural knowledge in a classroom setting.

Puppet Pals

For iPad, ages 5+

http://polishedplay.blogspot.co.at/

Using this iPad app, children create simple stories by selecting characters and backdrops and recording voice and audio to create animated movies.

Understanding Symbols

http://www.brainpopjr.com/socialstudies/citizenship/ussymbols/

On the website BrainPop Junior, a video and postviewing activities help K–3 students understand how symbols stand for things. Children learn the symbols that stand for the United States.

CIVIC ENGAGEMENT AND NEW LITERACIES: THE ACTIVIST AND TEACHER 2.0

Some teachers value digital and media literacy for how it enables active and creative participation both in the classroom and in the world.

Teacher 2.0 is the name we use for teachers who integrate literacy activities and participation in the classroom by using a variety of texts, websites, and frameworks so that students can make connections between classroom content and the kinds of participation that comes naturally at home and in social media environments.

Activists see the power of digital media tools and texts to change the world. They want to harness the power of online participation to foster students' emerging civic engagement at the local, national, and global levels.

Teachers who identify with the Teacher 2.0 motivation understand and imagine "texts" as a broad category, including visual, audio, and social media. These teachers make connections between film adaptations and their literary sources; they have their students create digital storytelling projects that manipulate words, images, and sounds to create new meanings; they are as likely to use cell phones, wikis, photographs, films, and games in daily warm-ups as they are an on-the-board exercise.

Jason Ohler, a highly talented Teacher 2.0, explains how digital storytelling across the curriculum offers a way to harness the tremendously persuasive power of the story form. He offers strategies that give kids the chance to perform stories in front of a green screen, discovering how to create "unreal realities" through chroma-key editing that lets them appear to be "in" any number of settings by manipulating the background and setting.[7] Teacher 2.0 types are drawn to digital and media literacy because of the creative power that can be unleashed by children's use of media technologies.

Activists, by contrast, conceptualize children's participation and engagement in a wider, more public context. Children and young people, working with teachers and parents, can help make society more equitable and just. Civic engagement and democratic participation are essential features of participation in society. But how can educators make students' participation in media meaningful in and out of school in a way that contributes to a healthy democracy? This is a central question for the Activist. By the time they reach high school, many students can become politically cynical because they do not believe that public life is relevant to them. But digital and media literacy can help students see themselves as citizens even at very young ages. Activists want students to see themselves as participants in democracy by addressing real and immediate needs in a particular community, using communication to make a difference in the world.

Various forms of media can be used to articulate and amplify the authentic concerns of young people. When Aggie taught her students about the news media, she wanted them to use their voices to talk back to mainstream news reports about violence. Nuala, another instructor, wanted her fifth-grade students to understand how the media shapes our understanding of the world through the representation of gender, race, and ethnicity. To accomplish this, she used youth media texts, from films to music, to inspire her students to take action.

However, it's not always easy for Activists to connect students to civic causes. Some educators and school leaders are hesitant to engage children in the exploration of political and social issues, including climate change, poverty, and social injustice.

Sometimes educators who explore these causes merely "go through the motions," not asking deep-enough questions of their subject matter. When David engaged his sixth-grade students in studying green roofs and environmental issues in 2009, he imagined that traditional civics would be an appropriate lens through which to think about the issues. But students were more familiar with these social issues in relation to personal actions, like recycling and littering. They had not yet explored environmentalism in a broader social or political context, despite already learning the basics of government, democracy, and taxation.

Conversely, sometimes teachers' concerns can be too complex for elementary students. When students have no personal stake in an issue or lack sufficient background knowledge to make informed opinions, they may compensate by parroting teachers' opinions. For example, Mr. Fitzgerald struggled to get his students to understand the soda tax, a hot-button issue in the Philadelphia community, before they made editorials about it. But Mr. Fitzgerald also had strong feelings about the issue himself, and his framing may have led some students to mimic his own views and argument style rather than consider for themselves the pros and cons of a tax on soda.

Today, teachers at all levels are pushing the boundaries of what counts as a text in the classroom. Gunther Kress and other scholars have observed that most of the symbolic material we encounter in everyday life skillfully blends different types of symbol systems together. Textbooks, newspapers, and other print media have words, photographs, illustrations, and graphics working in combination to express ideas.

To make sense of them demands an understanding of how to read different types of messages.[8]

The key factor that inspires teachers who affiliate with the Teacher 2.0 motivation is an understanding that the classroom is itself a space for culture to be enacted and embodied. Though these teachers may not be motivated by specific social or political causes in the way that Activists are, they likely see teaching itself as in need of a kind of transformation, one that expands both teachers' and students' conceptualization of what it means to be "literate" in a digital era.

REFLECTING ON YOUR MOTIVATIONS

Some of us enjoy reading astrological horoscopes or guides that purport to tell us about our personality, character, and values based on the date of our birth. Our list of teacher motivations is a little like this. You may find yourself identifying with more than one or two of these different motivations because they all have value and significance. On the website, you'll find some other teacher motivations, not mentioned here, that we've found are common among high school teachers and college faculty. We wouldn't want to carry these ideas too far, however—people are far too complicated to be reduced to simple labels.

But we believe that the process of reflecting and understanding our own motivations helps us become more metacognitive about the choices we make in the classroom. As teacher educators, we want to activate the strengths and energy of individual teachers' existing motivations. But because our work on teacher motivations thus far is in the beginning stages, we cannot yet claim to know if there are any "best" motivations, or which motivations are associated with which kinds of learning. Over time an understanding will emerge through the research process. In the meantime, we recognize that teachers are differentially motivated to use media and technology for teaching and learning. Now that you have reflected on your own personal motivations for exploring digital and media literacy, it's time for us to share what we learned from the many teachers who worked with us. In the next chapter, we will dig in to the instructional practices used by teachers in helping children develop their powerful voices through a combination of play and learning.

Lesson   Target Audience Music Remix

Lesson Description

Elementary students explore music composition using remix practices to consider their target audience and purpose while developing creativity and collaboration skills.

Objectives

Students will

- understand that popular songs have a purpose, a message, and a target audience
- label the basic structural elements of song lyrics: verse, chorus, and bridge
- strengthen creativity and collaboration through composing rhymes and performing new lyrics for an existing song

Vocabulary

Message

Audience

Lyric

Rhythm

Verse

Chorus

Bridge

Karaoke

Resources and Materials

✓ Instrumental (or "karaoke") backing track

✓ Original version of song

✓ "Teach Me Media" video available at powerfulvoicesforkids.com

✓ Chart paper

Activity

Access

✓ Explain to students that some musicians are like authors because they compose messages to create new songs.

✓ Play the original version of the song. Children may enjoy two opportunities to listen to the song, once with their ears and once with their bodies (through movement or dance).

Analysis

✓ Ask: What do you like about this song? What do you dislike? Encourage children to identify specific features of the song (beat, lyrics, chorus, instruments, melody, rhyme, etc.).

✓ Discuss: What are the key phrases and ideas (or the characters and story) of the song? Write these messages on the board. To get a full list of phrases, students might need to listen to the song again with this purpose in mind.

Composition

✓ Play the karaoke version, and ask students what is different about this version. Invite them to share what they already know about karaoke as a form of creative play.

✓ Introduce the activity: Create new lyrics for this song to communicate a specific message (about an upcoming school event) to inform and entertain a specific target audience.

✓ Show an example of work created by other students using the "Teach Me Media" video created by students at the Russell Byers Charter School.

✓ Small groups of students work together to develop their lyrics, working under deadline pressure. Invite different small groups to create lyrics for different target audiences (younger children, grandparents, boys, girls, mothers, teachers, teenagers, etc.).

✓ Use brainstorming and improvisation techniques to imagine new lyrics that fit with the music and rhythm of the original song by modifying the message and the purpose within the structure of the song to inform and entertain the target audience.

✓ Each team performs their work and records the new songs using simple audio or video production tools

Reflection

✓ Ask: How did your group's lyrics aim at your target audience? Encourage students to explain their choices.

✓ Discuss: What are some other differences between the new song you created and the original song? Write some of these ideas on the board.

✓ Some people might think that writing new lyrics to an existing song is not that creative. Other people might think it is an example of creative work. What do you think?

✓ What was fun about this project? What was challenging or difficult?

✓ What did you notice about how your team worked together?

Taking Action

✓ Explain that the process of using parts of other people's creative work to create your own messages is called *remix*. It is an example of the "fair use" of copyrighted materials. Remix is an important way to express ideas and can help people develop confidence in their capacity for creative work.

Source: Created by David Cooper Moore.

NOTES

1. Palmer, P. (2008). *The courage to teach.* New York, NY: Wiley (p. 10).
2. Kennedy, M. (2005). *Inside teaching: How classroom life undermines reform.* Cambridge, MA: Harvard University Press.
3. Grafe, S., Bergey, B., & Hobbs, R. (2012). *Does digital and media literacy support civic engagement?* Digital Media & Learning Conference, March 3, San Francesco, CA.
4. We asked instructors and teachers to reflect on their teaching in two ways: through conversation and in writing. In the summer learning program, at the end of each day, we met for 45 minutes for an informal but structured conversation about what we noticed in our own work. Teachers were also

asked to write in a wikispace set up as an online journal to respond to specific prompts at least once a week. We asked them to write about their practice at the end of a process during which they designed, implemented, and assessed a digital and media literacy learning activity. *Instructors* (identified by their first names) were undergraduate and graduate students, all new or first-time teachers, who participated in a summer learning program. You can learn more about instructors by flipping back to Resource D, at the back of the book. *Teachers* (identified by their surnames) were classroom educators who worked full-time with our partner school and participated in various staff development programs.

5. Kellner, D., & Share, J. (2007). Critical media literacy is not an option. *Learning Inquiry, 1,* 59–69.
6. Developmental psychologists have studied children's beliefs in the reality of supernatural beings (like Bugs Bunny, the Tooth Fairy, and Santa Claus) and their tendency to label certain events as "magic."
7. Ohler, J. (2008). *Digital storytelling in the classroom.* Thousand Oaks, CA: Corwin.
8. Kress, G. (2003). *Literacy in a new media age.* London, UK: Routledge.

Part II
Work With Intermediate Students

3 Connecting Culture and Classroom

In this chapter, you'll learn about

The Connections Between Digital Media, Mass Media, Popular Culture, and Learning Goals

- How can teachers use all of the resources in children's culture—including their media culture—to enrich learning experiences?

Promoting Intellectual Curiosity

- Children's talk in the classroom leads to surprises. How can teachers structure conversations to spark students' intellectual curiosity?

Getting Community Leaders and Media Professionals on Board

- How can teachers, community leaders, and professionals work together to help students experience the power of collaboration, communication, and civic engagement to make a difference in the world?

Imagining the City as a Classroom

- How can teachers use access, analysis, and creative activities to help answer children's complicated and difficult questions about the world around them?

Mona wanted to explore poetry and rhyme with her Grade 3 students, helping them appreciate language and recognize how sound and rhythm work together. After reading poems and music lyrics, children wrote their own poems. Mona regularly played her guitar for children and helped them set their words to music to learn more about rhythm and rhyme. But it was an unexpected visit from someone from outside the school—Caroline, a media professional—who inspired Mona to use the power of poetry to take on a community action project about littering.

The Powerful Voices for Kids instructors were encouraged to reach out to community leaders and media professionals specializing in the Internet, advertising, journalism, and film to come to the school to meet with children who were learning about the media. The idea: to bridge the gap between the classroom and the culture. Renee was inspired by the work of Marshall McLuhan, who wrote a book in 1977 called *City as Classroom: Understanding Language and Media.* McLuhan emphasized that learners were shaped by the total cultural environment, not just the pedagogical techniques of the classroom. McLuhan emphasized the educational role of the city as classroom, seeing much learning potential in the larger cultural environment that represented the increasingly interconnected world, the *global village.*[1]

Some instructors and teachers reached out to friends and colleagues while others made cold calls to those who worked in city government, local nonprofit organizations, or media businesses. One day, Caroline, a creative services professional from LevLane, an advertising agency in Philadelphia, came in to the school. David had encouraged her to talk to children in Mona's classroom about the city's new "Unlitter Us" public service campaign. In 2010, the City of Philadelphia's Recycling Office had sponsored the largest-ever anti-litter campaign using spoken word poetry compositions and street poet performances. Along with billboard advertising and TV public service announcements, the campaign included street poetry events, Facebook and Twitter presence, and block-by-block community mobilization.[2]

Caroline worked with children to brainstorm poetry about why a clean city is important to them. She and Mona led children in an activity in which they explored the idea that litter diminishes a community's emotional well-being. Could children inspire others by sharing their emotional response to litter and, in the process, activate behavior change and help create new social norms whereby littering is considered not acceptable?

When Caroline emailed the children after her class visit, she encouraged them to produce their own public service announcement video, which could then be used as part of the Unlitter Us campaign. Mona read aloud the email that Caroline had sent. As Mona remembers it, "The students practically had a mental breakdown when I read them Caroline's feedback. They were so excited! They got really pumped up about creating an ad."

In helping children appreciate what would be involved in creating their own public service announcement, Mona explained the sequence of steps involved:

- Get a clear understanding of the persuasive goal
- Brainstorm and compose the words to the poem
- Edit the poem, keeping the audience and purpose in mind
- Select specific locations to match the message of each line
- Practice setting up the camera and check the sound
- Rehearse by reading aloud in front of a camera
- Edit to include only the best shots
- Send the completed video to the advertising agency

As she explained this process, Mona decided that she'd take personal responsibility for editing the video in order to keep the total project time to only 2 days. She was familiar with iMovie software, she explained. But the children would need to be responsible for everything else.

To understand their persuasive goal, Mona introduced children to the genre of public service announcements. After watching some other video public service announcements created by media professionals for the Unlitter Us campaign, Mona asked the children, "What kinds of feelings do you get after watching these videos?" Children's responses included "I feel sad," "I want to encourage other people to keep the city clean," and "This makes me want to change something." Mona explained that their poem would need to activate the same type of feelings. Were they ready?

Of course they were. Children worked collaboratively with a partner to compose rhyming lines of poetry. Each child got to read a line, and the last line was spoken in chorus by the whole group. Mona explains what happened next: "We decided on shots, went out into the city, and they shot videos of each other. When we went back in class, we watched all the footage they took, and they actually critiqued each other!" Children offered thoughtful responses on the performances of their peers in ways that were helpful and supportive. It was a magical moment, as Mona remembers it. They offered meaningful peer feedback and coaching. The children were working as members of a team, so proud to be able to create something that would be visible to their family and community. The video was posted on the Philadelphia Unlitter Us Facebook page as a way to illustrate the power of all citizens—even the youngest ones—to make a difference in their community.

Unlitter Us

Video Public Service Announcement

Grade 3 Students

www.powerfulvoicesforkids.com

We need a big help or our city will yelp
This is our home, it can't be all gone
If it doesn't matter, our memories will shatter
If we don't take a stand, there will be no land
Come on, let's pitch in, don't you want this land to win?
If we don't litter, our city will glitter
If we're not mean, our city will be clean
And it will seem to gleam like a perfect dream
Keep Philadelphia clean! Unlitter us!

In the process of producing this particular video public service announcement, children were encouraged to think more deeply about both language and littering. This project was just right in scale, tone, and scope for young learners, with an authentic audience and real-world purpose.

Some researchers have found that when teachers experiment with digital media production in the elementary classroom, they may design and implement projects that can be overly ambitious, complex, and time-consuming, often as a result of their lack of experience with the medium. In a large-scale production, teachers may encounter technical difficulties that decrease their motivation to continue to experiment with new digital tools.[3] Unfortunately, some elementary-level video productions go uncompleted because teachers do not anticipate the level of challenges involved in even a very basic production. (We will talk more about learning opportunities and design challenges in different levels of media production in Chapter 5.)

For these reasons, the Unlitter Us project was a good model for an elementary-level collaborative media project that accomplished key civic engagement goals by tapping into an existing community initiative, using careful structuring of the production process by the teacher, and taking advantage of support from community leaders and media professionals.

LEARNING TO DISCUSS REAL-WORLD ISSUES IN AN EVER-WIDENING WORLD

Teachers know that a person's sense of responsibility for self, family, community, and nation and her or his capacity to act civically are strongly associated with socialization. One dimension of socialization is the practice of civic engagement in the elementary grades, which often takes the form of learning about social services offered in a community, participating in fundraising projects, and taking on simple social action initiatives that are sometimes tied to disaster news or other relevant news and current events. Through these activities, children develop skills and habits of mind, including tolerance for cultural difference, building community, and supporting collective action on common goals.

In his 1916 book *Democracy and Education*, philosopher and educational reformer John Dewey argued that we must not take for granted the formation of the habits and virtues required for democracy.[4] These habits of mind are developed by participating in democratic communities—places where groups of individuals join together around community interests and where there is dialogue among those holding differing views.

Not surprisingly, robust classroom dialogue and discussion turn out to be strongly associated with the quality of young people's civic engagement and their overall success in school. But although elementary educators greatly value discussion as an instructional technique, they may struggle with the many challenges of creating meaningful discussion with young learners. Many teachers comment on how much time it takes to involve all children in discussion. Mandated programs and the impact of standardized testing limit many creative activities, including time for conversation and dialogue with children.

But discussion skills need to be emphasized at every grade level.

Without explicit instruction, disruptive student behaviors may discourage teachers from using dialogue in the classroom. Generating good discussion among young children can be challenging when children fail to take turns, demonstrate poor listening skills, or display a lack of mutual respect for peers. Teachers recognize how differences in listening skills can affect the entire process.[5] And teachers may get frustrated or worn down by the "me, too" phenomenon, where one child's idea or comment inspires other children to make the same point over and over again, creating an echo chamber effect that deadens the quality and value of a discussion.

Teachers who model desirable behaviors consistently and provide guided practice on these skills can see real changes among their students within a just a couple of weeks. Other teachers have experimented with small-group experiences as a forum for informal dialogue. One elementary teacher explained, "With a large group, in order for everyone to share something, it just takes so much longer and you lose their attention. They are not as interested and engaged in the discussion in a large-group setting."[6] When teachers are prepared and active listeners, they demonstrate their own good listening skills and ask appropriate follow-up questions.

Guidelines for Speaking and Listening

When You Speak	When You Listen
Have a clear and original message.	Think about what the speaker is saying.
Take your time but let others have a turn.	Don't interrupt.
Say what you think.	Consider the speaker's words and feelings.
Say why you think it.	Keep your mind and heart open.
Build on what others say.	Use your eyes to show you're listening.
Pay attention to feedback.	Make a connection to what others say.
Ask questions when you don't understand.	Keep your body alert and attentive.
Be aware of the sounds in the room.	Respect each other's opinions.

When elementary educators introduce children to the practice of civic education, many use the concentric circle model of the ever-widening world. Children begin by learning about families and neighborhoods, then move on to explore cities, states, nation, and, finally, the world. In the 1920s, Harold Rugg, a professor at Columbia Teachers College and a co-founder of the National Council for the Social Studies, wanted children to think deeply about real-world problems in their families, neighborhoods, cities, states, and nations. He created educational materials for young children in the elementary grades that explored contemporary problems and their historical backgrounds.[7] At the time, this approach was thought to be radical in that it encouraged children to consider the real-world problems of the world around them, including issues like immigration, poverty, crime, and the economy.

It is sometimes called the *democratic method in action* model, with a focus on the fundamental practice of citizenship: gathering information, weighing the evidence and making decisions, and participating in collective community action. Today, it's common for children to learn about the real-world problems and issues that face their community at the local, national, and international levels. For children, concerns about violence, unemployment, homelessness, drug abuse, and the environment may be topics of concern.

DEVELOPING GLOBAL UNDERSTANDING

For all children growing up in a multicultural society, issues of immigration and cultural difference are important. Children deepen their cultural understanding of others through the use of mass media, photographs, and digital learning experiences. Working with the Wayne Elementary School in suburban Philadelphia, Renee and her graduate students collaborated with classroom teachers to create a variety of learning experiences to promote cultural understanding of the peoples and cultures of the Middle East. With support from an in-school mentor, Grade 3 and 4 children completed the following activities:

- Children identified inaccurate visual stereotypes of the Middle East that are embedded in children's films, advertising, news, and entertainment media.
- They asked critical questions about a message in order to analyze the author and purpose.
- Children learned about the many nations and cultures of the Middle East through the use of library resources and online databases.
- They viewed and discussed narrative films to understand contemporary life in the Middle East and increase a sense of emotional connectedness.
- Small groups created simple videos to represent their own cultural heritage and day-to-day family life to others.
- Using a simple wiki, children participated in an online asynchronous chat with young people from Kuwait in order to form social relationships across cultures.

This project used many of the learning outcomes that are shown in Resource A, including the practices of access, analysis, evaluation, collaboration, composition, and taking action. In measuring the impact of these experiences on young learners, we found that both students and teachers decreased their reliance on cultural stereotypes and increased their knowledge and appreciation of the peoples and cultures of the Middle East.[8]

In some communities, it's not easy to create classroom cultures where children learn to appreciate cultural difference. When classrooms are monocultural, this can be a particular challenge. One group of researchers used photographs to promote acceptance of diversity in elementary classrooms by leading discussions with children using photographs of disabled, Muslim, and poor children from around the world. In this study, students were able to form emotional connections between other children's lives and experiences. But several students felt threatened by the image of someone who was different. Some children lacked the frame of reference to understand the children in the photographs. When asked what he would say to a person who was culturally different from himself, one third grader answered that he would "tell them to get back where they came from. I don't want them here."[9]

Children have complicated and sometimes unpredictable responses to topics such as war, terrorism, and violence. No doubt about it: This work is challenging. Many classroom teachers are not used to classroom talk about controversial contemporary issues that tap into and activate some of the dialogue children may hear at home about social and political issues. Some classroom teachers are not comfortable when their students use examples from contemporary films, television, video games, and social media, especially if they lack knowledge about the specific references that children are making.

Teachers with firmly held beliefs about the innocence of childhood may feel the urge to protect children from certain media depictions. For example, in our work on exploring stereotypes of the Middle East as depicted in contemporary media, most Grade 3 children were eager to discuss the film *Iron Man*, a 2008 superhero film directed by Jon Favreau and starring Robert Downey, Jr. as an engineer who builds a powerful exoskeleton and becomes a technologically advanced superhero. But discussing this film posed a problem. Although most children had already seen the film, its PG-13 rating meant that the trailer could not be screened in class, not even as a means to stimulate discussion of Middle East stereotypes. The school had a strict policy: No films above a PG rating were permitted.[10]

Teachers who are unfamiliar with children's daily exposure to mass media culture may have distorted expectations about what kinds of film and media texts children are be able to use and understand. As we will show next, contemporary media texts enable children to access and explore important concepts they may not be able to access through written texts.[11]

> ### Teaching About Movie and TV Ratings With Assignment: Media Literacy
>
> *http://mediaeducationlab.com/elementary-school-unit-5-ratings-and-reviews*
>
> Watch a video that shows how people of different ages, from 5 to 50, interpret messages differently based on their life experience and knowledge of the world. Lesson plans help children understand the TV and movie ratings systems.

THE CITY AS CLASSROOM: GRADE 3 STUDENTS LEARN ABOUT HOMELESSNESS

Elementary children naturally view their school neighborhood as a place of discovery. When digital media is used to explore and represent their neighborhood, the unpredictable events of daily life can inspire teachable moments that can have lasting value for learners.

With her Grade 3 students, Rachel was determined to find a way to get children out of the building as part of a multimedia learning experience. She had begun exploring simple media production software called Comic Life, where users combine language, photos, and drawings to create graphic panels. Working with a small team, students had gone to Logan Square (sometimes called Logan's Circle), a small park only steps away from their school. They took photos of the historic Swann Memorial Fountain, a fountain sculpture by Alexander Stirling Calder, which features large Native American figures to symbolize the area's major rivers: the Delaware, the Schuylkill, and the Wissahickon. Numerous bronze animals, including frogs, turtles, and swans spout water toward the large water geyser in the center.

During one visit to the park, students took their Flip cameras to capture some photos of the fountain to complete their narratives. While there, Delia, age 9, approached Rachel and pointed across the square. There was a homeless man, sleeping on a park bench, and just behind him, a shopping cart from a local grocery store filled with his clothing and other belongings. An elderly woman was digging through the bags in a furious manner while the man slept. "What's going on, Miss Rachel?" Delia asked. "I think that lady is stealing from that homeless guy there."[12]

Rachel looked over, and indeed the incident did seem a bit unusual. As a somewhat new city dweller herself, Rachel realized at that moment that she actually tended to avoid looking at the actions of the more downtrodden residents on the streets of Philadelphia. But many children have not learned to avoid such incidents. Delia's eyes were riveted to the scene, and she kept saying, "Look, Miss Rachel, she's stealing from him!"

What should Rachel do? In the flash of the moment, Rachel had little time to ponder her options. She was feeling the burden of her role model identity as a teacher to make sense of the situation for her students, many of whom were now also looking at the curious incident. She could tell the children to look away and ignore the ongoing scene—but then, wouldn't she be encouraging her students to be callous bystanders? She didn't want her students to see the world as a place where we just turn our heads when we encounter other people's troubles.

Impulsively, Rachel went over to the homeless man's encampment in Logan Square and asked the lady who was digging through the shopping cart what she was doing. She said she was the wife of the homeless man and that she was trying to find her cigarettes. "He'll be OK in a couple of hours," she said about the man lying on the park bench.

Rachel returned to where the children had gathered and they walked back to the classroom. The children had so many questions: Why was he sleeping in the daytime? Was the lady really his wife? What was in the shopping cart? Could it have been dangerous for Rachel to approach them? Why are they so dirty? How do people get to be homeless? These were difficult questions indeed.

As she reflected on the situation, Rachel wondered if she had in fact done the right thing. With her students listening with rapt attention, Rachel acknowledged to them that she couldn't answer any of their questions because she didn't understand the problem of homelessness herself. At the end of the day, she announced to the children, "Maybe we can learn more about homelessness tomorrow."

The class launched into an exploration of homelessness. Rachel found a variety of resources for children to examine. They learned that on any given day, there are about 4,000 homeless people in shelters or on the streets in Philadelphia,[13] and across America, about 650,000 people, including thousands of children.[14] What causes homelessness? When people lack jobs, housing, and health care, when they are victims of domestic violence or have problems with alcoholism, substance abuse, or mental illness, homelessness may occur.

Of course, these were difficult subjects to talk about, but children seemed to recognize the seriousness of the subject matter and were eager to learn. Also, while they had a lot of questions, they also had a lot of information to share. One child talked to her mom, who told her that homeless people could sometimes be dangerous if they didn't have proper medications for their mental illness. Another student thought that even people with a good education could become homeless because he had seen the movie *Pursuit of Happyness*, in which Will Smith plays the part of an entrepreneur whose bad investments financially break the family apart, leaving him and his young son homeless, sleeping in a subway station and a homeless shelter. In the movie, we see that he is able to get a job and find a house for his family.

For several days, children's questions about homelessness became the organizing frame for the classroom, as Rachel helped them learn more about homelessness by using a variety of print, media, and online sources. She didn't feel comfortable having students work independently using the open Internet to explore this topic, however. Not only was she concerned that it would slow down the momentum of this particular project, but she was also concerned that children might stumble upon inappropriate content. When Rachel herself had used YouTube to search for videos about homelessness, she found videos of teens and young adults beating up homeless people as a form of entertainment. She naturally wanted to protect her students from content of this type.[15]

Instead, Rachel selected a variety of websites that she felt were appropriate for her students and displayed them to the children. The class did whole-group reading, interpretation, and discussion of content from news websites and from nonprofit advocacy organizations.

Rachel wasn't fully aware of how much value children were getting from this practice of reviewing information and ideas from websites she had selected for discussion until she invited an advocate for the homeless to come to the school to be interviewed by the children. He brought along a children's picture book about a snail who loses his shell. Actually, the book was a little "young" for children who had, by this time, already delved quite deeply into the topic. He was speaking metaphorically about the snail who lost his shell, while children were asking him questions like "How many homeless shelters are there in Philadelphia?" and "What do kids do if a member of their family loses their home?" The homeless advocate had not anticipated that children would have already learned so much about homelessness. He was surprised at the quality and depth of the children's questions.

When children were ready to create their comic, Rachel assigned children to work with a partner, assigning partners so that children with different kinds of ability were placed together. Each pair was responsible for composing a comic page about one of the topics the children had developed through their inquiry. One group explored the issue of media stereotypes about homelessness in the movies. Another group looked at why people are homeless. Still another group examined ways children can help those who are homeless. You can see a video that shows how the children worked together throughout the process at www.powerfulvoicesforkids.com.

During the production process, Rachel encouraged warm and cool feedback to help children discover how their work was being understood by other readers. *Warm feedback* offers information about features of the creative work that are valued and appreciated by readers, listeners, or viewers. *Cool feedback* offers ideas and interpretations about confusing or unclear elements of the creative work, enabling the creator to revise his or her own work. When warm and cool feedback are incorporated as a regular part of classroom instruction, it promotes awareness of the interpretation process and motivates the revision process.

Helping children understand and value revision is a fundamental early literacy competency. When the writing and revision process is understood as merely making written comments on texts, it is possible to overlook the context of the relationship between the author and the audience.[16] The particular quality of the caring relationship, as Nel Noddings has shown, influences how feedback is produced and interpreted. Promoting a climate of authenticity, respect, and trust is essential to nurturing the reciprocally dependent relationship between author and audience that supports the multimedia composition process.[17]

A TEACHER'S JOURNAL

Rachel's students created a comic titled *The Life of a Homeless Person*, which uses a combination of photographs, original drawings, dialogue, and writing. This collaboratively produced student multimedia project—a 14-page nonfiction comic book, created with a digital camera and simple multimedia production software—was shared with their families, civic leaders, and the school community.

While creating the comic with her students, Rachel kept track of how she used time in the classroom:

Day 1. Wednesday. We talked about our many questions about homelessness, and some of the children described their previous experiences with homeless people. We discussed how the comic form can tell fictional stories or tell true stories, and I showed examples of different types of comics and graphic novels. We then brainstormed ideas to create a homeless comic that would teach people about homelessness. Children worked in groups and wrote down some things that they were interested in learning about the homeless. After reviewing the entire list, teams of children decided what topics they wanted to explore in their section of the comic.

Day 2. Thursday. Each group read or viewed a short book, article, or video that I found for them. Each group took notes on the material and began writing 10 sentences (with their partner) to capture the main ideas. We discussed the similarities and differences of the materials we were using to gather information.

Day 3. Friday. We finished writing our 10 sentences and then did a whole-group feedback, edit, and revise session. We made sure that sentences did not repeat ideas or say trivial things (half of the groups had at least one sentence saying: the homeless don't have homes). Students then attempted to make story boards, but this went very badly due to lack of preparation on my part. I didn't structure it well. Plus, it's not a good idea to start something like this at the end of the week.

Day 4. Monday. I found about 30 images online of homeless people and projected them for the class to see. We discussed them, and children selected which ones they wanted to be in their comic. I asked "why" questions to help them reflect on their preferences. All the children wanted to have their own drawings in the comic as well as photographs, so today we began drawing the images. The rules for drawing images: no narration, no speech bubbles, because both will be added in when we put the whole thing together using the Comic Life software. They gained a sense of pride in learning to use the software tool to create their comic panels. The class was split into groups for this—so half the class drew while the other half worked with me on the board thinking up questions to ask the homeless shelter representative. We also worked on some simple storyboarding, where the students were asked to draw out the panels they wanted on their two pages, and put narration boxes in the panels, and plan out what image they looked at or what drawing they were going to use in the panels.

Day 5. Tuesday. We met the representative from Project HOME, who read a story about a homeless snail and then children interviewed him with the questions they wrote yesterday. It went well. The representative had some good things to say, and the kids were able to expand on their questions a little by carefully listening. We then continued to edit our sentences so that they reflected some things he had told us (especially about what we can do if we see a homeless person who needs help). Then children completed the drawings from Monday and began working in Comic Life to put together the comic.

Day 6. Wednesday. Children worked on producing their comic panels.

Day 7. Thursday. As a large group, we looked at all the children's panels and did a feedback, edit, and revise session. Children were working hard to make their panels compelling and attractive. We decided to add author information at the top of each page so the children were visually represented as the authors of their pages.

Day 8. Friday. We developed the cover page by thinking about our target audience and our purpose and then deciding on a title and a central image. Children practiced reading aloud from the 14 pages of the comic, standing in front of the image projected on a screen, as they prepared to give a final presentation about what we learned.

Day 9. Monday. We discussed the concept of target audience and predicted how parents, teachers, and other adults would respond to the comic. Children offered each other warm feedback about what they valued about other members of the team. It was a very warm session. Each child received a copy of the completed comic to share with family members, and children placed copies of the comic in the mailboxes of the school leaders and teaching staff.

Day 10. Tuesday. Children made a short presentation about their comic in an all-school assembly.

ELEMENTS OF EFFECTIVE PEDAGOGY

Five features of this instruction made the learning experience powerful:

- An improvisational decision to use the teachable moment to structure a full-fledged unit of instruction
- The teacher's openness to address children's difficult questions
- A clear focus on the information-gathering process
- Well-structured use of collaborative teams in the process of writing, creative media production, feedback, and revision
- Composing in a medium that combines language and images in sequential order with an easy-to-use software tool

Students in Rachel's class analyzed depictions in homelessness in some of the popular movies with which they were familiar. In Figure 3.1, a student compares the portrayal of homelessness in *Aladdin* to the more realistic depiction in the film *Pursuit of Happyness*. Use of copyrighted imagery from popular culture in their work was a frequent occurrence in the Powerful Voices for Kids program. We discuss teachers' and students' rights to repurpose copyrighted imagery in the classroom in Chapter 5.

The production of the homelessness comic helped children recognize that informational messages can come in many forms: fiction and nonfiction books, TV documentaries, video stories, youth media productions, and more. Children developed an understanding of the role of research and information gathering by reading, viewing, and discussing new information from a variety of sources and reaching out to community experts. The cycle of feedback and revision was absolutely central to the success of the homelessness comic. Through warm and cool feedback, these students understood the role and skills employed by an editor, felt more comfortable taking creative risks in front of their peers, and gained confidence and self-esteem.

Most important, children had frank conversations in order to understand some complex social problems: poverty, mental illness, and substance abuse. Classmates contributed their ideas to a meaningful issue that many people choose to ignore. Children increased their feelings of empathy and reduced their fear of homeless people.

Figure 3.1 The Life of a Homeless Person

The experience emerged as the result of an accidental encounter, witnessed by students, between their teacher and a homeless person. In the process of activating their curiosity, gathering and analyzing information, and representing what they learned, children were empowered to see the city as a place where learning happens. They exercised civic agency by individually and collectively engaging in society in order to address an issue of public concern: the causes and consequences of homelessness.

In this chapter, we've shown that media literacy classrooms are places where a great deal of child talk goes on. When learners do most of the talking, learning is dynamic and grounded, and yet sometimes unpredictable. One of the reasons media literacy pedagogy is so revolutionary in elementary education is that it creates rich, original moments of child-centered talk that makes it impossible to use the so-called *recitation script* in which brief recall answers and minimal (and often superficial) feedback are the norm.[18]

This form of dialogic pedagogy is especially useful in counteracting these potentially unproductive routines. Authentic dialogue can help teachers find the sweet spot for student motivation and engagement. When children are encouraged by their teachers to use the city and community as inspiration for learning that promotes civic engagement, they discover the social power that comes from turning thoughts and ideas into actions that make a difference in the world.

Lesson — Creating Realistic Dialogue

Lesson Description

Children learn about how to translate ordinary conversation into realistic written dialogue by creating a simple comic.

Objectives

Students will

- Participate in conversation
- Use an audio recorder
- Listen to and transcribe spoken language into printed words
- Edit and modify to create realistic dialogue
- Understand how the style of speaking affects an audience's reaction to dialogue
- Create a comic using both real and made-up dialogue

Vocabulary

Comic

Panel

Realistic-unrealistic

Speech bubble

Dialogue

Dialect/accent

Tone

Conversation

Character

Resources and Materials

✓ Samples of comic books (in print or online)

✓ Samples of dialogue from a book, script, or play

✓ Voice recorder—audio, video, or computer

✓ Comic drawing software (e.g., Comic Life) or paper and pencils

Activity

Access

✓ Explain that many stories start with an idea from ordinary life and ordinary conversation. Explain that an audio recorder creates a digital record of a spoken conversation.

✓ Select a pair of students, and have them discuss something they like together. Demonstrate how to use a voice recorder (maybe a video camera, a cell phone, or a computer) to record what they say. Let the students talk about whatever they want for 3 minutes. At the end of the 3 minutes, have the students listen to what they said on the recorder, and discuss what spoken language sounds like.

✓ Pick a small segment, and transcribe it word for word. As you do, discuss why this form of dialogue is considered "realistic" because it closely approximates how people really talk. Create a contrast by making up some "unrealistic" sentences that look good on paper but don't sound like real people talking.

Analysis

✓ When dialogue is written down, it becomes a script. Show different examples of written dialogue—in books, scripts, and comics. Explain how panels structure time by representing a sequence of actions through a series of boxes placed on the page.

✓ Have students look at the sample transcription and listen to the voices, and have them decide whether the dialogue is realistic or unrealistic. When speaking is depicted with words, writers have a lot of choices. They must decide how to represent nonverbal sounds like sighs, pauses, or stutters. They must decide how to capture slang, baby talk, accent, and the tone of voice. What changes to the written transcription would help it be more effective as a work of writing?

Composition

✓ Using the voice recorder, partners record 3 minutes of dialogue. Then they select an excerpt to transcribe. Each child should transcribe what her or his partner says. Then have the students make a comic that includes this written dialogue and adds drawings of characters and objects. But be sure to have them think about how their words can change meaning depending on the style of speech bubble and where it is placed on the page.

Reflection

✓ Have the students share their work, and hold a class discussion on what could happen next in the story that has been started. According to the style of bubble and content of the dialogue, what could happen to advance the plot?

✓ Why is dialogue on paper not generally just transcribed from an audio recorder? How does editing improve dialogue?

Taking Action

✓ Creative written expression can be inspired by the ordinary talk and actions that are all around us.

Source: Created by Rachel Hobbs.

NOTES

1. McLuhan, M. (1977). *City as classroom: Understanding language and media.* Agincourt, Ontario: The Book Society of Canada.
2. Smith-Teutsch, A. (2010, April 26). City of Philadelphia uses street poets to convey anti-littering campaign. *Waste & Recycling News.* Retrieved from http://www.wasterecyclingnews.com/atourdisp2.html?id=1272466729

3. Sadik, A. (2008). Digital storytelling: A meaningful technology-integrated approach for engaged student learning. *Educational Technology Research and Development, 56,* 487–506.

4. Dewey, J. (1916). *Democracy and education.* New York, NY: Macmillan.

5. Buchanan, L. (2011). Discussion in the elementary classroom: How and why some teachers use discussion. *Georgia Social Studies Journal, 1*(1), 19–31.

6. Buchanan. (2011, p. 29).

7. Bisland, B. (2009). Two traditions in the social studies curriculum for the elementary grades: The textbooks of Paul R. Hanna and Harold O. Rugg. *Journal of Social Studies Research, 33*(2), 155–196.

8. Hobbs, R., Yoon, J., Al-Humaidan, R., Ebrahimi, A., & Cabral, N. (2011). Online digital media in elementary school. *Journal of Middle East Media, 7*(1), 1–23. Retrieved from http://www2.gsu.edu/~wwwaus/JMEM_home.html

9. Lintner, T. (2005). A world of difference: Teaching tolerance through photographs in elementary school. *The Social Studies, 96*(1), 34–37.

10. Hobbs, R., Ebrahimi, A., Cabral, N., Yoon, J., & Al-Humaidan, R. (2011). Field-based teacher education in elementary media literacy as a means to promote global understanding. *Action for Teacher Education, 33,* 144–156.

11. De Block, L. (2010). TV talk and children's identities. In C. Bazalgette (Ed.), *Teaching media in primary schools* (pp. 1–21). London, England: Sage.

12. Hobbs, R. (2013). Improvization and strategic risk taking in informal learning with digital media literacy. *Learning, Media and Technology, 38*(2), 1–28.

13. Project HOME. (2006–2013). *Facts on homelessness.* Retrieved from http://projecthome.org/advocacy/facts.php

14. U.S. Interagency Council on Homelessness. (2011). *Opening doors: Federal strategic plan to prevent and end homelessness.* Retrieved from http://www.usich.gov/resources/uploads/asset_library/AnnualUpdate2011.pdf

15. Moore, D. C. (2013). Bringing the world to school: Integrating news and media literacy in elementary classrooms. *Journal of Media Literacy Education, 5*(1), 326–336.

16. Lee, G., & Schallert, D. (2008). Constructing trust between teacher and students through feedback and revision cycles in an EFL writing classroom. *Written Communication, 25,* 506–537.

17. Noddings, N. (1984). *Caring: A feminine approach to ethics and moral education.* Berkeley: University of California Press.

18. Nystrand, M. (1997). *Opening dialogue: Understanding the dynamics of language and learning in the classroom.* New York, NY: Teachers College Press; Alexander, R. (2008). *Essays on pedagogy.* London: Routledge (p. 93).

4 Asking Questions About Media and Popular Culture

In this chapter, you'll learn about

Asking Questions and Getting Answers

- What kinds of questions enable students to develop their powerful voices? How can children learn to identify an author's purpose?

What's Appropriate and Inappropriate

- When teachers connect to students' popular culture, they help create bridges between students' in-school learning and out-of-school lives. How can teachers engage, rather than ignore or deflect, the reactions and learning opportunities that arise when popular culture enters the classroom?

Dealing With Fame, Celebrity Culture, and Social Power

- Why do children sometimes imitate the behaviors and attitudes of famous people? How do teachers create meaningful conversations about social media like Facebook and decisions about information sharing?

The Role of Improvisation in Teaching Digital and Media Literacy

- How can teachers feel more comfortable responding skillfully to the here-and-now dynamics of intense social interaction among students and teacher?

Dee's students asked many different kinds of questions. They asked questions like:

"Why do they put toys in a Happy Meal?"

"Do you like Nicki Minaj's music?"

"How did you learn to play the piano?"

"How far away is Florida?"

"Can I ask my mom for a pet snake?"

"Will you show me how to make puffy letters like that?"

"Why do people get sick?"

"Why is chocolate your favorite flavor?"

"Did you ever watch Dragon Ball Z?"

Dee was proud of how she supported the speaking and listening skills of 7-, 8-, and even some 9-year-olds. She experienced the power of talk and dialogue to stimulate and extend children's thinking.[1] She offered praise to children who responded to questions in full sentences and to those who offered novel or unexpected ideas. She helped children construct more complex sentences by encouraging them to use reasoning and evidence to support their ideas. She recognized that the experiences children have both at home and in and out of school are highly significant to their development.

As an African American teacher working with children of the same ethnic background, Dee appreciated the complex lives and cultural experiences of her students—these children were diverse individuals living in families from many different neighborhoods in Philadelphia, and they were certainly not reducible to simple socioeconomic or demographic categorizations.

When Dee asked her students questions in order to promote speaking and listening, she distinguished between more routine forms of question-and-answer sessions or the listen-and-tell storytelling that is common in elementary classrooms. She knew that language development is fundamental to all learning and that, as children aim to make sense of their lives, active support from teachers and collaborative peer learning can promote *metacognition*, where children think about their own thinking through sharing, listening, reflecting, and taking action. So when children spoke, Dee listened actively, asked specific follow-up questions, and probed children's understanding.

Instructional practices should reflect the social context and lived experience of the learner. After all, pedagogies themselves are, as Robin Alexander has put it, a "cultural intervention in individual human development which is deeply saturated with the values and history of the society and community in which it is located."[2]

Every type of pedagogy described in this book consists of some structured form of talk and action—talk that "mediates the cognitive and cultural spaces between adult and child, between teacher and learner, between society and the individual, between what the child knows and understands and what he or she has yet to know and understand." [3]

ADDRESSING THE UNEXPECTED MOMENT

But sometimes children's unexpected questions may flummox even the best of teachers. For example, one day in Dee's classroom, the topic of Tiger Woods came up. As the highest paid professional athlete in the world, Woods earned $90.5 million from winnings and endorsements in 2010.[4] Dee's students had a lot to share on the topic.

One little boy, Tyson, asked, "Did he hit his wife or something?"

Another boy chipped in, saying, "And he was so scared."

One child added, "And his wife was screaming at him until he cried."

Dee was startled by the children's comments; she did not anticipate that her students would be following the particular news of the case. But Dee recognized that this was a topic that would be familiar in many households where African American sports celebrities were recognized and respected. In February 2010, Woods had delivered a televised speech from the PGA Tour headquarters in Florida, where he admitted that he had been unfaithful to his wife. He apologized for the hurt his behavior caused to his family, friends, fans, and business partners.[5]

Because Dee could see that some children were not aware of what was being discussed, she offered additional background knowledge to the children:

> Recently in the news, Tiger Woods has been getting media coverage for something bad he did. He cheated on his wife. Now he has never cheated in the game of golf, which is what he's known for. He did this cheating in his personal life. But since Nike gave him a lot of money to be a spokesperson, they wanted him to apologize. Being a spokesperson is a lot of responsibility.

Dee was in uncomfortable territory, and, as a result, she was structuring an interpretation of the event on behalf of her students. Her inner alarm bells were ringing. She just didn't feel right letting her students share what they knew and felt about this topic.

Then Zaiah piped up with a unexpected question. "Did he want to apologize?"

What a fascinating and important question it was. Zaiah wanted to inquire about the motivation and internal mental state of Tiger Woods, an act of imagination that may have elicited a lot of sharing of opinions and ideas, including questions about personal integrity, motives, and social responsibility. But Dee was not comfortable. These children were so young! This topic was so complex and messy. What should she do?

The Question Game

Two participants decide on a topic and generate as many questions about it as they can. One person starts with an open-ended question, then the other person responds with a related open-ended question. This goes back and forth as long as they can continue without making a statement or repeating a previous question. For example, the game might begin by exploring questions related to an object in the room, such as a light bulb:

A: Why is it important to have light?

B: Where does light come from?

A: What is the difference between sunlight and indoor light?

B: Can blind people see light?

A: Which do you prefer: summer days with longer light or winter days with less light?

When the players run out of questions, it's time to reflect: Write down the most interesting question and explain how you would learn more about it.

Source: Adapted from Youth Learn (www.youthlearn.org).

CURRICULUM AS TALK AND ACTION

When teachers set up interesting situations and children learn to engage in asking questions and giving answers, their questions will generate unexpected topics and ideas—and enable them to ask new and better questions. In fact, it is the act of *questioning* that makes dialogue different from mere conversation. What's especially important to consider is what follows from *answers*. As literary critic and philosopher Mikhail Bakhtin has written, "If an answer does not give rise to a new question from itself, then it falls out of the dialogue."[6]

Teaching through talk and action is one approach to pedagogy with a long and distinguished intellectual history stretching back to the ancient Greeks. In the 20th century, this approach was advocated by Jerome Bruner, a developmental psychologist who viewed human development as a continuous lifelong process, not a series of fixed stages.

Bruner believes that language enables and supports cognitive development and that learning is an active process in which learners construct new ideas or concepts based on their current and past knowledge. By selecting and transforming information, learners construct hypotheses and make decisions. Cognitive structures like language, symbols, schema, and mental models provide people with the tools to organize their experiences, enabling people to make inferences to "go beyond the information given."[7]

It was Jerome Bruner who, in *The Process of Education*, a book written in 1960, wondered whether *any* subject taught in primary school is worth an adult's knowing, and whether having known it as a child makes a person a better adult.[8] The relevance of digital and media literacy seems undeniable according to this argument—as it is an essential component of everyday life, work, leisure, and citizenship.

MANY TYPES OF QUESTIONS AND ANSWERS

Questions

Closed-ended questions can be answered with a simple yes-or-no or agree-disagree answer. *Open-ended questions* require language and explanation. There are three types of open-ended questions:

Factual Questions	Interpretive Questions	Evaluative Questions
These questions provide an explanation or information. Answers can be right or wrong based on the *quality* of information offered. • What is your date of birth? • When was the first children's cartoon broadcast on national television? • How do birds build their nests?	These questions depend on the respondent, who may answer in different ways, but the answers should be supported with *reasoning and evidence*. • How do you decide to share something in your lunch bag with a friend? • What are the qualities and characteristics of a hero?	These questions ask for someone to offer an opinion or express a point of view. The best evaluative questions help reveal the *personality and values* of the respondent. • What's your opinion of that new movie? • Who is your favorite character in the book? Why do you like him or her? • Why do you dislike peanut butter?

Answers

Answers come in three forms that reflect the author's purpose: *informative, persuasive*, or *entertaining*. In many cases, authors have complex purposes that blend several of these motivations.

To help recognize a message purpose, children can practice sorting messages into one or more of these three categories:

To Inform	To Persuade	To Entertain
The author's purpose may be to provide new information or to share ideas.	The author's purpose may be to change or reinforce a particular opinion, feeling, or behavior.	The author's purpose may be to express a mood or a feeling.

WHAT'S APPROPRIATE AND INAPPROPRIATE

So much of teaching is a form of *orchestrated improvisation*, which is a concept we define as the practice of navigating through a learning experience by skillfully managing the ordinary here-and-now dynamics of intense social interaction among students and teacher. It's an essential part of a constructivist classroom, because if the classroom is overscripted by the teacher, then students cannot co-construct their own knowledge.[9]

Here, in the split second of improvisational decision making in responding to the student's question, Dee faced the opportunity to engage, deflect, or ignore the child's question about Tiger Woods. If she had *engaged* with students on this topic, she would have asked children to weigh in on Tiger Woods's complex motives in making a public apology. If she had *deflected*, Dee might have shifted the conversation to the moral issues that underpin this issue, perhaps asking children to share their more general real-life experiences and observations about people's motives for lying, the consequences of lying, and the costs and rewards of admitting the truth. But instead, Dee *ignored* the opportunity and quickly changed the topic of the conversation altogether. Zaiah and the other children got Dee's message loud and clear: This part of the real world was not an appropriate topic for school.

Based on how adults respond, children gradually learn what topics are *appropriate* and *inappropriate* for the classroom. Unfortunately, by high school some students have overlearned what's appropriate and inappropriate and, as a result, may disinvest from the learning process, believing that nothing of genuine interest can be discussed in school. As this vignette reveals, each teacher must decide for himself or herself how much and what types of current events and popular culture references should enter the classroom. Many of these decisions are made at a moment's notice.

And it's likely that teachers' motivations for using media and technology, as we discussed in Chapter 2, have a substantial influence on these decisions. Indeed, this issue is one of Renee's seven great debates of media literacy: How should teachers respond to children's interest in mass media, news and entertainment, and popular culture?[10] When should we engage with children's media knowledge? With the real and imaginary worlds they learn about from watching TV, movies, YouTube videos, and playing video games? Which issues should we deflect and ignore?

Of course, it's probably impossible to create a learning environment where nothing is inappropriate—where *any* topic or issue can be discussed. But in aiming to promote a spirit of intellectual curiosity, most educators do try to be open and available to what students want and need to know. Because teachers can't predict how a discussion will turn out, decisions like this are made in the context of the particular moment. In blindingly quick moments of orchestrated improvisation, a teacher considers the needs of the children, the goals of the lesson, and the teacher's own motives and values. Learning to navigate the unpredictability of the media literacy classroom is an important skill that requires pedagogical practice.

When teachers take calculated risks to use popular culture and mass media in the classroom, the rewards can help children use their powerful voices to make meaningful connections between their in-school learning and out-of-school lives.

Asking Critical Questions

Assignment Media Literacy, Unit 1

http://mediaeducationlab.com/elementary-school-unit-1-asking-critical-questions

Five lesson plans for children in Grades 3–6 help them learn to identify the purpose, target audience, and techniques to attract and hold attention by analyzing TV ads, documentaries, and photographs.

CELEBRITY CULTURE IN THE LIVES OF CHILDREN

There's no doubt about it: Children are growing up with an awareness of what it means to be famous at a younger age. Lots of kids now grow up wanting to be famous musicians, athletes, or celebrities. With YouTube, parents may post videos of their babies and toddlers performing in front of the camera; children as young as 8 or 9 years old create and post online videos all by themselves.

Indeed, celebrity culture offers an array of both positive and negative features that may shape the lives of children and young people. In the city of Los Angeles, the capital of the media industry in the United States and globally, developmental psychologists conducted focus group discussions with 10-, 11-, and 12-year-olds about various types of values, including fame, benevolence, financial success, achievement, community connectedness, self-acceptance, and appearance. When they were asked to rank order these values, 40% of children listed fame as the most important. Fame is, of course, connected to money and attention, and many children see celebrity as a concrete, achievable path to future life success.[11]

Celebrity culture—with its focus on fashion, image, and social and sexual relationships—may promote a kind of narcissistic babble, where exhibitionism, vanity, entitlement, superiority, and a willingness to exploit self and others for personal gain are considered normative, and even attractive and desirable personality characteristics. We can all list numerous famous people—actors, athletes, musicians, and reality TV stars— whom we would not want children to view as role models.

However, celebrity culture may also offer children a sense of hope for the future. For some boys and girls, belief in a future in music or sports enables them to have personal power, money, influence, and attention. In a study of Australian children's hopes and aspirations for the future, Emily Bishop and her colleagues found that many young children want to be famous athletes, actors, singers, or models. In a survey of 1,170 children aged 5–12, about one third made reference to popular characters, both real and fictional, to craft their identities and hopes for the future.[12]

And who could be surprised by children's aspirations? Over the past 15 years, celebrity culture has become more unpredictable—and even accidental. Reality television and the rise of the gossip press as a veritable media industry have elevated unlikely everyday people like the subjects of documentary series *Duck Dynasty* to celebrity status. Now more than ever, popular culture must become not just a site for entertainment, but a site for questioning. Students have so many meaningful and difficult experiences with and through popular culture that educators can't afford to ignore it.

When popular culture was limited to a handful of television shows that were shared by mass audiences—the so-called monoculture of the 1950s through the 1980s—popular culture served as a shared site of recognition, something that everyone could casually nod to (or wave away) in the classroom. But in the digital era, popular culture connects students immediately and directly to adult situations and, in some cases, provides the potential to give some students an active role in popular culture itself, as is true of students who create videos that go viral or create classroom work featured, for better or worse, on national news programs.

Children enter into entire worlds through different genres and social contexts based on their interests, tastes, and incidental friendships in real life and online. The child whose parents do not listen to pop music, limit television use, avoid big-budget Hollywood releases, and read King Arthur stories to their children at bedtime will have a different cultural experience from the child who plays Angry Birds, watches Nick's *Victorious* and *iCarly*, and gets to see PG-13 action adventure films. Because not all popular culture objects are shared, teachers who assume one monolithic Disney or youth culture are doing a disservice to the diversity of media options that children and their families have.

Unfortunately, when popular culture is used as a component of teaching practice, it is often perceived as a break from normal instruction or as a form of entertainment. In one Massachusetts school, Renee observed a large group of 80 Grade 3 children watching *The Mouse and the Motorcycle* in a room. There had been no previewing or postviewing discussion. It was simply a matter of "plugging in the kids" on a rainy afternoon. This is a classic *nonoptimal use of media in the classroom*, where the full potential of media to engage students in dialogue or rich and meaningful learning experiences is missed.[13]

Children's Favorite Celebrities

More than half of the children in one school in Grades 3–5 named three favorite celebrities. Musicians were listed most often, followed by athletes and actors.

Musicians—45%	Athletes—26%	Actors—21%
Selena Gomez	Ryan Howard	Miley Cyrus
Katy Perry	Jimmy Rollins	Johnny Depp
Eminem	Chase Utley	Miranda Cosgrove
Taylor Swift		Anne Hathaway

Among students in this particular school, about one in four children (24%) did not name a favorite celebrity, athlete, or musician.[14]

ADULT ANXIETIES ABOUT POPULAR CULTURE

Depending on their motivations for using media and technology in the classroom, teachers have a range of different kinds of anxieties about children's popular culture.[15] Some educators may notice the impact that popular culture has on children's sense of fashion, taste, identity, and even values and beliefs, but they don't know how to, or don't care to, broach the topic with students. While popular culture can be a powerful educational resource, it may also be potentially harmful to children's sense of well-being and even their safety. We have seen students who, while mimicking pro wrestling moves, put other children in real danger. Celebrity behavior and popular culture may sometimes inspire the worst in all of us to be set free. For this reason, these distinct anxieties around popular culture are common among educators:

1. *Inappropriate Content or Behavior.* Some teachers are concerned that children will want to talk about sexuality, violence, bad language, and the questionable moral content that is a part of mass media and popular culture. Others are concerned about children imitating gestures or body movements that they may not understand but may be misunderstood by others.

2. *Lack of Knowledge About Popular Culture.* When children talk about the latest movies, music, or video games, it can sound like meaningless chatter. In an environment with 500+ channels, some teachers are simply not aware of the specific TV shows, movies, and music that their students enjoy, so they don't recognize what is being talked about.

3. *Dislike of Popular Culture.* Some teachers may actively dislike pop music, reality TV, and other media that their students value. They often can't resist offering their own opinions about the media children enjoy, including silly YouTube cat videos, stupid cartoons on Cartoon Network, or dumb reality talent shows.

4. *Alienation From Popular Culture.* Some teachers feel that they have nothing of real value to contribute to the conversation when talk turns to popular culture. Many teachers consider it unprofessional to talk about popular culture with their students because they don't feel it matches with their role and identity as teachers.

5. *Fear of Retribution From Parents or Administrators.* Some teachers are concerned that, when classroom talk includes references to popular culture, some children may misinterpret the point of the activity and share information with parents in ways that could lead to complaints. What if a child comes home from school and says to dad or mom, "Mrs. So-and-So told me I had to go see *The Dark Knight Rises*"?

All of these concerns have some merit. Especially in elementary grades, a sensitivity to adult content, violence, sexuality, and language is important not just for students' well-being, but for teachers' well-being. When parents and administrators are offended by a teacher's curriculum choices, professional integrity can be compromised. Teachers' ignorance, antipathy, or alienation from popular culture may reflect their own identities not only as teachers but also as people.

But students are in need of adults to help them express and reflect upon their complicated feelings, beliefs, and ideas about various forms of popular media. When David talked to a first-grade class at a Philadelphia school about documentary films—films with "real people" in them—for a Career Day, one 6-year-old was quick to tell him that her favorite show on television was *Teen Mom*, a reality show about the lives of teenagers who are pregnant in high school.

This is why the question-asking process is so crucial to using popular culture in the classroom. As we saw in Dee's example, children naturally have complicated questions about the world of celebrity and popular culture around them, and teachers can make it their responsibility to use interactions with popular culture just as they would other interactions in the world. Not only do such interactions have an impact on students, but teachers themselves can be a positive force in shaping the very way that students conceive of and use media in their everyday lives, as our subsequent example should make clear.

20 Questions

Question games encourage metacognitive thinking about the act of questioning. In this game, one person thinks of a person, place, or event. A group of people tries to uncover the answer in the fewest number of questions, but the questions they ask must be able to be answered with a "yes" or "no" answer. The game encourages children to think through their questions creatively, carefully, and strategically.

SOCIAL POWER AND FACEBOOK FAME

In most of the schools we worked in, children's use of Facebook exploded in Grade 5.[16] Our data parallel findings nationwide. One study found that more than one third (35%) of Grade 5 students have a Facebook profile. A *Consumer Reports* poll indicates that five million American kids under the age of 10 are using Facebook.[17] Some parents or older siblings create Facebook profiles on behalf of younger children to get around Facebook's age policy that prohibits access to children under age 13.

For both adults and children, one of the easiest ways to satisfy the need for fame is through Facebook. Many teachers recognize that Facebook plays a major role in children's lives in Grades 4, 5, and 6, when children are learning to deploy a variety of forms of *social power* to acquire friendships and develop communication and critical thinking skills. Social power is the degree of influence and authority you have in relation to your peer group. Learning to use social power is a developmentally normal part of growing up; it's why children sometimes talk back to parents and teachers and why they may experiment with bullying. Because communication is so powerful, it takes time for children to discover, gradually and through trial and error, how to use it to meet their needs.

Mr. Landis, a technology coordinator at Russell Byers Charter School who started his career as a PVK summer instructor, noticed that many of his older students had their own Facebook profiles, often in their own name but also, frequently, under pseudonyms. He wanted to engage them in a conversation about what kinds of information they might be able to trust or not trust on Facebook, in the same way they were expected to reflect on the credibility of results from search engines. But students who were already using Facebook, he found, seemed to separate what they said about it in class from how they seemed to use it in their spare time.

"What information do you feel OK putting on Facebook?" he asked the class in a lesson about online privacy. His goal was to have an open discussion about boundaries and limitations that students might employ to limit the amount of personal information they shared to a large online community. But the discussion didn't feel open. He felt as if kids were giving him the *expected* answer.

For example, one child said, "You shouldn't put *anything* on Facebook. You shouldn't even be on Facebook, really."

Mr. Landis knew this child had her own Facebook account. "Why not?" he asked.

"Because someone could stalk you. They could know where you live."

"Yeah, it's really dangerous," said another student who was also an active Facebook user, "because like someone could know everything about you and then they could even come and *kill* you."

Mr. Landis's first impulse in situations like this was to ask the class, "Do you *really* think someone would ever go through so much effort to murder a complete stranger?" He never acted on that impulse because of the disruption it might cause, but he sensed that students' responses were informed more by horror films—and horror stories both rumored and, though rare, occasionally real—than by any real experience online.

Mr. Landis wanted to get his students to go beyond just giving the socially correct answer. He was hoping to replace the superficial conversations about the Internet—the ones that happened only in school and focused on a common "stranger danger" approach to Internet safety—with a more reflective and authentic conversation that directly applied to their online lives.

Mr. Landis's students were still developing their online presence and were also developing their sense of comfort and boundaries with online communication. Although even at age 11 his students had obviously started to expand to social networking sites, blogs, and gaming sites, they were still struggling to figure out how they felt about being online, what concerns they had, and what actions they would take to address those concerns.

In many ways, the whole concept of online safety can be reminiscent of other sensitive subjects in elementary education, like health education and anti-drug education. Often two conversations happen about those topics, too—one in the sanctioned confines of a conversation appropriate for school and one more complicated, perhaps even transgressive conversation outside those confines.

Most teachers are aware of the extent to which their students talk, in free time, about their favorite media. How many times do young students debate the best superheroes, quote or sing along to popular songs, reveal all the cheat codes to their favorite video games, or talk about the coolest new websites? In each case, students are thinking about their home media use and shaping how they feel about it in conversation with their peers. But when left unstructured, this talk can often be heard as so much meaningless chatter, something off topic. How can teachers make students' home uses of media, in all of its messiness, fodder for a meaningful conversation and an opportunity for students to genuinely reflect on how media touches their lives?

Mr. Landis had commiserated on how difficult it was to talk about Facebook with other fifth- and sixth-grade teachers, who also expressed common and understandable anxieties about broaching the topic of students' popular culture with their students.

Draw a Website

Create your own website on paper. Make it as realistic as possible. You can make any kind of website you want, but make sure you include all four elements that every website has:

1. **Title.** What is says at the top.

2. **Address [URL].** Starts with http://

3. **Media.** Words, pictures, games—anything you can imagine.

4. **Links.** Click on these to see something else.

GOING ONLINE ON PAPER

Mr. Landis wondered what would happen if he tried teaching about social media to younger children. What if he talked to first- and second-grade students about online communication and social networks? Though they undoubtedly had some limited experiences online—the first-grade teacher in the school had instituted a rule that children could not use Google in the classroom for fear of inappropriate search results—were these experiences enough to create the kind of artificial reflections he was seeing from his older students? When one teacher polled her second-grade classroom informally during their recess in preparation for a short lesson in online safety, she found that nearly half of her 7-year old students had access to Facebook through parents' or siblings' accounts.

Mr. Landis decided to ask young children to use their background knowledge to draw a website on paper. He created a worksheet that outlined the four elements of every website. Mr. Landis knew that tablets, mobile media, and social networking websites were starting to threaten many of those elements; for instance, students frequently clicked around, using hyperlinks without noticing web addresses, and often knowing only one or two web addresses by heart—usually search engines.

Students took to the drawing activity with great enthusiasm, planning out websites about their favorite pets, about their favorite shows, and about their own lives. On paper, anything was permissible—including full names, addresses, family members, and phone numbers.

Then Mr. Landis asked children to write the name of one other student in the class on the paper—this was their *link*. When students shared their websites in front of the class, rather than call on the next student, the previous presenter would "link" to the new speaker.

Students' websites were highly inventive and often modeled on complicated gaming and popular culture websites the children used. When they were done with their presentations, they "clicked" their links ("Jazmyne!" "Rodney!") and other students presented their work.

After each student, Mr. Landis asked students to give warm and cool feedback: What did you like? What would make the work even better? Because many students did have background knowledge about websites, they also had opinions about the quality of their peers' sites. One child offered this feedback to a peer: "I really like your picture of a dog. I think that if you had more kinds of dogs, even more people who like different dogs could click those, and they would like it, too."

Then Mr. Landis presented the idea of sharing work with an audience. If you wanted to share this work with someone else you didn't know, what would you want them to know, and what wouldn't you be OK with them knowing?

Here students had a more genuine conversation about limitations than what Mr. Landis had experienced with the older students. You shouldn't put your home phone number, but what if there's a number you want people to call? Can you put that? You shouldn't put your full name, but what about your first name? One child said, "There are lots of Rodneys, why couldn't I still be Rodney?"

The class collaboratively came up with some guidelines. No last names. No home addresses or home phone numbers. No information that might tell people where you live or where you go to school. This caused a bit of a debate, as one child asked, "But can we say we're from Philly? Don't we want people in our city to know about it?"

Other than that, what was important was what you felt OK sharing. Now they were given new pieces of paper—these were their "profile pages." On their profile pages, students were asked to put things they would be OK sharing even with strangers. One child did not feel comfortable sharing her own first name, so she decided not to use it. One child did not feel comfortable using his dog's real name, so he changed it. Most students ended up putting names on their profile pictures that referenced their favorite celebrities or activities—like "Spongebob" and "Kittenlover." Others used their real first name, but not their last name.

After the revision process, Mr. Landis asked if they were satisfied and comfortable with everything that was in their new websites. They were. "OK," he said, "now I want you to flip your paper over. If you want this website that you've just drawn to go online *today*, as you made it, I want you to write 'yes.' If you do not want this website that you've just drawn to go online today, I want you to write 'no.' Either answer is fine—remember, this is what you feel OK about."

Mr. Landis was surprised to find that about half of the second graders were *not* OK sharing their work online. Students who had created elaborate designs for their websites with crayon, marker, and pencil were perfectly content with it staying away from the digital world. The other half of the drawings he scanned into separate image files and uploaded on the class website, which he created in Wikispaces (www.wikispaces.com), a free, educator-friendly blogging platform online.

Safe Search

www.google.com/preferences

Set preferences to screen out sexual content from Google search results.

The following week, the young students in class viewed their very own websites—their first foray into developing an online presence, carefully scaffolded and structured by adult support and supervision.

But there was something strange. When they looked at their class website, they saw the list of usernames—Avatarang, Beyonce, Spongebob, etc.—which, when clicked, took them to the hand-drawn profile pages they recognized.

"Who am I again?" asked one student.

Mr. Landis reminded them that they had to remember what their *Internet name* (their username) was going to be. Here Mr. Landis was drawing from his own personal history participating in online communities, which went back 20 years. In those days, you couldn't just sign up to a blogging system, social network, or other website with your own name and email address. You created a persona that sometimes was identical to your real identity but was often a pseudonym. He wanted to give his own students the choice that some online systems were denying them, to reflect on whether they wanted to use their own names online.

Next, Mr. Landis told the class that they needed to *comment* on each other's work. "When you comment on someone's page," he said, "it's just like giving warm and cool feedback in class. Except this time you'll give your warm and cool feedback with your Internet name."

Students were assigned a page to comment on, and quickly light bulbs began to go off.

"Wait a minute," said one student, "which one of you is Spongebob?"

Mr. Landis put up his hand, "Hold on—you don't need to answer that. Only tell people your real name if you want to."

"That's OK," said Jason, "I'm Spongebob."

"Mr. Landis," asked another student, "does that mean that we won't know whose page it is when we comment on it?"

"Not if they don't want you to know. That's their decision, just like it's your decision what information you want to use."

Students then shared their comments verbally ("Spongebob, your drawing is great!"). Afterward, one student, who had asked for Mr. Landis *not* to share her information, approached him at the door on her way to her next class. "Mr. Landis, can I still put my page online?" Mr. Landis told her that, if she felt comfortable, he would put her page online for next week's class. This group of young children had gotten a good sense of the function of public and private identities in an online environment. They were coming to realize that they have the power to decide for themselves how they want to participate in a social media environment.

Pranking Videos Create Conversational Space

Most 11- and 12-year-olds will have seen a YouTube "scary maze video." The most popular video has over 45 million views and depicts a young boy playing a computer game, when suddenly, a scary face appears with a blood-curdling scream. The video raises an ethical question: Is it OK to intentionally scare someone just so that someone else can laugh at them? Renee developed a lesson to help Grade 6 students explore the complicated relationship between the filmmaker, the subject, and the audience in YouTube pranking videos. Find it online at www.powerfulvoicesforkids.com.

ACKNOWLEDGING PLEASURE IN THE TABOO

Opening the floodgates to popular culture and mass media in the classroom can be fraught with ambiguity, frustration, and confusion. As a child, Renee watched certain TV shows at the neighbor's house because they weren't allowed at home. And David has fond memories of hiding graphic popular comic books in stacks of books in his bedroom at home.

Children's media worlds are complex places where they go to try out new identities, indulge in unknown and sometimes forbidden pleasures, and have raw experiences through the mediated world that are often inappropriate for other settings. Parental monitoring of media content is even more difficult today than it was a few years ago, because of the always-on nature of our broadband devices. Today, many children have constant Internet access on portable devices that are difficult for parents to monitor.

The fact that popular culture can be a catalyst for what some teachers see as *transgressive* behavior—behavior that pushes or crosses the boundaries of accepted classroom rules—is not something that can merely be wished away with classroom management techniques or rules.

Transgressiveness, whether it comes from inappropriate media content or inappropriate responses to content, is closely tied to how we take pleasure in some of our favorite kinds of media, as when we "root for the bad guy," watch embarrassing home movies or YouTube videos, or indulge in other guilty pleasures in private.

It's reasonable to think that exposure to transgressive media would inevitably bring with it transgressive behaviors from students. We can't blame children for repeating or reciting the messages they find in contemporary culture.

However, dealing openly and honestly with such material, student disruptions, and the complicated pleasures that students take in their media worlds requires both a teacher's sensitivity to how students make sense of media and a teacher's mind for improvisation. Teachers know that they must think on their feet when lessons don't go as planned or when technology malfunctions, and the same goes for when students provide unexpected or unwanted responses to classroom content.

Kids generally appreciate the opportunity to ask questions and receive frank and honest information about the unfamiliar, bizarre, or simply ambiguous messages that permeate popular culture. Jesse Gainer, a literacy educator, described an awkward encounter with his nine-year-old daughter, Clara, when they were singing along in the car to a song from the Black Eyed Peas, in which Fergie and will.i.am sing, "Whatcha gonna do with all that junk? All that junk inside your trunk?" When Clara asked about the meaning of the phrase, her father explained frankly that it was a colloquial reference to a woman's buttocks. The child's questions started a conversation about all the "dumb" things in mainstream media. After this, Clara began playing with gender and power reversals in pop music, reworking the lyrics of her favorite Avril Lavigne song to disrupt the fairy tale narrative.[18]

At school, these kinds of conversations are just as complicated, messy, and important as they are at home. When Mr. Fitzgerald's class did research for a commercial they were making for the school's book fair, they watched an IKEA commercial while reading its original shooting script to gain familiarity with the formal conventions of television ads. The commercial was hardly controversial—two women talk about their closet space like mechanics would talk about cars in a garage. The implication is that IKEA allows women to "geek out" about closet organization in the same way that men do about cars and tools.

The intention in the lesson was to talk about target audiences and the assumptions that the commercial might make about its target audience. What is IKEA saying about men and women, and how might someone interpret it differently or ask questions about its values? Then students would read the initial pitch and script for the commercial to see what the author's intentions were during the brainstorming phase. They would discuss whether the ideas the students generated matched the intent of the original author.

But Mr. Fitzgerald did not account for a sidebar feature of YouTube, which suggests "recommended videos" after the initial video finishes. The videos ran the gamut of inappropriateness. One video, called "IKEA GAY," had students snickering and shouting out uncontrollably. Another featured controversial imagery ("IKEA banned commercial!"). Still another, "IKEA HUNDSTOL, Dog high chair" was a unique challenge to maintaining order in a fifth-grade classroom—it featured an absurd picture of a yellow Labrador sitting in a baby's high chair. Kids couldn't help but giggle.

Quiet YouTube

When you find a YouTube video you would like to use, simply go to the address bar and type the word *quiet* in front of the YouTube in the address. This removes everything else from the page except the video itself. You can view the video with no ads, no comments, and no suggested videos.

Mr. Fitzgerald's lesson went on, despite these distractions. But the unpredictability of mass media and popular culture is both its biggest strength and its biggest liability in the classroom. When teachers take risks, they can find both challenges and rewards in the classroom, as Mr. Landis did in introducing Facebook to his students, and as, in other chapters, Rachel did in tackling the homelessness issue or Mr. Fitzgerald did in letting students bring controversial news stories to class.

Good teachers model how to talk and listen and share responses to a wide range of cultural artifacts. They're fearless, knowing that responsible communication is possible with every topic under the sun. Donna Alvermann and her colleagues talk about the flexible roles that teachers must adopt in bringing popular culture into the classroom: in balancing their own learning as they listen to children's interests and pleasures; in helping children identify and critique popular culture texts; and in assuming an authority position in protecting students while ensuring their pleasures are respected and questioned.[19] As we've seen from the teachers profiled in this chapter, there's no magic formula for learning how to do this except through creating a classroom culture of respect and trust, balanced with reflective practice.

Lesson   Celebrity You

Lesson Description

Students imagine themselves as celebrities and discover behind-the-scenes facts about real celebrities to realize that most are just people who worked hard to accomplish their dreams.

Objectives

Students will

- Play an online game to imagine themselves as a celebrity
- Use keyword search to find information about the background and early life of a celebrity
- Identify the authorship and evaluate the credibility of a web source
- Distinguish between different types of websites
- Learn how various information sources depict celebrities in different ways
- Learn how fans actively participate in celebrity culture using their own creativity

Vocabulary

Fame

Research

Fan

Official

Browser

Search engine

Keyword

Hyperlink

Result list

Website authorship

Resources and Materials

✓ Computer access, data projector, or computer lab

Activity

Explore

✓ On an individual piece of paper, ask children to draw someone who is "famous." Fame is defined as the state of being well known by others. Make a gallery walk of the drawings, and ask children to point out what the drawings have in common. Count how many children selected actors or actresses, athletes, musicians, reality TV personalities, politicians, authors, or others. Discuss: What's the difference between a famous person and a not-famous person?

✓ In the computer lab, ask children to play Celebrity You at My Pop Studio (www.mypopstudio.com). Children use language to depict themselves as famous by responding to questions such as "What new present have you bought yourself lately?" and "Your fans describe you as . . ."

Figure 4.1   Celebrity You

Source: My Pop Studio (www.popstudio.com).

Access

✓ Working with a partner, children develop a list of keywords to search for information about a celebrity. Their goal is to find accurate information about the person's childhood and life before becoming famous. Students should use Google search with "Safe Search" enabled. Encourage them to read the result list carefully before they click on a hyperlink.

As they explore, ask children to be sure to look for what type of website they have found.

- Is it an independent source, like Wikipedia, *People* magazine, or TMZ?
- Is it an official celebrity website, created by the celebrity or the people who work for her or him?
- Is it a fan website, created by people who pay attention to celebrities?

✓ You may need to help children find the "author" of a website. It's sometimes as simple as looking for an "About" page, but other times it can be challenging to find the author. If they find information but cannot find an author, don't let children use this information in the activity.

✓ Explain: Information on a website might not be trustworthy when the author chooses to be anonymous.

As children find specific facts, encourage them to organize the information they find into these categories:

Magazine, TV, or Independent Websites	Official Celebrity Websites	Fan-Created Websites

Analysis

✓ After completing the research, discuss these questions:

- What was the most interesting information you learned?
- Which information source was most useful in your research? Why?
- Which sources were most trustworthy and believable? Why?

Composition

✓ Invite students to write a summary of what they learned about the celebrity. To document their research, ask students to keep track of the URLs where they found information and list these at the end of the summary.

Reflection

✓ Discuss with children the pros and cons of life as a celebrity. As a class, create a chart to depict the advantages and disadvantages. Encourage children to go home and ask their parents to share their own opinions about the pros and cons of being famous.

Taking Action

✓ Invite children to talk to their parents and grandparents by asking this question: What are the advantages and disadvantages of being famous? Families can share their values on the complex and multifaceted role of fame and celebrity in modern society.

Source: Created by Renee Hobbs.

NOTES

1. Alexander, R. (2005, July). *Culture, dialogue and learning: Notes on an emerging pedagogy.* Keynote address at the International Association for Cognitive Education and Psychology 10th International Conference, Durham, UK.
2. Alexander, p. 2.

3. Alexander, p. 3.
4. Mahler, J. (2010, March 24). The Tiger bubble. *New York Times Magazine,* p. MM30.
5. Stanley, A. (2010, February 19). Vulnerability in a disciplined performance. *New York Times,* p. D1.
6. Bakhtin, M. (1986). *Speech genres and other late essays* (Trans. V. W. McGee). Austin: University of Texas Press (p 168).
7. Bruner, J. S. (1961). The act of discovery. *Harvard Educational Review, 31,* 21–32.
8. Bruner, J. S. (1960). *The process of education.* Cambridge, MA: Harvard University Press.
9. Sawyer, R. (2004). Creative teaching: Collaborative discussion and disciplined improvisation. *Educational Researcher, 33*(2), 12–20.
10. Hobbs, R. (1998). The seven great debates in the media literacy movement. *Journal of Communication, 48*(2), 9–29.
11. Uhls, Y. T., & Greenfield, P. M. (2011, December 19). The value of fame: Preadolescent perceptions of popular media and their relationship to future aspirations. *Developmental Psychology.* Advance online publication. doi:10.1037/a0026369
12. Bishop, E., & West, M. (2010, December). *Celebrity and performance in the hopes of children.* Paper presentation at Enfancee et Cultures colloque international, Paris, France. Retrieved from http://www.enfanceetcultures.culture.gouv .fr/actes/bishop_willis.pdf
13. Hobbs, R. (2007). Non-optimal uses of video in the classroom. *Learning, Media & Technology, 31*(1), 35–50.
14. Hobbs, R., Cipollone, M., Bailin, E., Moore, D. C., & Schlesinger, M. (2011, June). *Young audiences and new authors in a multimedia landscape.* Unpublished manuscript, Media Education Lab, Temple University, Philadelphia, PA.
15. Moore, D. C. (2011). Asking questions first: Navigating popular culture and transgression in an inquiry-based media literacy classroom. *Action in Teacher Education 33,* 219–230.
16. Hobbs et al.
17. Consumer Reports survey: 7.5 million Facebook users are under the age of 13, violating the site's terms. (2011, May 10). *Consumer Reports.* Retrieved from http://pressroom.consumerreports.org/pressroom/2011/05/consumer-reports-survey-75-million-facebook-users-are-under-the-age-of-13-violating-the-sites-terms.html
18. Gainer, J. (2007). Social critique and pleasure: Critical media literacy with popular culture texts. *Language Arts 85*(2), 106–114.
19. Albermann, D., Moon, J., & Hagood, M. (1999). *Popular culture in the classroom.* Newark, DE: International Reading Association.

5 Making Media

In this chapter, you'll learn about

New Ways to Make Media in the Classroom

- How do teachers create learning environments that enable children to balance style and substance as multimedia authors?

Finding Your Comfort Levels and Pushing Your Boundaries

- How can teachers, regardless of their media production expertise, use their interests, passions, and strong learning goals as a foundation for simple media production activities?

The Delicate Balance Between Order and Chaos

- What strategies help create classrooms that have the right level of classroom management combined with positive energy, excitement, and creative chaos?

Mr. Fitzgerald, a Grade 6 teacher who has taught in Philadelphia public schools for decades, was struggling with his PowerPoint presentation. He couldn't change the font size or figure out how to embed an image. As he worked to complete his own project, he noticed that his younger colleague was using transitions—with words whizzing and whirring by in a stunning visual sequence. "How did he do it?" Mr. Fitzgerald wondered. The process of adding transitions to a PowerPoint presentation was a mystery to him.

Mr. Fitzgerald was focused on generating good ideas for his presentation. As part of a professional development workshop, teachers were invited to create a six-slide PowerPoint presentation to depict their own love-hate relationship with print, visual, sound, or image-based media. As an avid news watcher and lover of classic TV news editorials by Walter Cronkite and Edward R. Murrow, Mr. Fitzgerald wanted to use his slide show to discuss the varying points of view of CNN and FOX, two different 24-hour cable TV news stations. His younger colleague, Mr. Marino, was exploring the action film genre. But for the colleague, the assignment was really just a springboard to create animated transitions and sound effects that displayed his creative prowess with PowerPoint.

When teachers presented their slides to the group, Mr. Marino's presentation certainly got laughs and some mild wonderment at both the choice of topic and the razzle-dazzle features. But Mr. Fitzgerald's presentation on the differences between CNN and FOX, which was functional, plain, and reliant on simple statements with well-chosen still images, sparked a real dialogue between participating teachers about point of view in news broadcasting. Teachers had a lot to say in response to Mr. Fitzgerald's presentation. In that moment, we realized that teachers struggle (as much as or even more than students) with both the technology learning curve and the natural tension between style and substance.

BALANCING CREATIVITY AND NEW TECHNOLOGIES

Today, the distinction between author and audience is being erased as nearly everyone, young and old, is engaged in both sending and receiving messages. While once upon a time only a small number of creative professionals created media, today nonprofessional creativity is becoming one of the defining features of contemporary society, something the futurist Richard Florida has called *the creative class*, as more and more jobs and cultural practices involve knowledge production or knowledge sharing.[1]

Just a couple of generations ago, writing composition was hardly evident in the curriculum at all. Even when Mr. Fitzgerald was in school, the main form of creative written expression was the ability to craft a five-paragraph essay.

Every generation's creative work reflects a legacy that's quite specific to the time period and historical context in which it takes place. In 2013,

Mr. Fitzgerald's younger colleagues now highly value the practice of making videos, writing blogs, and composing music. In their eyes, to accomplish these forms of cultural expression is to make something of real value.

New forms of expression continue to emerge because everyone in the society, not just a narrow group of mass media providers, is participating in creating and sharing messages using digital tools and technologies. According to some scholars, the ease of both creating messages and accessing them has led messages to become more multisensory, multimedia, chaotic, unapologetically mimetic, and playful.[2]

When people comment on a blog, videotape a conversation and post it to YouTube, or send Twitter messages about their favorite pop star, their participation in media culture reconfigures the relations between authors, industries, and audiences and between message production and consumption. Today, the increased representation of ordinary people as authors (and, occasionally, temporary celebrities) has led to a whole generation of *do-it-yourself* (DIY) media makers. As digital media's ease of use makes it more accessible, creating media becomes a part of everyday cultural life. For many of us, it's part of the way we express our identities and experiences to ourselves and the people around us.

Where to Watch Online Videos Created by Kids

Jacob Burns Film Center

www.youtube.com/burnsfilmcenter

The Jacob Burns Film Center is a nonprofit cultural arts organization that offers a range of media education programs for children and youth.

The One Minutes Junior

www.theoneminutesjr.org/

A collection of youth media videos from around the world curated by the United Nations Children's Fund (UNICEF).

Children's Media Project

http://blip.tv/childrensmediaproject

This nonprofit art and education group in Poughkeepsie, New York, offers workshops that empower at-risk youth through the media arts.

SchoolTube

www.schooltube.com/category/31/

Teachers have posted examples of videos produced in elementary school here, with samples of storytelling, morning news, science experiments, dramatic performances, and more.

WHEN IT'S TOO EASY TO CREATE

The concept of *digital storytelling* emerged from the work of Joe Lambert, founder of the Center for Digital Storytelling, in the mid-1990s to describe the process of involving children and young people in the creation of narratives built with words, pictures, and sound into a linear sequence.[3] Digital story-telling is a workshop-based composition process by which ordinary people create their own short autobiographical or narrative audio or video programs that can be streamed on the web or broadcast on radio or television.[4]

When young children make digital stories, these are generally around 1–2 minutes long and use written scripts that are recorded as voiceovers, combined with pictures or photos, usually drawn by hand or brought in from home. Using a video editing application such as Adobe Premiere or Apple's iMovie, it is possible for nearly anyone to produce a digital video that is of sufficient technical quality for web streaming, broadcast, or DVD distribution.

According to Jean Burgess, an Australian educator, it's the simplicity of digital storytelling, with its particular formal characteristics and creative constraints, that matters because it

> leads to the production of high-impact stories by people with little or no experience, with minimal direct intervention by the workshop facilitator. The personal narrative, told in the storyteller's unique voice, is central to the process of creating a story and is given priority in the arrangement of symbolic elements. Narrative accessibility, warmth, and presence are prioritized over formal experimentation or innovative "new" uses for technologies.[5]

When we attend conferences where K–12 educational technologists showcase the latest fancy and sometimes expensive digital tools and technologies, we can't help but feel that the gap continues to widen, leaving classroom teachers feeling both overwhelmed and energized by all the new ways of using technology.

But nearly every educator recognizes the *style-over-substance* problem as one of the biggest challenges to student media production practices across all grade levels, from kindergarten to college. One researcher, Jamie McKenzie, warned that the ease and simplicity of digital tools can lead to the emergence of poor instructional practices. When it's too easy for students to create, they may take shortcuts that substitute snazzy visual effects for meaningful content. For example, in one classroom he observed two fifth graders as they presented a PowerPoint report on tigers that employed every known transition and special effect the software offered. Mr. McKenzie noted there was very little content and "even less information than we have come to expect from one of those time-honored encyclopedia-based reports."

But, my, the special effects were impressive! Unfortunately, it seems, the children were unable to find a picture of a tiger. So they substituted a picture of a lion. Even more remarkable, Mr. McKenzie noted, no one seemed to notice or care, not even the teacher. The bells and whistles of the moving images on the screen had interfered with everyone's attention to the informational content of the message.[6]

To assist educators in solving the style-over-substance problem, teacher-librarians can serve as an indispensable resource in elementary education. A large number of research studies have shown clear evidence of the connection between student achievement and the presence of school libraries with qualified school library media specialists.[7] That's why it's one of the deepest sources of shame that the funding for elementary librarians has been drastically compromised in so many schools. Unfortunately, U.S. Department of Education data reveal that in the 2007–2008 school year, 40% of elementary school libraries had no full-time or part-time professional staff, and only about half of the 3,560 public charter schools had a school library.[8]

Whenever we have had the fortunate opportunity to work with school librarians, we realize how their work ensures that both students and staff are effective users of ideas and information. Teacher-librarians assist school staff and students in gaining access to high-quality materials in all formats. They stimulate intellectual curiosity and independent learning through reading, viewing, and using information and ideas. By guiding children toward self-discovery and self-direction, teacher-librarians help children develop skills and attitudes that are essential to academic and personal development.

Addressing the Style-Over-Substance Problem

The style-over-substance problem can occur when students make very pretty, visually stimulating messages that feature poor-quality, weak, or inaccurate content. Evaluation rubrics can be used to help learners distinguish between these two distinct features of a message:

Ideas and Content	Expression and Form
The ideas and information in the message are clear, accurate, and trustworthy.	The expression and form of the message are appropriate to the purpose and target audience. The style complements the main ideas and content.
The ideas and information are superficial, random, unorganized, of questionable quality, or even incoherent.	The stylistic choices distract from paying attention to the content and ideas.

THE NEVER-ENDING LEARNING CURVE

It's not easy to keep up with the continual changes in media and technology tools. Most of us learn only the technology we really need to use, such as email, word processing, shopping, banking, or keeping track of friends on Facebook. Many people are not deeply invested in creating messages using digital media. For these reasons, when we work with teachers in professional development settings, we find that learning new technology and media production skills can be a formidable barrier for some.

For all the changes wrought by the transition to a digital and online media environment, comfort with changing technologies and modes of communication remains the most noticeable—and the most varied— among elementary educators.

Some teachers just aren't that interested in media and technology. Others adamantly refuse to learn new forms of media-making, like social media, digital comic creation, video editing, or podcasting, wanting step-by-step guidance or throwing their hands up in defeat before they've even gotten their feet wet.

However, for other elementary teachers, work with digital media is a snap. Some have technological skills that far outpace our own. For example, we have had the experience of helping one teacher figure out how to save a file to its appropriate folder while another teacher is creating custom templates and transitions, skills that confound even us on occasion.

Learning to use new digital media and technology is just another version of *learning how to learn*—and like anything worth doing, it takes time. There is no automatic way to learn to use digital tools, no magic bullet technique that can replace a teacher's ability to explore, practice, and gain familiarity and comfort with technology. But teachers don't always need to be experts with digital media to create meaningful digital learning experiences for their students.

Talking About Copyrighted Images Builds Language Skills and Creativity

www.youtube.com/watch?v=FtX8nswnUKU&feature=youtu.be

In the YouTube video titled *Kittens Inspired by Kittens*, a 5-year-old girl introduces us to the book *Kittens*. She comments on the pictures in the book and makes up little stories about them, pretending to be the voices of the kittens. This popular video illustrates how children's active reading of images spurs imagination, creativity, and the development of language skills. It also demonstrates why educators cherish the fair use of copyrighted materials, as we see that new ideas build upon and extend other people's creative work.

STARTING EARLY: MAKING A VIDEO WITH GRADE 1 STUDENTS

Some very simple production activities can have quite a powerful educational impact with young children. One Powerful Voices for Kids (PVK) instructor, Kate, developed a simple video production activity with her

Grade 1 students. These children weren't ready to use iMovie since most of them had only minimal familiarity with a computer. So Kate focused instruction on the design and planning processes as her young students participated in creating a video titled *How to Take Care of Your Pet*.

First, she helped children recognize that they knew something that other people might value: all the work and effort involved in caring for a dog or cat. Then she helped them understand a particular *genre* (the public service announcement: "a persuasive message that helps people"), a *target audience* (people who needed to learn about becoming a pet owner), and the *message* (the ideas and information they wanted to convey).

In the preproduction phase, each child developed a particular piece of advice for a young pet owner by answering the question, "What is involved in taking care of a dog or cat?" In deciding how to visualize this advice, children discussed whether they could bring their own pets to school to film certain scenes. After a robust and lively conversation, children ultimately decided to use stuffed animals to represent their pets because the youngsters understood and could imagine many potential problems that could result by using real animals in an in-class production.

After Kate set up the camera and microphone, children worked with a partner to act out the advice, with one child setting up the scene with a stuffed animal and the other filming it. When it came time for postproduction, Kate uploaded the footage, edited the video, and exported the film to DVD and the web (see Figure 5.1). It wasn't hard work, but it took some

Figure 5.1   Kate's *How to Take Care of Your Pet* Still

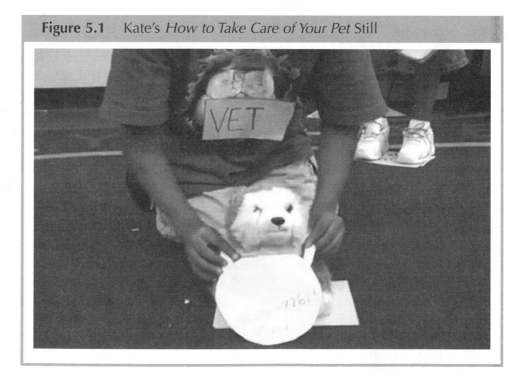

time. Kate completed the project in the evenings and on weekends, behind the scenes, editing the video herself and showing her students only the end result. Watch the children's video at www.powerfulvoicesforkids.com.

A Five-Step Process: Creating a Video

1. **Identifying Your Goals.** Figure out your purpose, target audience, genre, and message.

2. **Preproduction.** Using brainstorming, develop creative ways to express your ideas with images, language, and sound. Write a script and plan the sequence of images.

3. **Production.** Rehearse and practice, gathering video footage and recording audio and paying careful attention to image and sound quality.

4. **Postproduction.** Assemble your image and sound, and edit so that the project makes sense to the target audience.

5. **Distribution and Promotion.** Develop ways to share, display, or present your completed work to an audience.

MULTIMEDIA COMPOSITION: A GATEWAY TO 21ST CENTURY WRITING

Certain general communication competencies are activated when children create messages using media tools and technologies. It begins in early childhood, when children communicate a personal reaction and point of view, speak to an individual and demonstrate listening skills, or use writing and images to inform, persuade, and entertain.

There are also competencies and skills that are specific to each medium of expression. For example, to compose a photographic image, you need to select, crop, and sequence images for a specific purpose and target audience. To make a video, you must use a video camera to record images and sound, and then select and sequence images, language, and sound to accomplish a specific purpose and reach a particular target audience. To create a performance, you must use heartfelt emotion, voice, and body to convey feelings and ideas; demonstrate creativity and imagination; participate as a team member or leader in a performance; and use time well throughout the process of idea development, planning, rehearsal, and performance. Although it takes time and practice to master these competencies in the elementary grades, partnerships between teachers, librarians, and media professionals, working both in and out of school, are proving to be effective.[9]

A Map of Media Composition Competencies

General Composition Skills

- Communicating a personal reaction and point of view
- Speaking to an individual and demonstrating listening skills
- Speaking to a large group and responding to feedback
- Using writing and images to inform, persuade, and entertain
- Composing in a variety of formats, including email, review, report, film script, music lyrics, webpage, nonfiction, fiction, and other literary genres
- Composing for a variety of audiences, including peers, family, educators, special interest groups, government leaders, and members of the general public

Medium-Specific Skills

Performance as Composition

- Using heart, voice, and body to convey feelings and ideas
- Demonstrating creativity and imagination
- Participating as a team member or leader in a performance
- Using time well throughout the process of idea development, planning, rehearsal, and performance

Image Composition

- Creating a photographic image
- Selecting, cropping, and sequencing images for a specific purpose and target audience

Audio Composition

- Using technology to create an audio recording
- Being highly aware of sound, noise, and tone while recording
- Selecting and assembling audio and musical excerpts

Video Composition

- Using a video camera to record images and sound
- Selecting and sequencing images, language, and sound to accomplish a specific purpose and reach a particular target audience

Social Media Composition

- Thinking about audience and purpose while composing
- Attracting and holding audience attention
- Respecting privacy
- Being socially responsible and sensitive to others

Digital Media Composition

- Using software tools to create messages in a variety of forms (wiki, blog, podcast, interactive multimedia, etc.)
- Learning how to learn programming software and understanding how it works
- Using a process of iterative problem solving throughout the creative process
- Sharing information appropriately and respecting privacy
- Understanding copyright and applying the fair use reasoning process appropriately

BASIC MEDIA PRODUCTION: SCREENCASTING

One PVK instructor, Emily, was finding it difficult to deal with what she would later recognize as the fourth-grade slump. Many of her students had had unsuccessful experiences in Grade 3 and been selected for academic remediation. Their previous experiences in school were leading them to believe that school was not worth the effort.

The fourth-grade slump has been attributed to an excessive focus on textbook reading, where children get fewer opportunities to read materials of interest to them. When children can self-select what to read and write about, they increase their motivation and their vocabulary skills and become more confident in reading more challenging materials.[10] For these reasons, popular print media like magazines and newspapers and online digital resources can be powerful learning tools for young readers and writers.

Emily struggled to get her students to read and write on a regular basis. But she found that engaging them in popular culture, particularly talking about favorite music and celebrities, opened up opportunities for reading, writing, and critical thinking. For example, children enjoyed the opportunity to read magazine articles and discuss the then-controversial trade of NBA player Lebron James to the Miami Heat.

Emily also noticed that students listened to popular music and talked about how it made them feel, what the lyrics meant, and how the production, beats, and rhythms moved them. But when it came to writing, the students were still hesitant.

Emily was effective at opening up space for students to share, reflect, and think aloud; however, these conversations often seemed to stop there, at conversation. Was there a simple way to engage student conversation in a way that would enable them to practice their writing? She knew that merely recording the conversation wouldn't be sufficient. Having experimented with the writing process, she could see that for many children, writing on its own did not capture the full depth and complexity of their ideas. Emily wanted children to feel powerful, proud, and confident in expressing themselves using language.

Emily decided to use *screencasting*, a process through which anything on a computer screen can be recorded, with or without a simultaneous voiceover. Examples of screencasting software include free web-based tools like Screenr (www.screenr.com) or downloadable tools created by TechSmith, including Snagit and Camtasia.

The effect of a screencast is that of director's commentary about a film or television show. You can hear the creator's commentary while you see whatever is on the computer screen. Since her students were interested in exploring classic hip-hop music videos by artists like Queen Latifah and Public Enemy, Emily asked the children to analyze these, first spontaneously through conversation, then in an extemporaneous form; these short speeches, timed to accompany the visual images of the music video, were planned and organized in advance. Students had detailed written notes, but their responses were not written out word for word.

This activity took less than an hour, and by the end of it, the simple media production had yielded some interesting analysis and added value to the conversations students were having in class. For example, one group of boys noticed the socially empowering message in Queen Latifah's 1991 music video for her song "U.N.I.T.Y.":

> **Andrew:** I got from this song that women should stand up for themselves and don't let men abuse them.
>
> **Byron:** I did not like how men were hurting the women. If you put your hands on a woman, you are a punk.
>
> **Charles:** I like how Queen Latifah was boosting up girls' self-esteem.

It didn't take long to create these screencasts. First came the brainstorming to find the best ideas. Then an informal script, or set of talking points, was written. There was a rehearsal process, and then the screencasts were performed and recorded in a matter of minutes. Students were able to translate their spontaneous analysis of popular culture to a clear product that also required a bit of formal writing. Because they were not intimidated by an essay format, students could develop brief but powerful ideas using a combination of both written and spoken language. You can see samples of this and other student screencasts at powerfulvoicesforkids.com.

When screencasts are demonstrated to teachers, it's often depicted as a top-down technology, a way for the teacher or expert to demonstrate, model, convey, or deliver a message to learners. Many of the videos from the Khan Academy (www.khanacademy.org) are like this, simple screencast tutorials by good teachers who explain concepts like addition or multiplication in an engaging way.

Recently, screencasting has inspired educators at the high school and college levels to explore the *flipped classroom*, where students view instructor-created screencast lectures or slide shows at home, as homework outside of class, so that classroom time can be used for answering questions, working with small groups, and guiding the learning of each student individually.

But we like screencasts for a different reason: They offer opportunities for students themselves to be authors, simultaneously strengthening their communication and critical analysis skills through media production.[11] Screencasting is an authorship tool that requires students to observe and listen carefully to the media they hear, see, and interact with and then comment on it in both spontaneous and planned ways through listening, speaking, and writing. It captures structured dialogue between students but can also be used as a formal mechanism to introduce even young children to identifying a variety of different components of messages.

LEARNING TO REVISE: CREATING SCREENCASTS TO EXPLORE FOOD AND NUTRITION POLITICS

Mr. Fitzgerald, the teacher who struggled with PowerPoint, wanted to increase his own comfort with technology tools by using screencasting in his classroom. As an experienced public school teacher in Philadelphia, Mr. Fitzgerald was keenly aware of the sensitive politics of teaching diverse urban students about complex topics. In recent years, he had turned his attention to childhood nutrition. He had followed reports about initiatives by Michelle Obama to publicly address childhood obesity at the national level. He had begun teaching his students about the intersections between nutrition and public policy, discussing high-profile local issues like the implementation of a soda tax to benefit Philadelphia public schools.

The day after Mr. Fitzgerald discussed the soda tax with his Grade 5 students, they came up with an idea of their own about the politics of food. While watching the local TV news, one student had learned of a group called Corporate Accountability International that was putting pressure on the McDonald's Corporation to stop using their colorful clown mascot, Ronald McDonald, to sell unhealthy food to children.[12] Mr. Fitzgerald's class had strong reactions to this news story. Some students thought that "little kids" (their younger brothers and sisters) were attracted to Ronald McDonald and Happy Meal toys without realizing that McDonald's might not be a healthy choice. Others believed that it was up to parents to feed their children with healthy options and that getting rid of Ronald McDonald and Happy Meals would be devastating for kids who loved those aspects of McDonald's.

Mr. Fitzgerald used two strategies to capitalize on students' engagement. First, he split the class into a "pro" group and a "con" group. One group would do some online research to develop an argument about why McDonald's should consider retiring its mascot and Happy Meals. The other group would develop an argument about why McDonald's should be able to keep those components of their marketing to children. Students who were unsure of which position they agreed with, or who wanted more structure in the assignment (e.g., "I agree with it, but I'm not sure why") were given a specific position to research—for example, a city council member, a concerned parent, or a McDonald's company spokesperson.

After gathering information on this issue using online research, Mr. Fitzgerald decided to encourage his students to create a screencast, even though he had only one prior experience with creating one himself. He was a little nervous about trying out this idea in class. But his fears about the project started to recede as children began their search for simple news reports, newspaper articles, and websites that supported their position. Mr. Fitzgerald realized that what they were doing was a digitally enhanced version of a timeless debate activity, where students use role-playing and personal opinion to guide the research process. When viewed that way, the technical requirements seemed less daunting.

Where it differed from a standard debate, and in ways that Mr. Fitzgerald did not foresee, was when it came time for students to revise their research projects, which they had written in the five-paragraph essay form, to meet the demands of a screencasting production activity. Because they had selected media texts like newscasts and commercials to illustrate their ideas, some children found that their five-paragraph essay structure did not transfer perfectly to the screencast genre, which is ultimately a short oral presentation matched with visual images. Indeed, students hadn't thought very much at all about the relationship between the words and the pictures.

So during the rehearsal phase of the production, as children read their scripts aloud, many were frustrated that what they were trying to say didn't seem to fit with the images they had selected. Spontaneously and independently of formal instruction, children began to revise their essays, rearranging words, sentences, and even paragraphs that didn't concisely get across the points that were most important.

And after students heard their own voices recorded on the first take of the screencasts they had created, they realized that even more revision was needed. They had still other ideas about word choice, argument structure, and delivery that might strengthen their presentation. Although a few students decided ultimately to read their original five-paragraph essays in their original form, most students revised their pieces radically, creating something more like a brief position paper or editorial.

Mr. Fitzgerald, who grew up with TV news editorials that were marked as such and separated into their own section of news broadcasts, was pleased to see that his students' work had begun to transform into a classic television format that, he felt, had been lost in the evolution of the 24-hour cable news cycle.

Because his students felt safe exploring, testing, and revising, Mr. Fitzgerald himself felt more comfortable approaching his curriculum the same way. And he also knew that, though he wasn't technically a technology expert, his own brand of expertise in helping students engage with a meaningful contemporary public debate had far more impact on the children's learning experience than the specific technology skills required for the production itself.

Some higher education scholars, including Cathy Davidson of Duke University, have explored using blogs, video, and other simple technology tools to develop students' writing. Davidson notes that the quality of writing her students sometimes produce in blogs exceeds the quality of their formal research papers, in part because their more natural engagement translates to students writing more than they may think they are writing.[13]

The potential of simple media production to enhance the learning process may be even more pronounced as students are just beginning to develop their confidence in their print writing skills. This principle applies to the discoveries made by Mr. Fitzgerald. Screencasting allowed his students to match the passion of their extemporaneous arguments to an informal writing style, and actively encouraged students not only to write but also to revise and rewrite to improve their work.

PLAYING WITH REMIX AND PARODY

As children get nearer to puberty, they face new pressures to depict themselves in ways that are aligned with the norms presented in the culture. Many boys become more interested in demonstrating their competence in sports; many girls seek to be thin, to sing or dance, or to wear trendy outfits. Children recognize that getting attention through music, performance, and athletic ability is highly valued in American culture.

At the end of the school year in 2011, many children and teens were talking about a previously unknown teenager from Orange County, California, who unexpectedly became one of the most popular new celebrities in the pop music scene despite having no performing experience, record label, or any connections to the world of professional music production. It was the kind of a fantasy-turns-reality that Andy Warhol once predicted when he noted that, in the future, everyone would have 15 minutes of fame.

When Rebecca Black turned 13, her mother paid a company called Ark Music Factory—a cross between an amateur music production team and a pop singer fantasy camp for young women—to write, produce, and create a music video for her daughter to have what we might call an immersive digital and media literacy experience.

It's likely that Rebecca Black's mother had some key media literacy questions for her daughter in mind: What is it really like to produce your own pop song? How hard is it? Can anyone be famous? The result of the collaboration between Rebecca Black and Ark Music Factory was "Friday," a song that became an overnight Internet sensation, getting over 100 million views on YouTube in only 45 days. In the weeks after it was released, Rebecca Black became a genuine celebrity, appearing on talk shows, on news broadcasts, and in cameo roles in professional music videos for the hottest contemporary pop stars.

But not everyone liked the young girl's foray into stardom. Within only a few days of the song's release on YouTube in March 2011, it became the most talked-about topic on Twitter, receiving more than 3 million "dislikes" as compared with 450,000 "likes." Rebecca Black's so-called haters took delight in being mean-spirited, making remarks like "Worst singer ever," "I hope you cut yourself," and "I hope you get an eating disorder so you look pretty." Some even sent her death threats![14]

That spring, in fact, it seemed that a lot of children were taking a lot of pleasure in formulating strong opinions about the song. Mr. Marino's students, a group of sixth graders, had divided and intense opinions about the song. Many found its chorus to be catchy and memorable, a legitimate addition to their own personal canon of favorites. Others found it irritating—they disliked the vocals, the production, and the lyrics. They protested to their teacher, "*We* could make a better song than that."

It was the end of the school year, a time when it's hard to start any new serious work as the rising sixth graders were in their last days at the elementary school. Mr. Marino saw in his students' engagement with the Rebecca Black debate an opportunity for a *remix* activity that, he thought, they could feasibly complete in a week or two, using little of the time set aside for formal instruction. A remix is defined as an alternative version of a recorded song, made from an original version. Sometimes this term is also used as a verb, describing the process of altering a variety of media, including stories, books, movies, video games and other aspects of culture to create something new.

Students begin the process of remixing by identifying what aspects of the song they might change to create their own message and then remix the song, using the original music to sing their new lyrics over the old beat.

As something of a tech expert, Mr. Marino was eager to figure out how to produce this type of project. He immediately imagined the technical components of the project: purchase a karaoke version of the song, which had already been created in response to the song's popularity and was available on websites like iTunes; use a microphone connected to a classroom computer to record students singing at the tempo of the original song; edit the vocal and music together in a simple audio editing program like Audacity or Windows Media Maker. Voilà!

What Mr. Marino could not foresee were the ways in which this seemingly simple technical exercise would take on new, meaningful dimensions for students as they navigated the production process, even in brief sessions that did not conflict with classroom instruction. The entire process took them through the entire production cycle—the preproduction phases of brainstorming, planning, and writing; the production phases of recording and rerecording; and the postproduction phases of editing and revision.

In their first brainstorming session, students quickly thought of the subject matter they wanted to address in their remix: they would change the title of the song from "Friday" to "Wednesday," referring to their last day of classes as elementary schoolers, which was quickly approaching in a little over 2 weeks. Lyrics came quickly as students repeated verbatim from memory the song's original lyrics and then modified them to be specific to their own school culture. They had informal conversations about rhyme schemes, syllables, and using an economy of language to get across their ideas in the song.

Next, students discussed the production of the song—what is usually referred to as the beat or the music. Opinion was divided: Lots of students enjoyed the original beat of the song, but others found it amateurish and corny. Mr. Marino and his students decided to devote their final few music classes to working with their music teacher to re-create the music for their own purposes. The music teacher used a combination of electric and live piano and a computer-generated beat to create a close copy of the original song.

Throughout the process, students offered specific suggestions about how to improve the beat: the drums and cymbals shouldn't be so loud; a real piano should be used instead of a keyboard; could it be a little faster?

Finally it was time for students to record their own voices over the recorded beat provided by the music teacher with the lyrics they had written in class. They learned about singing directly into a microphone and saw what the sound waves of their voices looked like in the free audio editing program Audacity. They played with effects, observing how their voices sounded with more reverb ("It's like an echo!"). They listened to the song in their headphones and, confident that it would sound exactly as they imagined, they began to sing. But when the music and words came together, students were frustrated. A chorus of voices echoed:

"Why do our voices sound like that?"

"That's not on the beat!"

"You can't even hear our part!"

"Please, can we do this again?"

Their attentiveness to its quality surprised Mr. Marino. These were students who rarely excelled in peer critique of written work and often had little warm and cool feedback for each other's work. But for this performance, nearly every student had an opinion—noticing a missing detail here, a mistake there. Students *insisted* on revising their performance.

The "Best Work" Test

Teacher-librarian Sue Dahlstrom knows that children between the ages of 7 and 12 are keenly aware of professional standards in media production. When children create short formal or informal media productions, she asks them, "Is this your best work?" It's a question that often spurs reflection and revision. When children choose to revise, they deepen their personal investment in a project, sometimes reworking entire projects from conception to completion.

Writing composition teachers are enthusiastic about the promise of digital media because they've discovered that learners value the revision process when they're working with familiar genres. When students are engaged in media production activities, they often show a willingness to think critically about their work in a way that can be difficult in forms of media with which they are unfamiliar. When students write book reports, letters, informational brochures, and other forms of print media that are embedded in the elementary curriculum, they often have little basis for judging the quality of their own work. But children are familiar with the codes and conventions of popular music, television, films, websites, and video games. They can use this knowledge to make real-world comparisons to their own work.

Mr. Marino's students were easily able to respond to an existing work and create a parody by activating home and cultural knowledge. But educators must interrogate the parody in terms of its educational value. David Buckingham warns that sometimes children's parodies can serve as an easy out to a more nuanced understanding of issues, particularly issues surrounding popular culture.[15] In all media production exercises, there is a balance between fun and learning. As we see it, Mr. Marino's project was a classic end-of-year activity, good for strengthening student engagement, building on teamwork and collaboration, and highlighting the role of revision in the composition process. But it was not so useful as a means to promote critical thinking or creativity.

Simple engagement with cool tools and fun media production projects can be appealing to teachers who use media production in the classroom. But it shouldn't be a substitute for learning. How can teachers balance learning goals with the inevitable exploration, troubleshooting, and fun that go into most media productions?

BALANCING PLAY AND LEARNING

When media production is paired with inquiry-based learning, students are actively involved in formulating questions, investigating widely, and then building new understandings, meanings and knowledge. This new knowledge may be used to answer a question, to develop a solution, or to support a position or point of view. The knowledge is usually presented to others and may result in some sort of action. The work of one of our summer PVK instructors provides an illustrative example of how to achieve the balance between play and learning that is critical to the success of inquiry learning.

Osei had long worked with disenfranchised teens in creative media production activities, generally in informal learning environments. But he had never worked with elementary school students prior to the Powerful Voices for Kids program. He went through the same process as Mr. Marino—students talked about some of their favorite songs and then identified a theme or message that interested them. In Osei's class, the students had decided that their overarching theme was "Stop the violence in the Philadelphia community," based on discussions the students had about the differences between how the world is represented in popular music and how they experience it in their lives.

After deciding on a theme, students recorded a new vocal track over the instrumental for a popular song, "Hold Yuh," by reggae artist Gyptian. To do this, they needed to compose lyrics, which included both singing and rapping. Most substantive learning happened when students explored the formal conventions of popular music and tried out different ways of creating songs, beats, and rhymes.

Students had to think carefully about both the *form and content* elements of their piece. What did they want to say, and how did they want to say it? How would they rhyme their words—would they use multiple rhymes per line, like many of their favorite rappers, or keep it simpler? And what kind of stories did they want to tell in their own song?

Of course, to record the song, the teacher needed some familiarity and comfort with editing sound with music software tools. As a musician himself, Osei was intimately familiar with the hidden and unexpected technical hurdles in music production. Issues like microphone quality and placement, sound effects, and equalizing volume levels can be challenging for novice teachers to address. Fortunately, children who possessed natural singing talents enjoyed sharing their vocal gifts with the class, while students who had never rhymed or rapped before discovered newfound talents and new ways to express themselves.

The lyrics that students worked on over the course of the week were evocative, poetic, and powerful:

> Why be a victim, a criminal, a drug dealer
> You could be a hero instead of a stealer
> You rob and you shoot people, you think you bad
> That ain't nothin' compared to the life we've had
> Where I'm from, people shoot first, ask questions later
> Block block, chop chop, like a zombie slayer
> If you get in his way, you're gonna catch the worst of it
> And please, promise me you'll never forget

When other teachers listened to the song, they were struck by the poignancy of the message: These children were singing about the various representations and realities of life in tough urban neighborhoods, warning others about the dangers of the so-called gangster lifestyle. Children had decided to select a specific instrumental track of music and develop a new message through the writing and revision process. This process led to quite an exceptional song. In both its form and content, it's thrilling to imagine that a group of 11-year-olds created it. You can listen to the song online at www.powerfulvoicesforkids.com.

What we noticed was that this media production experience unintentionally encouraged students to continue writing lyrics and poetry in their spare time. Evidence from one student's journal shows her and a friend trading turns writing new rap lyrics for songs that did not yet exist. Their writing was playful but well constructed. It might have been mistaken for an off-task excursion in frivolous note-passing unless you took note of some of the same formal principles Osei taught to his students in action, as they numbered each rhyme and compared the construction of their song to lyrics by the OMG Girlz, a girl group that includes the daughter of rap star Lil' Wayne.

1. Ciara and Jamelia they call us CJ Productions
2. We fly and we ballin I'll tell you about my passions
3. Yeah we the best I'll tell you about my fashions
4. 1st of all we in charge salute to your captains
5. We walk up in the spot we be amazin you
6. We number one but you can be number two

More research is needed to better understand how the process of students transforming favorite media into their own creative work may build competencies of digital and media literacy education. Scholars of hip-hop education, including Ernest Morrell, Chris Emdin, and Marc Lamont Hill, have begun to explore this rich and complex terrain.[16] Anecdotal evidence from the Powerful Voices for Kids program shows that lessons learned in this activity translated to other creative writing work that students did independently and voluntarily.

At its core, however, the songwriting project was not primarily a technology activity. It began with a need to "stop the violence" in social relationships. In expressing this set of values through song, children gained a sense of themselves as advocates for social and political change.

MAKING VIDEO GAMES: CHOICES AND CONSEQUENCES

Some teachers use their own advanced knowledge and skills as media producers themselves in order to develop a particularly challenging media production. Our colleague John Landis has a wealth of expertise in media production and computer programming. As a summer PVK instructor, John knew that his students should understand the choices that go into the design of video games and have at least a basic understanding of computer programming in the creation of the websites and games they loved. He was familiar with the academic field of video game studies, in which scholars like James Gee have made the case that video games exemplify an integral component of new literacy practices.[17] Douglas Rushkoff even claims that students, by about age 10, should learn to program their computers or "be programmed" by them.[18]

John knew that actual programming, like learning how to type or write in cursive, requires technical skills that can take months if not years to develop. He wanted his students to understand not the technical language of computer programming, but rather the features of video gaming that create meaning in his students' lives. He identified the opportunity for players to *make choices* as essential to that understanding.

In the summer of 2010, many Philadelphia schoolchildren were being told by guidance counselors, administrators, teachers, and parents that they needed to make better choices—especially when it came to forming *flash mobs*, impromptu gatherings of teens in public spaces. Media outlets portrayed the 2010 flash mobs that were spontaneously occurring in Philadelphia as violent mobs. They focused on vandalism, property damage, and in some cases, arrests of young men and women who participated.

John's students had another perspective. They were too young to participate in the flash mob events but old enough to know people, including family members and neighbors, who might be involved. They knew that some people made poor choices but that flash mobs were a complicated phenomenon. Some kids went because their friends pressured them to. Some might get in trouble with their parents if they did go but would be in worse trouble with their peers if they didn't. What kind of media would help them express these complicated points of view on the subject?

John used his knowledge of computer programming to teach the students Scratch, open-source video game software developed by the MIT Media Lab. Scratch uses a kid-friendly jigsaw design to help students understand the *process* of creating a video game. For instance, a student might imagine a scenario in which a character has to choose whether to go to a flash mob. If you click "go," you end up at the flash mob. If you click "don't go," you end up in your bedroom.

The hardest part of this process, John discovered, was not the programming itself. During summer instruction, he had ample time to let his students explore the software, and what's more, some of his more avid gamers in class used spare time to intuitively figure out more about the software. What was more difficult for *all* students, though, was the level of preproduction required in developing the video game. Students created flow charts and other organizational tools to help them visualize the world of their game on paper before they began to work with the software. John had to unexpectedly redo a lesson on flowcharts when, after their first lesson, some students were still struggling to think through the various choices available to users in the games they were creating.

He knew what his media production activities were *for*—he wanted his students to think not about programming in and of itself, but about ways of making media that told stories not only in its content but in its very structure. When students created their flash mob video games, they were simultaneously deepening their understanding of how choices work in interactive media and reflecting on a pertinent social issue.

Professional media-making abilities can be both an asset and a liability in the classroom. Renee has written about common issues in youth media production at the middle and high school levels, including superficial use of mass media tropes and stereotypes, unfinished projects, more time spent on perfecting the style than mastering the content, and other common pitfalls.[19] In some ways, these concerns can be even more acute for elementary educators, who have to deal also with students' developmental levels in working collaboratively and sustaining interest in a project that may take days or even weeks to complete.

Scratch

www.scratch.mit.edu

Scratch is a programming language that makes it easy for people to create their own interactive stories, animations, games, music, and art—and share these creations on the web. As young people create and share Scratch projects, they learn important mathematical and computational ideas, while also learning to think creatively, reason systematically, and work collaboratively.

THE DELICATE BALANCE BETWEEN ORDER AND CHAOS

We once gave a workshop to experienced youth media and community media producers to talk about the delicate balance of order and chaos in an elementary or secondary classroom or afterschool program where collaborative media production activities take place. We asked participants to "raise your hand if you have had a project seriously compromised because of problems resulting from classroom management chaos."

Every hand in the room went up.

Creative classrooms are often noisy places. We observed a consistent tension between order and chaos in the classrooms where children were creating media and using technology. Progressive educators who use inquiry learning methods have long noted this phenomenon. In creative classrooms, it is often "hard to distinguish between apparent chaos and creative disorder," says open classroom education veteran Herb Kohl.[20]

Walking the hallways of the Powerful Voices for Kids program, an observer would generally see small groups of children in a classroom, talking, writing on the blackboard, dancing, or acting out a scene. In one room, children might be musically improvising, with a small digital piano, drums, and plenty of hand clapping and singing. In another room, an observer would hear a spirited conversation going on, led by a teacher who might be frequently interrupted by students calling out ideas. In another room, children might be working at tables, drawing out a storyboard, or writing in a journal. At the computer lab, children might be surfing the Internet, uploading and manipulating photos, or using a drag-and-drop computer programming tool to create simple interactives. Teachers are not always comfortable with learning environments like this.[21]

Educators and learners often underestimate how much time is required for media production. Nearly every instructor we observed wrestled with the effort involved in getting a group of children to complete a media production project. For example, Mr. Fitzgerald thought his Grade 5 students would be able to create a public service announcement in 1 week, but it actually took 3 weeks to complete. Even very simple projects, it seemed, took more time than expected.

The delicate balance between order and chaos and the time-consuming process of media production are phenomena that are little discussed among theorists in the field of digital media and learning. There is a gap between theory and practice that we are trying to address in this book. As PVK instructor Emily described it,

> Coming to Powerful Voices for Kids every single morning was such an exciting thing. I am very familiar with a lot of theory and a lot of studies that have been done but I've never seen it actually in action, so that's been incredible. I mean it started at 6 a.m. when I was up and it, you know, ended maybe at 10 p.m. when I would go back to sleep at night. It was just the adrenaline kicking in.

Despite the heroic efforts of Emily and the rest of the staff, some projects developed by Powerful Voices for Kids students did not get finished. Some lessons even bombed within the first 10 minutes. Others bore the unmistakable mark of the teacher who did some late-night heavy lifting to edit video or polish up websites.

Classroom management issues arose because new learning activities (like viewing and discussing) were unfamiliar to some children. Many children in the program had not previously experienced classrooms where movies, videos, and YouTube were used as educational resources. Most children grow up thinking of media as fundamentally part of out-of-school playful fun. To create a learning environment where children could have actual dialogue about popular culture, music, movies, video games, websites, apps, television, and other media, for example, teachers had to develop and practice precise routines for managing discussion. Teachers explicitly modeled how to share responses, one at a time, and how to look at people while they are talking, showing your level of listening and understanding through nonverbal indicators.

We learned that it takes time for children to approach viewing activities with a certain level of seriousness, since long before they enter school at age 5, children have already learned to see video viewing as simple entertainment—something you do for fun, not learning.

When PVK instructor Val led children through a viewing and discussion of the children's film *Cheaper by the Dozen,* with Steve Martin, children struggled with detaching themselves from the narrative in order to have a discussion. They clamored, "Don't stop the movie!" and "Let's keep watching!" which created tension in the classroom as Val tried in vain to activate children's interpretations of the film by asking questions.

Sometimes the creative ideas that children share inadvertently lead to classroom management challenges when teachers become uncomfortable with the unique and sometimes unpredictable perspectives of children, who fuse together personal life experiences and media experiences as they create their own messages.

When PVK instructor Dee was leading a conversation about heroes, victims, and villains in storytelling by asking children to create characters, one of her Grade 2 students read from her story:

> My character is bad because, when she was a young little girl, people always used to pick on her and she got tired of it. Her childhood was really bad, and then when she was a grownup, since people did all that mean stuff to her, she's gonna do it to other people, even though she don't even know them.

Indeed, this child had created a character who was both a villain and a victim, but Dee wasn't sure how to respond to the child's story. Was the child inspired by media experiences to generate this idea? Or by personal experiences? As she hesitated in deciding how to respond, the hubbub of response from the other children led to some confusion and the loss of classroom momentum.

Other issues arose from children's lack of comfort with a creative space, where creative activities, like brainstorming, involve certain kinds of verbal and sometimes physical playfulness.

For example, when David's students wrote and produced their own pop song, they wanted to create the beat, the chorus, and the dance simultaneously. Coming into the classroom, an observer would see a cluster of students standing at the whiteboard, fighting for the dry erase marker, as they collaborated on writing and revising song lyrics. Other students were working on the computer, using GarageBand to create their beats. Still other students had pushed aside the classroom chairs as they worked out the choreography to the dance. For parents, educators, and school leaders who expect learning to happen in quiet classrooms where children are seated at desks, this kind of learning environment can be startling, to say the least.

CREATING A CLIMATE OF MUTUAL RESPECT

Media production and analysis activities are intensely social. As a result, we saw many examples of respect, kindness, and generosity among children that fueled their creativity, but we also observed some learning situations that included interpersonal aggression and meanness that interfered with the quality of learning and the quality of student-teacher relationships.

Some days, it seemed that the classrooms were bubbling with one-upmanship and "one-downmanship" of social power—among children and between students and teachers. Again, some part of this was clearly linked to the lack of experience on the part of teachers in creating a respectful learning environment. To help beginning teachers, we offered support and structure to address classroom management issues by using Doug Lemov's book *Teach Like a Champion*.[22]

PVK instructor Nuala worried that her Grade 5 students engaged in sometimes aggressive and mean-spirited behavior that might lead teachers to lower their expectations of learners:

> One of my biggest fears [is] that teachers, some teachers, might give up on them. Sometimes I just want to say, "You can't act like this! You can't act like this because if you do continue to act like this, I'm afraid that teachers might give up on you, you know."

From these experiences, we wondered:

- How might media exposure contribute to children's emerging understanding of what's right and wrong when it comes to social relationships? Does this behavior reflect the impact of the kind of hurtfulness and power games that are so much of contemporary culture, including entertainment culture—the normalizing of insulting creative efforts we see on *American Idol*, or the backstabbing and two-faced lying on the reality shows?
- How do we nurture and cultivate the values that really matter— creating trust, respect, warmth, and caring in a community where people have shared goals?

These questions remind us of why educators need professional learning communities. Thank goodness that there were so many instances in which kids and teachers came together for productive work and learning, so that even when disruption occurred, these moments were offset by other very human moments that occurred spontaneously when we encountered each other as human beings, in all our frailty and with all our limitations.

Lesson   Screencasting the Critical Questions

Lesson Description

Students learn to ask critical questions about popular culture using the five critical questions and demonstrate their critical analysis, reading fluency, and vocal performance skills by creating a short video screencast to document their interpretations.

Objectives

Students will

- Appreciate the value of asking critical questions as a way to analyze the meaning of a message
- Understand that all media messages are constructed by people who make choices
- Strengthen writing and revising skills
- Improve vocal fluency and performance skills
- Use screencasting to create a video that documents their work

Vocabulary

Screencasting

Clip

Reasoning

Inference

Imagination

Respect

Deadline

Feedback

Resources and Materials

✓ Clip sample (see the links below)

✓ Data projector or computer lab

✓ Screencasting tool like Screenr, SnagIt, or Camtasia

Activity

Access

✓ Encourage children to exchange opinions about a TV program that many are familiar with, like *American Idol* or *iCarly*. Demonstrate respectful listening and using a nonverbal signal to indicate when you agree with the speaker.

✓ Explain that it is important to appreciate that people have different ideas about what they like and dislike and that every person may find something valuable or important in many different kinds of media. What's important is the ability for us to explain why we think and feel in certain ways.

Analysis

✓ Introduce the Media Literacy Remote Control, and show the video about how it works (http://mediaeducationlab.com/what-media-literacy-0). Offer a specific example of kids who use the critical questions by showing this clip (www.youtube.com/watch?v=DdWQv1JaSYs&feature=plcp; cue to 1:27) featuring children analyzing a department store commercial.

✓ Practice using the critical questions by showing children an *iCarly* clip about teachers and technology (http://youtu.be/R6LN1vE3n-8). As a whole group, discuss possible answers to each of the five critical questions:

1. Who created this message, and what was the purpose?

2. What techniques are used to attract and hold attention?

3. What lifestyles, values, and points of view are shown?

4. How might different people interpret this message?

5. What is left out?

✓ When students give answers, write them on the board. Encourage children to elaborate and offer reasoning by asking *why* questions. There can be many different answers for the same question.

✓ Critical questions require some educated guesses or inference-making. It's OK if children aren't sure or don't know. Encourage them to use their imagination and their reasoning. Many will be familiar with the program and have knowledge about the characters or situations that they can use in their explanations. Point out that good reasons make an answer better and more powerful than answers without reasoning or evidence to explain or justify an opinion.

✓ Play the clip a couple of times to encourage children to look and listen carefully to the images, language, sound, music, and editing. By considering the choices that the producer made in creating the message, students can analyze and evaluate these choices and make inferences about the message purpose.

Composition

✓ Model the process of creating a script and making a screencast, explaining to children that they will be doing this on their own after they learn how to do it.

✓ Use the phrases and ideas generated by students to compose a simple script, using this structure:

My name is _____ and the media I am analyzing is _____. The first question is, "Who is the author and what is the purpose?" I think the author is _____ and the purpose is _____ because _____. The second question is _____.

✓ Demonstrate how to make a screencast by selecting a still image from the media message and recording your voice reading the script.

✓ Play the screencast video, and ask students to offer warm and cool feedback about what they like about the video and what could be improved.

✓ Review and discuss a screencast made by a team of three children who analyzed music videos from the 1990s (http://youtube/M5EoHOArrk4).

✓ Divide the class into partner groups (two or three children to a group), and encourage them to select a video to view and analyze using the critical questions. Give students some deadline pressure to complete the task. Make sure students compose a script to plan what they intend to say as they talk about the video.

✓ You may choose to assign students a clip to analyze, select from a group of clips you have chosen, or even let them select one for themselves.

✓ Review the students' work and, as a group, ask students to offer warm and cool feedback to each team.

Reflection

✓ Discuss: What did students notice about how asking critical questions changes the way they see TV and video? Explain that all TV images are made by people who make choices. When students analyze a message, they notice these choices and pay attention to them.

Taking Action

✓ When children listen to music, use social media, read books, or watch movies and TV shows, they can notice the choices made by authors and be inspired to create their own messages.

Source: Created by Renee Hobbs.

NOTES

1. Florida, R. (2002). *The rise of the creative class.* New York, NY: Basic.
2. Kleinsmiede, H. (2002). Multimedia challenging epistemology: Epistemology challenging multimedia: Noting this reciprocity for multimedia design. In R. Earnshaw & J. Vince (Eds.), *Digital content creation* (pp. 60–78). New York, NY: Springer.
3. Lazorchak, B. (2012, May 8). *Telling tales: Joe Lambert From the Center for Digital Storytelling.* Retrieved from http://blogs.loc.gov/digitalpreserva tion/2012/05/telling-tales-joe-lambert-from-the-center-for-digital-story telling/
4. Burgess, J. (2006). Hearing ordinary voices: Cultural studies, vernacular creativity and digital storytelling. *Continuum: Journal of Media & Cultural Studies, 20,* 201–214.

5. Burgess (2006), p. 207.
6. McKenzie, J. (2000). Scoring power points. *From Now On: The Educational Technology Journal, 10*(1). Retrieved from http://www.fno.org/index.html
7. U.S. National Commission on Libraries and Information Science (2008). *School libraries work!* Washington, DC: Author. Retrieved from http://www .scholastic.com/content/collateral_resources/pdf/s/slw3_2008.pdf
8. National Center for Education Statistics. (2009). *Characteristics of public and Bureau of Indian Education elementary and secondary school library media centers in the United States: Results from the 2007–08 Schools and Staffing Survey* (NCES No. 2009322). Washington, DC: Author.
9. Barack. L. (2012, November).The league of extraordinary librarians. *School Library Journal.* Retrieved from http://www.slj.com/
10. Sanacore, J., & Palumbo, A. (2009). Understanding the fourth-grade slump: Our point of view. *The Educational Forum, 73,* 67–74.
11. Moore, D. C. (2010). Pause, point, rewind: The use of screen capture software for media analysis. *Recherches en Communication, 24,* 115–127.
12. Jargon, J. (2011, May 18). McDonald's under pressure to fire Ronald. *Wall Street Journal.*
13. Davidson, C. (2012). *Should we really abolish the term paper? A response to the* NY Times. Retrieved from http://hastac.org/blogs/cathy-david-son/2012/01/21/should-we-really-abolish-term-paper-response-ny-times
14. ABC News. (2011). Rebecca Black: "Don't think I'm the worst singer." *Good Morning America.* Retrieved from http://abcnews.go.com/GMA/video/ rebecca-black-dont-think-im-worst-singer-13164800
15. Buckingham, D. (2003). *Media education: Literacy, learning, and contemporary culture.* London, England: Polity.
16. Morrell, E., & Duncan-Andrade, J. (2002). Promoting academic literacy with urban youth through hip-hop culture. *English Journal, 91*(6), 88–92.
17. Gee, J. (2003). *What video games have to teach us about learning and literacy.* New York, NY: Palgrave Macmillan.
18. Rushkoff, D. (2010). *Program or be programmed: Ten commands for a digital age.* New York, NY: OR Books.
19. Hobbs, R. (2011). *Digital and media literacy: Connecting classroom and culture.* Thousand Oaks, CA: Corwin.
20. Kohl, H. (1969). *The open classroom.* New York, NY: Taylor and Francis (p. 39).
21. Moore, D. C. (2011). Asking questions first: Navigating transgression and popular culture in an inquiry-based media literacy classroom. *Action in Teacher Education, 33,* 219–230.
22. Lemov, D. (2007). *Teach like a champion.* San Francisco, CA: Jossey-Bass.

6 Everything Is Social

In this chapter, you'll learn about

Taking Action in the World

- How can teachers link literacy practices to the community and help their students discover the power and social responsibility of taking action in the world?

Literacy, Ethics, and Social Relationships

- How can educators create digital and media literacy learning environments where students trust and respect one another and develop an active stance toward messages?

Exploring Advertising and Celebrity Culture

- How can teachers engage children's intellectual curiosity so that they want to learn more?

How Media Literacy Supports Print Literacy

- How can viewing and discussing media and popular culture and creating multimedia productions develop children's reading comprehension skills?

When a Philadelphia fifth grader wrote a letter to the president of the United States about her experience being bullied, it was a surprise to most of her peers. Most children who experience harassment from their peers don't tell anyone. There's a lot of shame associated with the experience of bullying. It takes courage even just to talk about it to a close friend.

But the pain Ziainey had experienced as the target of teasing and name-calling in school inspired her to write to the president when she learned about another student who had committed suicide after suffering from years of bullying.

Her dad mailed the handwritten letter to President Obama—and lo and behold, the president wrote back to her, thanking her for the letter and offering encouraging words that inspired Ziainey to start a support group with other children at her school. Through these empathetic and courageous actions, Ziainey discovered the power of literacy to change oneself—and the world.

Throughout this book, we have been using the term *literacy* to mean *the sharing of meaning through symbolic form*. There are two powerful elements of this definition. One is that meanings are shared through many types of symbols—nonverbal elements like facial expressions, tone of voice, and body language; spoken and written words; but also images, graphic design, moving images, sound, rhythm, and interactivity. The other is that literacy is also framed as a social practice: We share meaning through symbols in order to get things done in concert with others.

Literacy is tied up with our social relationships with people near and far. When children recognize how relevant, useful, and powerful literacy practices are in relation to their daily life experiences, they are motivated to want to develop those skills in order to use them to gain social power and influence.[1]

That's why the everyday practices of literacy—speaking, listening, reading, writing, analyzing messages, and sharing meaning using images, language, and technology tools—are so fundamentally linked to ethical conduct. Ziainey Stokes used writing to take principled action to address an unexpected problem in her own life. There was certainly something therapeutic in describing her troubling experience in writing, but there was also some substantial unpredictability in how others would respond. That's why the act was courageous.

Her parents, for example, could have berated her for not being tough enough to withstand the social pressure inflicted by the bullies. Her siblings could have humiliated her for expecting to receive a response to her heartfelt letter. Or her actions might have received no response at all, disappearing into invisibility. Any of these options (and numerous other possibilities) could have been the result of Ziainey's decision to write to the president.

As Hannah Arendt has explained, when it comes to taking action in the world, there is boundlessness to it, because we can never fully know the relationship between actions we take and the reactions that result.[2]

So when Powerful Voices for Kids (PVK) instructor LaShon saw the newspaper article about Ziainey Stokes, she brought the article to class for children to read. It launched an intense discussion about bullying. Children had a lot of strong, emotional reactions to the story. One of LaShon's Grade 3 students, Caleb, decided to write his own letter to President Obama. After composing it, he practiced reading his letter out loud.

Inspired by the suggestion that a YouTube video about bullying might help other kids gain confidence in sharing their stories, Caleb presented his letter as a formal video presentation, where, looking directly into the camera, he said:

> Dear President Obama, I would like to talk about bullying. Kids get bullied almost every day, in every school. Bullying is a real serious matter. When I was in third grade, I used to get bullied. One boy used to tease me about my head, my height, and my teeth. Another friend used to hit me for no reason. My friend Joshua has a problem with bullying and he told his mother, but she didn't do anything about it. Bullying should not be in school or outside. If a child gets bullied, they should tell an adult. I would like to stop bullying.

Caleb's powerful voice was clearly evident in his well-organized message, effective choice of examples, confident delivery, and earnest tone. You can see his letter and video performance at www.powerfulvoices forkids.com.

Our belief in the value of digital and media literacy is based on the provocative gap to be explored between teaching children both about *the world as it is* and *the world as it should be.* The natural idealism of youth is a renewing force in the world. As children discover the power of literacy, they gain courage in taking communicative action.

Because literacy practices are inextricably bound up in a web of social relationships, it's important for educators to create learning environments where trust and respect are the norm, where learners feel comfortable being themselves. When children have the expectation that they will be respected, they gain confidence in self-expression. They become more willing to take the risks that are an inevitable part of the creative process.

The Power of Self-Disclosure

Self-disclosure is the practice of letting another person know about your own wishes, desires, hopes, and fears.

When watching young children struggle with their complicated emotions, we sometimes say "Use your words" because we want them to have the courage that self-disclosure requires. When children encounter literature, poetry, and music, they can be invited to consider how much courage it takes *to make oneself visible* by using symbols to share meaning. Self-disclosure is a fundamental dimension of being an author. Even more important, self-disclosure is what makes social relationships authentic and meaningful.

THE SOCIAL CONTEXT OF LANGUAGE AND LITERACY DEVELOPMENT

Children's literacy skills do not develop in a vacuum but exist in relation to the specific dimensions of the particular social world around them. The contemporary social world is deeply inflected by media-related experiences—watching TV, reading books, listening to music, playing video games, and using the Internet.

Literacy scholars note that two key components are most strongly associated with reading comprehension. The first is *oral language* skills (listening comprehension and vocabulary). Early childhood educators know that *talking* is central to literacy development. Varied experiences (including music, reading and art activities, nature walks, field trips, author visits, games and dramatic play, and a variety of screen media messages) provide children with the content for talk. By telling stories, asking questions, offering opinions, and explaining what they know, children develop oral language competencies. Word play and rhyming help children notice the patterns in sound-letter relationships. Talk also helps children develop a good sense of the rules of social interaction, including the habits associated with active listening and turn taking.

The second literacy component involves a deep understanding of both the *alphabetic code* (letter-sound recognition) and the *text structure* (page turning, left-to-right reading, graphic design layout, sentence and paragraph structure). But these components don't just apply to children's understanding of the function of books. Children also need to understand the codes and structural characteristics of all forms of symbolic expression in their daily life: other print material, pictures, graphics, film, TV and video, websites, apps and games, and social media.

For these reasons, we wonder why some literacy educators neglect the power of mass media, popular culture, and digital media to promote children's literacy development. Some elementary educators are suspicious and fearful of children's engagement with mass media and digital media. Some treat *nonprint texts* as second-class citizens in the early childhood classroom (for example, by emphasizing the superiority of the printed word in relationship to photographs or illustrations). Too many teachers dismiss or trivialize children's use of television and movies. When emphasizing the importance of making connections between home and school, educators may ask parents to provide children with plenty of books and urge them to restrict or limit their exposure to film and television. They don't point out to parents the value of talking with children about their favorite TV shows, video games, and movies as a means to support oral language development.[3]

While we are sensitive to the genuine concerns of educators and parents about the volume and scope of children's exposure to mass media, we don't want those concerns to interfere with the practice of media literacy education. Whether we like it or not, children and their families do spend hours watching television, playing with apps, listening to music, and using the Internet. Because these practices are meaningful and significant, they deserve to be explored through inquiry.

Many parents are unaware of how *family social interaction* promotes literacy development. In 2010, the American Institutes for Research conducted extensive focus groups and survey research with low-income families in 20 communities. Because most parents are focused on supplying basic needs for their family, not all parents see themselves as their children's teacher. Most parents have very little time to be involved in their children's activities. Many poor and low-income parents do not know that simple behaviors, like rhyming and letter recognition games, can help their children get ready to read. Some parents do not read to their kids every day because they do not have time, do not read well, or cannot read English. However, parents are willing to try activities with their kids if they can easily fit them into their schedules.[4]

Researchers tell us that talk about television may support the development of listening, reading achievement, and attitudes that promote literacy. Preschoolers who watch and discuss *Dora the Explorer, Blue's Clues, Arthur, Clifford,* or *Dragon Tales* increase their vocabularies and have higher expressive language scores than children who don't view these programs.[5] The impact of viewing on specific reading skills such as inference making, comprehension, and vocabulary acquisition has also been explored; we must see television viewing (and cell phone and Internet use) as situated literacy practices embedded within family life.[6]

In many families, television, the Internet, and other forms of media actually expand children's knowledge and exposure to story genres. In fact, media and technology use may foster children's interests in various topics in ways that can support literacy development. Encounters with multiple perspectives through media can support critical thinking. Rather than being in competition, the entertainment and educational purposes of television, video games, and digital media may have a complementary, synergistic relationship in enhancing children's literacy and learning.

1-MINUTE MEDIATORIALS SUPPORT THE PROCESS OF ACTIVE REASONING

LaShon wanted to better understand her Grade 3 students' experience with television, movies, and video games and provide them with an opportunity to talk with confidence about something that was important to them. And she loved making up new and creative words as a way to illustrate to children the plasticity of language.

So she created a weekly activity she called the "Mediatorial," in which children made simple 1-minute videos where they talked about their favorite TV programs, musical artists, and books. Gradually, children gained confidence in sharing their ideas, offering increasingly polished on-camera performances to describe their in-home media use preferences. Here are some examples of their presentations:

Jacob: Hi, my name is Jacob. My favorite artists are Usher and Michael Jackson. My favorite TV show is *The Boondocks* but I'm not supposed to watch it because it's a little inappropriate.

Zaiah: Hi, my name is Zaiah. My favorite artist is Justin Bieber. When I first heard him, I cried. When I grow up I want to be a singer because I have a beautiful voice.

Karina: Hi, name is Karina. My favorite artist is Alicia Keys because I like her songs and she seems like a good person. My favorite book is the My Weird School series because they make me laugh.

In an activity she called Humanizing Celebrities, LaShon found images of 20 celebrities her students had named as important to them. She posted these images around the room. Each day, she stood near one of the images and read to children a short 2- to 3-minute article about some aspect of the celebrity that featured his or her childhood or adolescence. At the end of the week, she created a competitive quiz game for children to play. She had written 20 statements about the celebrities on index cards (e.g., "Who am I? I was teased incessantly in grade school about my big ears."). She placed the index cards face down on one of the desks, and two teams competed to answer the most number of questions correctly.

As LaShon explains it, this activity gave children a chance to practice listening comprehension skills, work as a team, and respect the ideas of their peers. Plus, it contributed to a certain level of demystification of celebrities. As LaShon puts it, "All of the questions are aimed at humanizing the celebrities who are oftentimes put on pedestals by children."

ACTIVE REASONING: A PRECURSOR TO MEDIA LITERACY

There are some important differences among children in *how* they talk about television, music, and video games. Some kids are virtual blabbermouths, with plenty of ideas and information to offer about why they like certain shows, musical artists, movie genres, and video games; others say very little. With her colleague Michael RobbGrieco, Renee conducted research to better understand how children develop metacognitive thinking about media.

They asked two groups of children to respond to a simple prompt: "What is your favorite television show, video game, or song, and why do you like it?" They compared a group of gifted and talented African American children ages 9–11 with a group of students who were not identified as gifted.

What they found was that high-achieving students use *active reasoning* instead of just reacting to media messages. When writing about their favorite television programs, video games, and music, these children demonstrate active reasoning—they seem to be thinking about media's content and form. When children use reasoning like this, they may or may not be "critical viewers," but they are able to articulate ideas about what they enjoy and value. For younger children, this ability is a precursor to media literacy.[7]

For example, when asked to explain why they like their favorite TV show, examples of children's active reasoning responses included the following:

"I like *Naruto* because it is about a boy who will follow his dreams no matter what. It has a lot of action."

"It is about a teenager who is a rock star and it shows me that even a kid can be famous and a star. It was her dream and even if it was hard, she accomplished it. It shows me that I can do that too."

"It's funny and the cartoons can sometimes be so clueless and at other times can be so evil."

When asked to explain why they liked their favorite video game, two children who used active reasoning offered the following thoughts:

"It has awesome graphics, great characters, and cool super attacks."

"I like it because it feels like you are really playing sports."

When describing why they liked their favorite popular music, a couple of students who used active reasoning responded with these answers:

"I like the beat of the song and I like the theme and setting of a hospital."

"It is appropriate and does not have any profanity in it. It's more of a gospel song than a rap song."

Active reasoning is evident when children make these types of high-quality answers; they stand in sharp contrast to other answers from children who simply reacted, generally offering a status label or a simple emotional evaluation. Renee and Michael found that many children in their study did not demonstrate active reasoning. These children responded to the question about why they liked their favorite show, video game, or music by generally writing, "It's funny." Other answers were descriptions of how frequently they watched, played, or listened. When asked to explain why they liked various media, many only claimed:

"It's my favorite."

"It's cool."

"It is the best."

High-achieving 9-, 10-, and 11-year-olds were found to use more active reasoning about favorite media than students not labeled as gifted. They offered more well-elaborated answers in responding to a question about television programs, video games, and music. Of course, it's possible that the gifted children simply had better control over language and were thus able to offer more rich description about their media preferences.

But it's also likely that the reasoning and using evidence to support ideas and opinions are central components of critical thinking that emerge differentially in childhood.[8]

These competencies generally develop in a *dialogic environment* in which children are encouraged to talk and listen, where they use language to provide support for their ideas, conclusions, and choices. And while most students have the ability to develop reasoning and argumentation skills, children need guidance and a supportive environment where reasoning is valued and appreciated.

Parents and teachers both play a crucial role in the development of these competencies. Children's use of reasoning and argumentation in relation to everyday activities in the family, like media consumption and technology usage, may be leveraged to support success in the classroom.[9] We believe that all students have some knowledge and expertise related to popular media that can be used to stimulate and engage the sort of active, engaged, and analytical thinking that schools would like all of their students to develop.

Look Again

Teachers in Great Britain have benefited from the many curriculum resources developed by the British Film Institute. *Look Again* is designed for teachers of children 3–11 years old to help them extend and improve the way they use and teach about moving image media. The guide offers basic teaching techniques that work with any type of film or video text, including the following:

Freeze Frame

Use the video pause button to help the class discuss each shot of a short moving image text by looking at and discussing:

- What they can see in the "frozen" image, how the elements of the image are positioned in the frame, how lighting and color affect what is seen
- Distance between camera and subjects, camera angle, movement of the camera during a shot
- How many shots there are and how the sequence of shots builds up information and ideas or impressions

What Happens Next

Show a short clip from a moving image text with a clearly identifiable genre (reality TV, competition show, science fiction, romantic comedy), stopping before the climax. Based on their knowledge of the genre, students make predictions about how the scene will end. After the real ending is revealed, children should reflect on the reasons for their predictions.

Free download available: http://old.bfi.org.uk/education/teaching/lookagain/

READING ADVERTISING

Children are constantly reading and comprehending visual and media texts, often without even knowing they are doing so. In an informal learning situation when children were learning about advertising, PVK instructor Aggie asked her students to find food ads in magazines. She handed children a large pile of magazines to explore. They did so with evident pleasure, enjoying the opportunity to handle the magazines, read, and look at them. When a student found a food ad, Aggie asked the child to read the ad aloud and discuss the words used. And while children enjoyed this fun activity, it also served an important purpose.

For those kids who don't associate reading with activities that happen outside the classroom, Aggie reflected, "As children read aloud and interpret, they begin to understand how text and image work together. They understand that words are conveying a message, that they are serving a purpose, that they are a part of the larger intention behind the work."

This activity not only generated productive talk about advertising and persuasion, it also created plenty of new vocabulary words that went up on the board and got defined and used in class. Such activities help support both reading and writing composition skills. After reading and discussing food ads, Aggie decided to have children create their own ads, because, as she explained, "When children create their own advertisements, they think carefully about which words to use, where to position the words, and how to craft a catchy and pithy slogan that will encapsulate their product's strengths."

Both reading and writing skills develop in the contexts of social relationships. Aggie described two of her students, Matthew and Quintin, who were writing a rap to accompany a cereal advertisement they were creating. The boys were working together on a script, explaining, "Try Special Kare. It will make you have a better day. You wanna know how? Let us explain it to you now." Michael wanted to talk about how Special Kare will give you energy because it is made of whole grains. He wrote, "Special K will give you engery. It's made of whole greens."

In reviewing their manuscript, Aggie pointed out that *energy* was spelled wrong. Michael fixed the error. Then Quintin continued to proofread. He laughed. "Whole greens!? It's whole grains!"

"What are whole grains?" Matthew asked.

The teachable moment had arrived because a child asked a simple but meaningful question of another child. At the computer, Aggie and Matthew began to search using the keywords "whole grains" to see what a grain looks like and to learn a bit about why it is important to eat whole grains. As they played The Question Game, more questions followed, and the boys continued to explore:

What are the health benefits of grains?

What kinds of grains are used?

What happens if you don't eat enough grains?

How do whole grains get turned into cereal?

Another of Aggie's students, Jane, had found an ad for Coke in a magazine. This ad utilized a Coca-Cola bottle as an image. Playing The Question Game about the ad, Aggie and her students were discussing why the shape of the bottle evokes a certain kind of feeling. Students realized that the bottle was probably older than the can and so conveyed a more "classic" feel.

One of Jane's questions was: "When was the Coke bottle invented?" Kids seemed curious about this question. Jane enthusiastically offered to search for it, which meant she had to generate proper search terms and sift through several websites, reading for comprehension enough to discover the answer. After some time exploring, she was thrilled to discover an article about Coca-Cola's design competition held in 1915 that resulted in the distinctive shape of the bottle. How proud she was to share what she had learned!

Not only did Jane get to practice her research and reading skills, but her self-confidence grew by leaps and bounds as a result of this informal inquiry learning experience. Why? The student *controlled the learning process*—in both generating the question and finding the answer. These kinds of media-rich activities spark intellectual curiosity.

STRUCTURED LEGAL DIALOGUE ABOUT CELEBRITY CULTURE

Henry, another PVK instructor, used an ongoing celebrity controversy in contemporary popular culture to help Grade 5 children develop confidence in using reasoning and evidence to support their opinions and ideas. He started by digging into a topic they were already talking about informally, during the lunch hour and on the playground: the case of Chris Brown, the chart-topping pop singer who made headlines in the summer of 2009 when he was convicted on charges of domestic abuse for beating his girlfriend, fellow pop star Rihanna.

After analysis of the news event, and working from some of his students' earlier requests to play judge and jury, this lesson culminated with a student-produced mock trial. Ultimately, the purpose of the trial was not to determine Chris Brown's guilt or innocence with regard to the assault charges, since Brown had already pled guilty and posted an apology video on YouTube. Rather, Henry challenged the children to understand and analyze the event as a series of media phenomena, each with its own stake in informing, entertaining, or persuading an audience. With this understanding, the mock trial functioned as an opportunity for the students to evaluate some of the ethical and rhetorical dimensions of this event.

For example, to develop the mock trial, after discussion of the Chris Brown case, children investigated the genre of the courtroom drama. In order to compare and contrast fictional depictions of courtrooms with actual courtrooms, Henry showed his students examples from episodes of *Judge Brown* and *Judge Judy*, and then he invited one of his friends, a law student, to come into class as a guest speaker to offer basic information about the practice of law.

What was accurate and inaccurate about the judge shows on TV? Not surprisingly, children had lots of questions—and lots of misinformation—about the legal system.

Most of what children learn about the world comes from a combination of media exposure and incidental information learned from parents and family members. In the process of generating questions about TV judge shows and the Chris Brown case, children learned about the differences between civil and criminal court and the distinction between local, state, and federal law. Children discussed the differences and similarities between fictional and real courtrooms, comparing and contrasting the messages that entertainment media presents about the law to other types of information sources.

Henry then encouraged students to gather some information on the facts of the Chris Brown domestic violence case, a topic that was widely being discussed in families and the community in the summer of 2009. Although every student in the class had some familiarity with the details of the news event, knowledge among students was naturally divergent, with different students having awareness of different aspects of the case.

Henry used class discussion, with a particular emphasis on listening skills, to promote the sharing of knowledge and opinions about the case. The class then watched Chris Brown's YouTube apology. Henry led students in a discussion of the clip, asking the class to identify Chris Brown's purpose in posting this video, and whether Brown's words and choice of setting served that purpose. Children were invited to place key phrases from the video on the board; these were phrases that children recognized were designed to be both persuasive and informative.

Finally, it was time for the culminating activity. Now that they had all this knowledge, children wanted to "put Chris Brown on trial." Henry gave children a template of a trial, complete with "All rise," opening and closing arguments, and other formal dimensions. Children wrote out key statements and then energetically performed the roles of judge, prosecutor, defense attorney, witnesses, and jury, reenacting a jury trial about whether Chris Brown abused his authority as a celebrity by offering a false apology.

One student, Sabina, got to play the role of Rihanna, and after swearing to "tell the whole truth and nothing but the truth," she responded to questions from both the prosecutor and the defense attorney, using information the children had researched from newspaper accounts.

The children pulled out all the rhetorical stops in making their best case to the judge. "My fans have the right to know that I am a good man," pleaded Jon, the student playing Chris Brown. Still, in Henry's Grade 5 classroom, the student judge found him guilty of using the domestic violence incident as a publicity ploy and sentenced him to a $1,000 fine and 5 years' probation.

Same Language Subtitling (SLS)

Dr. Brij Kothari, the president of PlanetRead (www.planetread.com), developed a fascinating technique to support reading and literacy development. Called Same Language Subtitling (SLS), it's the use of videos with a format similar to karaoke, where captioned text changes color in synchronization with audio. The purpose is to encourage reading and increase reading proficiency. Students are able to hear the words being spoken or sung and read the words being spoken or sung at the same time. Music, poetry, audiobooks, and famous speeches are used in SLS captioning.

In one experiment, teens with learning disabilities (with average reading scores at about a fifth-grade level) were randomly assigned to participate in activities in which teachers used songs from three Broadway musicals that contained lyrics above the students' reading levels: *Les Miserables, Cats,* and *Big River.* For 6 weeks, students engaged in viewing and response activities for 15–20 minutes per day at the beginning of class, during which they completed cloze-style worksheets and responded to comprehension questions while viewing. During the last 6 weeks of the intervention, they also spent 90 minutes per week listening to music and using free digital software tools to create their own subtitles for songs. Students in the control group had their school's regular curriculum.

Students' reading comprehension was measured before the program, immediately after the program, and in a delayed posttest when students returned from their summer break. Reading skills were measured using the STAR Accelerated Reading assessment, a computer-adaptive instrument that is used to identify the reading level of a student, measured in terms of grade equivalents. Evidence from the study shows statistically significant gains in reading comprehension as compared to the control group, and the gains in reading persisted over time.[10]

HOW DIGITAL AND MEDIA LITERACY
SUPPORTS LITERACY DEVELOPMENT

The declining interest in reading and the gradual disengagement with school that may occur in the elementary grades is disheartening to parents and teachers alike. This malaise is not confined to children in Grade 4. It may happen as early as second grade or as late as sixth grade. Some scholars think it happens because of the "teaching to the test" mentality that leads to repetitive drill-and-kill school tasks in order to meet Adequate Yearly Progress goals.[11] Teachers in the Powerful Voices for Kids program also noticed significant differences in the behavior and attitudes of children in Grades 1–3 as compared to children in Grades 4–6. Except for a few children with emotional challenges, the younger kids were intellectually curious and easy to engage in nearly any activity. But older children could be more resistant, disengaged, or chaotic at times.

Some critics believe that disengagement happens because all the fun gets sucked out of school when grades and assessments create new kinds of pressure for children to perform. Teachers may use leveled readers that don't hold much appeal for children, who are intellectually curious about the world and able to process information from visual and digital sources without the laborious effort that decoding the printed word entails.

And when adults in the home aren't doing much reading, then reading doesn't appear to be a tremendously useful skill from a child's point of view. The consequences are profound: Approximately 6 million kids (70% of all eighth graders and 65% of all twelfth graders) read below grade level.[12]

Researchers have found that children's attitudes about reading—attitudes that lead a learner to approach or to avoid an academic or recreational reading opportunity—are strongly associated with reading skills.[13] Ironically, an all-reading curriculum in the early grades, with its focus on decoding and phonics, may leave less time for science, art, music, and social studies, which provide exposure to rich content, background knowledge, and inquiry learning that supports the development of abstract thinking and vocabulary development. And since primary-level teachers generally rely on narrative (story) texts, children may enter Grade 4 with little understanding of the form and structure of other genres of texts, including video documentaries, websites, newspaper and magazine articles, and expository text, especially those they encounter in the world outside the classroom.

For these reasons, experts recommend these strategies to promote literacy learning:

- Use student-generated questions and inquiry to inspire children with a real need to get information from written texts.
- Offer young children more exposure to expository texts and discourse, including information from multimedia sources such as newspapers and magazines, videos, documentaries, websites, and social media.
- Give children the opportunity to select their own reading materials and use school time for independent reading.
- Use instructional practices that activate students' emotional engagement, participation, and social interaction in the classroom.[14]

In this chapter, we've shown that such strategies are effective with children in the elementary grades.

Children need *daily practice* in gathering information, knowing how to use keywords and search engines, understanding search results, and critically evaluating information. We need new measures of literacy to assess children's ability to engage in *online literacy skills*. We are encouraged by research like that by Professor Julie Coiro at the University of Rhode Island, whose work helps educators better assess student learning as they fully integrate digital media for teaching and learning into the elementary and secondary grades.[15]

A new generation of elementary educators and literacy scholars have begun to recognize that reading comprehension cannot be confined to the medium of the printed page. Pictorial images, TV shows, newspapers, magazines, websites, music, video games, and social media experiences all involve a type of reading comprehension that, if used well, may activate the full panoply of literacy skills, including accessing and analyzing information, composing messages, reflecting, and taking action, which are all at the heart of this book.

Lesson   Bootleg Cola: Pro and Con

Lesson Description

In this simulation activity, students gain firsthand experience as advertisers and advocates by getting mixed up with Bootleg Cola, a new soda and energy drink that contains some harmful ingredients.

Objectives

Students will

- Play and interact appropriately in formal and informal situations
- Brainstorm and generate ideas in a creative team
- Gather information about health and nutrition using the Internet
- Analyze information and develop a point of view
- Recognize power relationships that shape how information and ideas circulate in culture
- Understand the economic context of information and entertainment production

Vocabulary

Researcher

Distributor

Advocacy

Lawyer

Economic

Arsenic

High-fructose

Caffeine

Aspartame

Taurine

Activity

Access

✓ Children will enjoy telling you about the most memorable ads they've seen. They will also be able to describe ads for products that they don't fully understand, including pharmaceutical ads, Red Bull, and FreeCreditReport.com.

Analysis

✓ Now the class becomes a role-playing game where the teacher is the head representative of a new product called Bootleg Cola. Will the children help create an ad campaign for the new product? Here are the facts:

1. Bootleg Cola has high levels of sugar in the form of high-fructose corn syrup.

2. Bootleg Cola contains 8 times the recommended daily amount of caffeine.

3. Bootleg Cola contains two chemicals to research: aspartame (found in diet sodas) and taurine (found in Red Bull).

✓ Only one of these facts has been singled out by the government: All advertisements for Bootleg Cola must, in some part, include a reference to the above three facts.

Reflection

✓ Students are asked if they would like to advertise this product: Why or why not? Should children aged 7 to 12 be a target audience for Bootleg Cola? Why or why not? Encourage students to give reasons for their answers.

Composition

✓ After discussion, teams now split into PRO and CON sides.

> **PRO Team.** The Bootleg Cola Company. This is a group of advertisers trying to get various target audiences to buy the soda. As a team, they design an advertisement for Bootleg Cola that attracts target audiences by leaving out bad information and hiding the government-required label.

> **CON Team.** Anti-Bootleg Cola Action Committee. This is an advocacy group devoted to spreading awareness about the harmful effects of Bootleg Cola.

✓ Further divide the class into teams of three or four students to work best on this project. Students should work together but be responsible for certain tasks that are assigned to specific roles. For example, the **Researchers** gather information about the unfamiliar terms like *taurine* and *aspartame*, sharing this information with the team. Keywords to search: Red Bull, children, taurine, caffeine, aspartame, arsenic, health, risks. **Artists** develop the words and pictures to help convey the message, getting ideas and feedback from the team. **Distributors** develop an action plan for where and how the message will reach various target audiences, getting ideas and feedback from the team.

✓ As they gather information and develop ideas, each team will need to think carefully about the specific message, the target audience, and the intended action they want the audience to take. You can use deadline pressure to create a "work-like" environment where children understand they have limited time to come up with their ideas. After all, this is a simulation of the media workplace environment!

Reflection

✓ Each group gets a chance to develop their ideas about what message they will communicate to what audiences and how they will reach those audiences.

✓ Discuss: Did your opinions about the product change as you worked on this project? Why or why not? Is it OK to advertise a product that may have harmful ingredients? Why or why not? Do children know of any products on the market today that have harmful ingredients? What new questions did this simulation raise?

Taking Action

✓ People can use media messages to make a difference in the world. Check out the news at the website of the Campaign for Tobacco-Free Kids (http://tobaccofreekids.org). Then explore the "It's My Life" PBS website (http://pbskids.org/itsmylife/body/smoking/article7.html), which lists a variety of action steps that children can take to spread the word about the dangers of smoking.

Source: Created by David Cooper Moore.

NOTES

1. Leu, D., & Kinzer, C. (2000). The convergence of literacy instruction with networked technologies for information and communication. *Reading Research Quarterly, 35,* 108–127.
2. Arendt, H. (1958). *The human condition.* Chicago, IL: University of Chicago Press.
3. Strickland, D. S., & Riley-Ayers, S. (2007). *Literacy leadership in early childhood: The essential guide.* New York, NY: Teachers College Press.
4. American Institutes for Research. (2007). *Focus groups with Ready-to-Learn families.* Washington, DC: Author. Retrieved from http://www.air.org/reports-products/index.cfm?fa=viewContent&content_id=1208
5. Linebarger, D. L., & Walker, D. (2005). Infants' and toddlers' television viewing and language outcomes. *American Behavioral Scientist, 48,* 624–645.

6. Neuman, S. B. (1995). *Literacy in the television age: The myth of the TV effect* (2nd ed.). Norwood, NJ: Ablex.

7. Hobbs, R., & RobbGrieco, M. (2013). African-American children's active reasoning about media texts as a precursor to media literacy in the United States. *Journal of Children and Media, 6,* 502–519.

8. Roychoudhury, A. (2007). Elementary students' reasoning: Crests and troughs of learning. *Journal of Elementary Science Education, 19*(2), 25–43.

9. Seiter, E. (2005). *The Internet playground: Children's access, entertainment, and mis-education.* New York, NY: Peter Lang.

10. U.S. Department of Education, Institute of Education Sciences, What Works Clearinghouse. (2013). *WWC review of the report "Same-language-subtitling (SLS): Using subtitled music video for reading growth."* Retrieved from http://ies.ed.gov/ncee/wwc/pdf/single_study_reviews/wwc_sls_010813.pdf. See also McCall, W. G., & Craig, C. (2009). Same-language-subtitling (SLS): Using subtitled music video for reading growth. In G. Siemens & C. Fulford (Eds.), *Proceedings of World Conference on Educational Multimedia, Hypermedia and Telecommunications 2009* (pp. 3983–3992). Chesapeake, VA: Association for the Advancement of Computing in Education. Retrieved from http://www.editlib.org/p/32055

11. Grant Compliance/Title I Office. (2013). *AYP status report.* Philadelphia, PA: School District of Philadelphia. Retrieved from http://webgui.phila.k12.pa.us/offices/t/title1/programs—services/adequate-yearly-progress/school-improvement/ayp-status-report

12. Alliance for Excellent Education. (n.d.). *About the crisis.* Retrieved from http://all4ed.org/about_the_crisis

13. McKenna, M., Kear, D., & Ellsworth, R. (1995). Children's attitudes toward reading: A national survey. *Reading Research Quarterly, 30,* 934–956.

14. Sanacore, J., & Palumbo, A. (2009). Understanding the fourth-grade slump: Our point of view. *Educational Forum, 73,* 67–74.

15. Coiro, J. (2011). Predicting reading comprehension on the Internet: Contributions of offline reading skills, online reading skills, and prior knowledge. *Journal of Literacy Research, 43,* 352–392.

Part III

Work With Primary Children in Grades K–2

7 Media Literacy for Young Learners

In this chapter, you'll learn about

Identifying and Addressing Gaps in Children's Understanding

- How can educators help children recognize the nuances of what's real and what's imaginary when it comes to the messages found in movies, TV shows, and other media?

Creating Characters and Stories

- How do teachers support children's development as authors and storytellers? How can learning targets help children self-assess their learning?

Small Steps for Younger Learners

- What kinds of learning experiences in digital and media literacy are developmentally appropriate for preschool and primary children?

How do kids learn that a cartoon is a cartoon?

Maria's question was posed to a circle of exhausted but talkative instructors who met after the end of each day in the Powerful Voices for Kids (PVK) program to discuss their experiences in the classroom and reflect on their choices as educators. The group reflection was designed as an informal professional development experience in which instructors could share ideas and generate strategies for meeting students' needs.

Maria had been surprised earlier in the day when she showed kindergartners a clip from *Kung Fu Panda*, a slapstick animated comedy film starring the voice of comedian Jack Black. Her intention was to help children use descriptive language to discuss various features of the animation—how it looked, why it was funny, and how characters are portrayed. After watching the clip, the 5- and 6-year-olds shared what they liked about the characters and the scene—using language to describe the characters.

Then one student commented, "The man in the panda was silly." Thinking that she had misunderstood, Maria responded, "Yes, the panda is very silly."

"No," said the child. "I mean the man in the suit there," pointing to the screen paused on the Kung Fu Panda. "He's funny." This child seemed to think that the cartoon was a kind of digital skin with a person inside.

Maria didn't know how to respond. In the reflection circle, Maria shared her thoughts about how to address this child's confusion about the genre of animation. Was it good, at least, that the child recognized that it was a representation and not a real animal? "I'm wondering now," she said to the others, "when did I learn that a cartoon is a cartoon? The hard part is going backward and saying, 'How do I *teach* someone that a cartoon is a cartoon?'"

Instructors were continually discovering gaps in children's understanding of mass media, popular culture, and digital technology. Many had experienced something similar to what Maria was describing. The PVK instructors had adopted a hand gesture from their students to indicate a sense of connection; it's a *hang-loose* gesture that you point toward another person to connect to what they're saying. As Maria asked her questions, there were nonverbal gestures of hang-loose connection all around the room.

Kate built on Maria's experience and reflected on her own experiences as a young child, saying, "I think I understood that Julia Roberts and Richard Gere were actors in *Pretty Woman*. But I refused to believe that they weren't really romantically involved together in real life. I don't know why; I just refused to accept that."

John commented on the ambiguity of animation in an age of special effects, noting the challenges children face in sorting out the *unreal realities* continually presented in film, video games, and television: "It's that much harder when everything's so realistic. I mean, you watch the film *Avatar*, and they're really trying to make it look like a seamless version of reality. That's much harder to figure out than cartoons and puppets."

We still have much to learn about working with the youngest, and perhaps most vulnerable, age groups with a high level of sensitivity to their needs, their developmental abilities, and their sense of magic and wonder in the media landscape, where sci-fi avatars, Julia Roberts, and Kung Fu Panda can exist in a nebulous space between reality and fantasy.

What a Difference a Few Years Can Make

Fours and Fives

- Have trouble understanding the visual/auditory code of television: fade, cutting from one shot to another, switching of scenes, zooming from long shot to close-up, splitting the screen, faceless narrator, canned laughter, events not shown on screen, changing channels
- Confused about fantasy versus reality
- May be frightened by fantasy content
- Confused about the difference between programs and commercials
- Pay attention to sounds, body movements, and special effects
- Frequently don't understand emotions of characters
- May have trouble understanding the central plot

Sixes and Sevens

- Understand the difference between fantasy and reality
- Are more frightened by news and reports of real violence than fantasy violence
- Generally distinguish between programs and commercials
- Begin to understand the persuasive intent of commercials
- Understand simple and complex emotions of characters
- Increasingly understand adult programs
- Understand the central plot of narrative stories presented on TV

Source: Adapted from Hesse and Lane (2003).[1]

MEDIA AND TECHNOLOGIES CHANGE, BUT DO CHILDREN CHANGE WITH THEM?

Market researchers and media producers involved in children's media are rumored to say that they're lucky that "they get a whole new audience every 3 years." The quote points to a complicated component of teaching digital and media literacy to younger students, particularly those in kindergarten and early grades.

Children's access to media and technology is indeed expanding and changing rapidly. While most young children encounter *Sesame Street* by watching TV, one survey of parents found that one in five American preschool children first watched it not on television but by seeing it on a computer, using YouTube or PBS.org. In 2012, 27% of households with a preschooler living at home had an iPad, with 40% of those families reporting that the child used the device.[2] However, when we see YouTube videos of babies intuitively figuring out cell phones or talk with a young child who can recite the stories of his or her favorite movies, TV shows, and online games, we may see children as hypercompetent, and we may not appreciate the misunderstandings that they can have about mass media and digital technology.

In working with 5-year-olds, Maria saw firsthand the complicated balance between the intuitive nature of new technologies and developmental changes that happen in early childhood when students, who know and love very complicated films laden with digital special effects, still struggle with basic distinctions between reality and fantasy.

As early as the 1970s, developmental psychologists exploring media literacy identified these distinctions as crucial to teaching media literacy to young children.[3] Understanding the differences between different visual media forms—cartoons versus puppets, cartoons versus live-action television shows, or photographs versus illustrations—is a recurrent concern for teaching young children, one that reasserts itself in new generations.

At times, the teaching of visual symbol systems in photography, film, television, and online is referred to as *demystification*. This may have a negative connotation to many early childhood educators, who associate revealing the how-to of media production with a violation of the magical thinking that's characteristic of early childhood. To some, it might seem that explaining to a young child that Bugs Bunny is not a real rabbit is like explaining that Santa Claus is the product of our social imagination.

But we have found that we can honor children's imagination and creativity and also help them understand how media represents reality by respecting their own boundaries around understanding "real" and "fake" and providing opportunities for them to understand and create visual stories themselves. Visual storytelling has many advantages for young children who are still learning the basic mechanics of print literacy. The saying tells us that a "picture is worth a thousand words." But a picture also conveys these meanings to us in ways that may help engage children's *verbal fluency*, their ability to share their ideas in language.

Kindergarten and first-grade teachers are particularly sensitive to the developmental needs of their students. Compared with educators who work with older children, educators who teach the youngest grade levels have far more negative views about media and popular culture and are less likely to use media like DVDs, the Internet, and television in their own teaching practices.[4]

Kindergarten teachers may distrust exposure to television in particular. Early childhood educators often recognize the potential and actual negative effects of early television viewing on young children. Indeed, a variety of meaningful risks are associated with some kinds of media exposure, including aggressive behavior, materialism, attitudes about nutrition, and language use, as well as gender, race, and occupational role stereotyping. Some developmental psychologists have studied the relationship between heavy TV exposure and the development of attention skills. For example, researchers have found an association between the type of programming preschool children watch and their classroom behavior. In one study of low-income 4-year-olds, parents were asked to report their children's media viewing habits, and teachers were asked to observe that population of students to report classroom behaviors, including hitting and fighting with others, problems with paying attention, being nervous or tense, and being restless or fidgety. The results of the study reveal that viewing of inappropriate content (defined as watching PG-13 or R-rated videos/movies) was associated with higher hyperactivity and aggression scores and a lower social skills rating.[5]

But kindergarten teachers also recognize and use the positive power of media as a tool for learning. One such example is the Ready to Learn program, administered by the Public Broadcasting Service through a cooperative agreement with the National Institute on Early Childhood Development and Education in the U.S. Department of Education. Since 2005, at many local public television stations, Ready to Learn coordinators have conducted 20 or more workshops each year with parents, childcare providers, and early childhood educators. The PBS Kids Raising Readers program has demonstrated significant gains in word recognition, phonological awareness, vocabulary acquisition, verbal expressiveness, and overall school readiness among children ages 2–8. For many low-income children, the program helps close some of the pervasive achievement gaps between students from high-poverty backgrounds and their peers from wealthier families.[6]

Super WHY!

Preschool children who watch *Super WHY!* develop alphabet knowledge and letter recognition fluency skills.[7] Developed by Angela Santomero and Samantha Freeman Alpert, the program features a character called Whyatt who enrolls a group of Super Readers into a story. As each story develops, the characters encounter obstacles, which can be solved by applying their literacy skills to change the story. *Super WHY!* helps children learn the fundamentals of reading through interactive storybook adventures.

The show's characters embody the early literacy practices of phonemic awareness, phonics, fluency, vocabulary, and text comprehension. Alpha Pig, for example, has alphabet power, and each of his games focuses on identifying letters, while Wonder Red has Word Power and games that focus on word decoding. Princess Presto brings spelling power and games that center on letter sounds, spelling, and handwriting skills into the mix, while *Super WHY!* brings skills together, imparting valuable lessons on comprehension and vocabulary.

Children's media researcher Deb Linebarger found that preschoolers who watched *Super WHY!* over an 8-week period showed significant gains in alphabet knowledge, phonological and phonemic awareness, symbolic and linguistic awareness, and comprehension.[8]

RECOGNIZING THE SYMBOL SYSTEMS OF VISUAL MEDIA

When Renee introduced digital and media literacy concepts in a preschool classroom, she began by bringing in her digital video camera. She recorded the morning activities using short 5- to 12-second shots, creating a simple in-camera montage about 3 minutes in length. After about an hour, the 4-year-old children gathered to review the video footage, thrilled to see images of themselves and their classroom teacher going about their routines: entering the classroom, putting their coats in the cubbies, playing at the clay table, making structures with blocks, figuring out puzzles, drawing, and dramatic play.

"Did this movie show everything that happened this morning?" Renee asked the children who had gathered around the TV monitor to review the footage.

"Yes," the children said in unison. Renee probed, "What did you see?" Children talked about the scenes they had seen in the short film.

Exploring Visual Representation With Young Children

Help young children understand visual messages and visual storytelling with these activities:

Inside and Outside the Frame. Select a small group of photos for discussion. Children use "I see . . ." statements to describe what they see in each photograph. Encourage many different responses about a single image. This helps children understand and appreciate how different people pay attention to various elements of a photo. Then invite children to imagine what's outside the frame. What *might* they see if they were present at the location where the image was created? Encourage them to use their imagination. Discuss the difference between probable and improbable possibilities. And remember: There's always a photographer present!

Illustration Versus Photograph. Bring in samples of illustrations and photographs from print and online media. When children distinguish between realistic drawings and photographic representations of objects, they recognize that people create images using a variety of different tools. Encourage children to look at a variety of images and then create drawings and take digital photos. Discuss: What is special about a drawing of an object and the picture of the same object? How are they similar and different?

Animation Versus Live Action. Children enjoy learning about how cartoons are made (many drawings are edited together to suggest movement) versus how live-action media is made (a camera records real people and things). Show a sample of different types of children's media. Discuss: How are shows with real people made? How are cartoons made? What do you enjoy about watching TV shows or movies that have real people in them? What do you enjoy about shows with animation? Children can create simple videos using their own drawings along with dramatic performance of the character voices.

Character Versus Actor. Children may best be able to distinguish between a character and an actor when they themselves engage in pretend play. After pretend play, children can talk about their own pretending and how the actors they see on television are sometimes pretending, too. For example, Anne Hathaway is the name of the actress who pretends to be Mia Thermopolis, a princess in the movie *The Princess Diaries*. Sometimes, we see actors when they are not pretending to be a character, as in shows like *Entertainment Tonight* and *TMZ*.

"I saw Tyrone putting his coat on the hook," one child said. "I saw Wendy playing with the blocks," another said. Renee repeated the original question, "Did this movie show everything that happened this morning?"

Shyly, William raised his hand. "It didn't show *me* putting my coat on the hook," he said. "That's right," Renee acknowledged. Another child said, "It didn't show *me* climbing on the ladder."

Renee explained that, when it comes to media messages, all *messages are selective and incomplete*. By understanding video as a text, created by an author who makes choices, even young children can recognize that video is a representational system. When children understand visual symbol systems used in illustration, photography, video, and digital media, they begin a process of abstract thinking long before they have the decoding and comprehension skills to understand printed texts. Just as children can infer complex meaning from stories that are read to them, they can also make inferences from pictures they see, videos they watch, and websites they view.

TELLING DIGITAL STORIES IN KINDERGARTEN

Technology coordinator Mr. Landis was struggling to figure out how to integrate digital and media literacy with kindergartners. He had great ideas for projects with older children that developed their computer and digital literacy skills while offering them storytelling opportunities making websites, writing songs, and finding images for class assignments. He made active use of *learning targets*, those statements written in language that helps children self-assess their performance as learners. You can see a list of learning targets used in the Powerful Voices for Kids program at the back of this book, shown as Resource A.

But Mr. Landis also recognized that younger children had some developmental blocks to digital media production activities. Their manual dexterity was unpredictable. Some of his first-grade students had difficulty double-clicking a computer mouse. And perhaps most challenging, since he saw children in his technology classroom only one day per week, each lesson needed to be self-contained.

His collaborating teachers had worked together in the PVK professional development program, where elementary teachers developed approaches for integrating digital and media literacy into their lessons. Some of the activities that the teachers of older students were doing (talking about civil rights and environmentalism, and telling fiction and nonfiction stories) were all well and good for third-, fourth-, fifth-, and sixth-grade students. But what was appropriate for kindergartners?

The kindergarten teachers decided to concentrate on how students make inferences about stories from images. They were learning about beginnings, middles, and endings of stories and often used picture books to infer a narrative from a series of drawings. In one activity, children selected images of objects that had been cut out of magazines and glued them on paper in left-to-right sequence. After assembling the paper montage, children used them to help tell a story. Images can help children anchor memories to words, helping them build narrative, creative authorship, and comprehension skills.

In considering how to design a learning experience for the youngest students in his computer lab, Mr. Landis found himself watching some of the children's media that *he* had found useful in understanding a variety of media messages when he was a young boy. He was particularly taken with a 1984 clip from *Mister Rogers' Neighborhood* in which Fred Rogers takes viewers through the entire process of making his television show. A wide shot revealed the television studio. Rogers explained how his puppets were made and how someone else provided the voice. Viewers were invited to meet the "neighbors" in the television studio—the producers, directors, camera operators, musicians, and others responsible for the hard work of creating a television program (see Figure 7.1).

How could Mr. Landis translate these ideas to make sense for his own younger students? He identified two key messages that he thought would be valuable and developmentally appropriate for his students. The first was that puppets, like all fictional characters, are constructed by their creators to have particular characteristics and *points of view*. A point of view is the perspective from which a story is told. Second, many puppets and other fictional characters are framed on television so that you cannot see how they are manipulated. Understanding the *frame*, then, was deeply connected to understanding the process through which people and characters are represented in visual media.

With these two ideas in mind, Mr. Landis developed a simple script template that his kindergarten and first-grade students would use to create a unique character, develop that character by having it interact with another child's character, and then film this interaction in front of a fixed frame. Here's a summary of the process he used:

Step 1: Develop the Characters

At ages 5 and 6, children are still developing manual dexterity. This means that manipulating a computer mouse may be more difficult for some children than for others. Mr. Landis gave his kindergarten and

Figure 7.1 Mister Rogers Makes a TV Show

first-grade students time to explore moving the mouse on the painting program Tux Paint, a close relative of the graphic art program Kid Pix.

When children had developed their familiarity with moving the mouse, using different colors, and, in some cases, using "stamp tools" for patterned effects, Mr. Landis provided them with a gingerbread-man template on which they could design a character. At this point in the process, it was essential for students to learn how to *undo*. Young children can be frustrated when they cannot carry out ideas that they can imagine; the undo function of a computer is an elegant way for students to fix mistakes without having to start over from scratch. In some ways, learning how to undo was one of the most useful and important takeaways from the lesson.

To help them design their characters, Mr. Landis told students to imagine giving their character a name. This might look something like [profession] [name]—Bus Driver Tammy, Cowboy Ben, or Princess Latoya. Many children used the names of their favorite characters from popular culture, like Batman, Hannah Montana, and Ben-10. In these cases, Mr. Landis was sensitive to children's need to express themselves through familiar characters; he knew that he could no more prevent children from using Batman or Barbie than he could prevent them from modeling characters on their family members, teachers, and members of their community.

Soon, the class had 24 characters that would enact 12 scripts (one per pair of students). Mr. Landis observed some common characteristics. Many girls chose princesses and girls' dolls like Barbie and Bratz as inspiration for their characters, while many boys used superheroes and athletes. Many children used the names of friends and relatives, while others made up "nonsense names" that they imagined. And some children defied expectations, as when a boy in class created a Hannah Montana character or a girl created a variation on Spider-Man. It was important, Mr. Landis thought, to honor the many ways that students both embraced and challenged expectations or stereotypes from popular culture.

Step 2: Write the Script

For children still developing basic print literacy skills, any writing can be a daunting prospect. In this exercise, children did a minimum of print writing—limited to writing their character names—but were still engaged as budding storytellers. Mr. Landis developed a flexible six-line script template that all children could understand and change according to their own ideas and their understanding of their character. In this particular script, one character is sad, and the other character suggests an activity that might make him or her happy again.

Another feature of the lesson was the way in which established popular culture characters and original characters alike responded in inventive ways to their problems. Superheroes, princesses, and bus drivers could all use a feature of their identity to solve the problem. When a princess was sad that she lost her tiara, a bus driver offered to drive her to get a new one. When Batman lost his jet pack, an astronaut offered to give him a ride in her spaceship. Established characters took on new features imagined by students through improvisation, while original characters developed personalities based on their profession or, more simply, through the imaginative leaps of their young creators.

No doubt about it: Even at age 5, children's perception of gender roles and a consumer-oriented approach to solving problems with "stuff" were both entrenched in many of the children's emerging understanding of the world. Not surprisingly, children often framed problems as coming from a lack of resources (clothes, food, money, or technology) and solutions as the supply of these resources. For example, in children's stories, happy characters comforted sad characters by offering to buy them gifts. Girls were often offered jewelry or clothing, while boys were offered technology and toys. Again, Mr. Landis needed to be sensitive to children's improvisation; although he made it clear that violent solutions were unacceptable, more complicated matters of representation sometimes required him to honor students' lived experience even when their stories betrayed social values (like materialism) that he personally found troubling.

Step 3: Frame and Film the Scene

The concept of the *frame* is a foundational one in photography and video production. The frame is what we see when we watch a television show or movie, when we play a video game or watch a video on YouTube. In the video production process, making a frame determines what aspects of the world around us will become part of our film. You can make a frame right now: Simply form a rectangle between the thumb and index fingers on both hands.

For young students to understand the way framing works, they might consider frames on paper first. Mr. Landis had created special backdrops with different settings (forest, city, and fantasy) that he tacked to the wall. He put blue paper tape around the frame so that its boundaries were clearly drawn. Then students placed their popsicle stick gingerbread figures in front of the paper. He instructed them: "Make sure your character stays in the frame."

However, for young children, translating one medium of expression to another can be a challenging cognitive task. It was not necessarily intuitive to all students that what they were seeing on paper would also be the movie they were making once the camera was turned on. Mr. Landis's solution to this problem was to set up a monitor on which they could view their frame in real time. They would see that every movement of their hands changed the way their figure appeared on the screen.

Mr. Landis's students performed the scripts they had written just below the frame line of their shot. They had to think about several different aspects of production simultaneously. They needed to speak loudly and clearly; they needed to hold their characters still, moving them as intentionally as possible to "walk toward" other characters; they had to be careful not to get their own hand in the shot. When a student's hand did enter a shot, other students in the class would whisper excitedly, "I can see his hand! They need a do-over!"

Step 4: Perform and Receive Audience Feedback

When David observed Mr. Landis working with a group of children to produce a set of scripts, it was clear that he not only engaged his students

Scripting Templates for Storytelling

By creating a template script with a *problem* and a *solution* that young children could understand, Mr. Landis ensured that every kindergartner could create a unique story.

> CHARACTER 1: Hello, <u>CHARACTER 2</u> .
>
> CHARACTER 2: Hello, <u>CHARACTER 1</u> .
>
> CHARACTER 1: I feel sad because _____ .
>
> CHARACTER 2: I could make you feel happy again by _____ .
>
> CHARACTER 1: Thank you, <u>CHARACTER 2</u> .
>
> CHARACTER 2: You're welcome, <u>CHARACTER 1</u> .

When teachers identify competencies involved in activities and ask children to self-assess specific learning targets, even simple activities can support fundamental dimensions of media literacy learning:

Competencies	Learning Targets
Brainstorming and generating ideas	I listen to others and contribute ideas that add value and relate to the topic.
Composing creatively	I draw images and use spoken and written language to create.
Working collaboratively	I work with a partner to get something done.
Giving and receiving audience feedback	I share my reaction to the work of others and learn things when people share their reactions to my work.
Editing and revising	I make changes to my work based on feedback.
Using appropriate distribution, promotion, and marketing channels	I take pride in sharing my work with others.
Playing and interacting appropriately in formal and informal situations	I play and learn in ways that are respectful of others.

as storytellers but also engaged them as *audience members*. Mr. Landis helped children think about how different types of audiences might respond in different ways.

While the children performed, the other children were asked to role-play a particular kind of audience. A polite audience gave presenters a soft golf clap. An older audience was encouraged to shout "Huzzah!" after each performance. There was even a dog audience who barked or howled with approval after a performance. This kept students engaged in listening attentively as they considered how their new audience role might be expected to react to each performance.

The project was successful because Mr. Landis structured the activity using the competencies and learning targets of the Powerful Voices for Kids program. Children were able to self-assess their own ability to meet the learning targets for this activity. But Mr. Landis also noted some limitations of the activity. Young students' imagination seemed to be limited after their initial brainstorming and character drawings. As we noted earlier, media production can be extremely time-consuming when there are 20 to 25 students working together. The possibility of losing students' interest in the tedium of production is a real one—all the more reason why it is so important to develop students' understanding through mini-lessons in areas like framing, creative choices in video-making, and giving a performance during recording.

PLAYING SPOT THE SHOT

It's not obvious how film and television are actually put together. That's why young children (and even some older children and adults) might believe that a 30-second video takes 30 seconds to create. Kate, another PVK instructor, wanted her Grade 1 students to recognize that film and video are constructed of short segments that have been assembled together through montage.

She introduced the concept of the *shot*, the duration of a frame between video edits. Shots can also be defined by how close the subject is to the camera: close-up, medium, and long. To depict a romantic relationship, a traditional shot and reverse shot pattern from classic Hollywood film might be used, where we might see Humphrey Bogart's face, then Ingrid Bergman's, then Humphrey Bogart's again—three shots. Christian Metz, a French film theorist, argued that cinema is structured like a language where shots are fundamental building blocks. Unlike language, however, film does not use a strict grammar and syntax equivalent to that of the written or spoken word. Instead, individual cinematic texts construct their own meaning systems.[9] Particular shots derive their meaning from their relationship to the content and the form of the images that precede and follow them. The French word *montage* is used to describe the process or technique of selecting, editing, and piecing together separate shots to form a continuous whole.

To help her students understand how all videos contain a series of shots, Kate brought into the classroom some footage she had taken of her pet dog. On a FlipCam, she had filmed the dog in a variety of camera angles and shot lengths. One was a close-up of the dog's face. Another was a long shot of the dog walking through the park. A third was a medium shot of the dog's feet moving on the ground. Would children recognize that the images were all taken to represent her dog from different places? As it turned out, they did.

To play Spot the Shot, students are instructed to watch a short video and pay attention to shot changes. They clap their hands together whenever they notice a new shot. In this piece, each shot lasted about 4–7 seconds. Shot of the dog's face—CLAP. Shot of the dog's whole body walking—CLAP. Shot of the dog's paws—CLAP.

Digital Resources for the Youngest Children

TOON Books

http://toon-books.com

Comics support the literacy skills of emerging readers in this engaging online resource, which includes both a "toon reader" and a "cartoon maker" that enables young children to create and share their own simple cartoons.

International Children's Digital Library

http://en.childrenslibrary.org/

This website offers a variety of children's literature from all over the world in more than a dozen languages.

One More Story

http://onemorestory.com

Students can access both new and classic children's books digitally in an interactive read-aloud format. Each story has lots of opportunities to pause and ask questions about stories and images.

Kate played Spot the Shot with her students using advertising (47 shots in 30 seconds—whew!). They discussed how a rapidly paced ad, with so many shot changes, forces viewers playing Spot the Shot to pay very close attention. At first, children had trouble noticing the shot changes. But after a few games like this, their ability to recognize frames and shots seemed to stick. David was particularly amused to enter the classroom one day to find Kate showing her second graders the final poetic scene in Michelangelo Antonioni's 1969 film *Blow-Up*, in which two mimes mimic a game of tennis. Close-up of the mime's face—CLAP! Wide shot of the tennis court—CLAP! Cut to the face of the protagonist—CLAP! How charming for children to get their first exposure to a classic Italian film director—if only the few developmentally appropriate scenes from his work—in primary school!

SMALL STEPS FOR YOUNGER STUDENTS

Mr. Ivery and his teaching partner Ms. Al-Muid, two kindergarten teachers, were interested in incorporating visual storytelling with their students after developing ideas in our professional development workshop. The story of how their project evolved is a nice illustration of why digital and media literacy can help students expand their creativity and critical thinking, even at very young ages.

Mr. Ivery teaches his prekindergarten students how to go to school, which is a complex set of social practices that involve speaking, listening, taking turns and creating with art and language. For Mr. Ivery, helping students control impulses and emotions, remain calm, and take turns is just as important as teaching them fundamental knowledge about letters, words, and numbers.

Like many preschool and primary-level teachers, he takes a conservative approach to the use of media and technology in his classroom. The National Association for the Education of Young Children has reported that this is true for many early elementary educators, who are more reluctant than their colleagues working with older students to use media like television shows, DVDs, the Internet, and computer games.[10] When students may be struggling to sit still, or may be developing the fine motor skills necessary to handle scissors, Mr. Ivery doesn't find much value in examining TV shows, video games, commercials, or websites. He occasionally told us that these kinds of exercises seemed too advanced for his students.

But we knew that when Mr. Ivery taught early and preliteracy skills, he often used picture books and other visual imagery to activate his students' abilities to tell stories and make inferences. Asking predictive questions ("What might happen next?"), for instance, is equally applicable to print and nonprint sources; it activates students' abilities to infer information from a text, a skill that supports and may even strengthen their ability to read.[11]

Ms. Al-Muid had a different set of strengths in the classroom. An avid popular culture fan and a contributor to Philadelphia's independent music scene, she recognized how even the youngest children engaged with popular culture and mass media. She was excited to use FlipCams, comics, and other media in the classroom with the kindergarten students.

Mr. Ivery's initial plan was to present a story and have students put a selected group of images in cause-and-effect. But Ms. Al-Muid had a different idea. Sensing an opportunity to activate students' creativity, she suggested letting different students put images in any sequence that made sense to them, so that they would become the storytellers themselves.

We are not sure which approach was more developmentally appropriate. We recognize that young children are not only capable of creating original stories of their own but are hungry for opportunities to develop the kinds of personal narratives in school that they do when they play with their favorite toys, dolls, and action figures at home.

As they planned and worked together to create this activity, Mr. Ivery and Ms. Al-Muid decided to use a story that had one image sequence, but they asked students to then change the story in their own words, using the same image sequence to try to tell *different* stories. They used the children's comic book *Silly Lilly*, a volume in the TOON Books children's series that commissions prominent comics artists to create developmentally appropriate cartoons and comics for K–3 classrooms. Their learning target was "I can create a new story by changing the *beginning*, *middle*, and *ending* of the story."

We were pleased to see that these kindergarten teachers had used the professional development workshop to reflect on both the kinds of texts and the kinds of questions they could incorporate into their own teaching.

Too often professional development workshops encourage teachers to use radically new instructional practices in their classroom in their efforts to integrate technology tools. We were heartbroken to see two experienced kindergarten teachers in another partner school struggling with a SMART Board that had been installed against their wishes in the middle of their whiteboard space. These teachers were new to PC technology, and delays and confusion from inadequate professional development support for new technology had a detrimental effect on their teaching practice as they struggled to do basic daily learning tasks like changing a date from one day to the next or recording the weather outside. In our professional development programs, we try to honor the small steps teachers of the youngest learners take to find modest but meaningful ways to integrate media and technology into their early literacy instruction.

One reason we advocate small steps is due to the very limited knowledge that is available about the role of media and technology in the lives of young children. The American Academy of Pediatrics recommends no screen media time for children under the age of 2.[12] There are countless YouTube videos that show parents ignoring this advice, instead displaying precocious children, some still in infancy, exploring new screen technologies. One famous example comes from the young child who tries to swipe a print magazine like a tablet device, to the amusement of her parents. Still, there is very little evidence to support the value of media and technology that is marketed as educational for preschool children, like the Baby Einstein videos.[13]

Educational leaders don't need to be hostile or dismissive toward teachers who are cautious and strategic about how to use media and technology with young children. Instead, we should aim to understand teacher motivations using the typology we introduced in Chapter 2. Part of the conservative stance that some early elementary educators may take regarding media in the classroom stems from a combination of Spirit Guide and Watchdog motives, which pairs a deep respect for children's lives with a skepticism of the value of technologies that have been heavily promoted, like LeapFrog. This company offers e-readers, educational videos, and computer programs for sale, claiming that they give very young children a leg up intellectually. These persuasive claims may appeal to the most vulnerable parents who are desperate to make sure their children are not disadvantaged. But these parents may not be aware of the simple, inexpensive and nonmediated ways to support early learning for children.

We have found that professional development in digital and media literacy for early elementary educators can be most useful, and perhaps most effective, when we trust teachers' expertise about their young students while gently pushing at the boundaries of their comfort levels with media and technology.

Some important developing competencies in early literacy—including visual, oral, and early print literacy storytelling in a variety of forms—can be enhanced and expanded when we expand our conceptualization of literacy to include visual, audio, and interactive forms. A story is, after all, still a story, and the many stories that students can imagine and share can be developed across a wide variety of media, even with the youngest learners.

Lesson · The Ant and the Grasshopper

Lesson Description

Children watch an episode of *Super WHY!* to make predictions about characters and discuss ideas about visual stereotypes.

Objectives

Students will

- Consider how our expectations affect the way we believe characters (or people) will look based on their personality
- Understand that stories are created by storytellers
- Understand that storytellers construct characters and messages
- Understand that characters do not necessarily reflect people in the real world or people in the way that we know them

Vocabulary

Visuals

Dialogue

Audience

Character

Predictions

Resources and Materials

✓ *Super WHY!* episode "The Ant and the Grasshopper" cued to 8 minutes

✓ Paper

✓ Crayons

Activity

Access

✓ Your class is full of characters—every child is a unique character that we can describe using words. Get children ready to watch the episode by asking them to pay attention to the different characters.

✓ After viewing, ask children to name and describe the characters. Discuss the character of the ant. What makes him seem "smart"? Children will recognize the glasses and vocal accent as signifiers of intelligence.

✓ People who make TV shows use certain visuals or dialogue to let the audience know about a character. But are they always right? Are all people with glasses smart?

Composition

✓ Ask children to draw a person who is "mean."

Analysis

✓ When children have completed their drawings, post them up and ask children to point out some similarities between the drawings. Are there more boys or girls depicted? What common facial expressions and clothing are shown?

Reflection

✓ Discuss examples from media characters in TV shows, movies, and video games that might influence children's drawings of "mean" characters.

Taking Action

✓ Make sure children understand that not all mean people "look" mean. It's best not to judge people by the way they look.

Source: Contributed by Sherri Hope Culver.

NOTES

1. Hesse, P., & Lane, F. (2003). Media literacy starts young: An integrated curriculum approach. *Young Children, 58*(6), 20–26.
2. Jensen, E. (2012, December 16). Apps give preschoolers a first look at TV shows. *New York Times*, p. B1.
3. Singer, D. G., & Singer, J. L. (1991). *Creating critical viewers: A partnership between schools and television professionals.* Available from The Pacific Mountain Network, 1550 Park Ave., Denver, CO 80218.
4. National Association for the Education of Young Children & Fred Rogers Center for Early Learning. (2012). *Technology and interactive media as tools in early childhood programs serving children from birth through age 8.* Retrieved from http://www.naeyc.org/files/naeyc/PS_technology_WEB.pdf
5. Conners-Burrow, N., McKelvey, L., & Fussell, J. (2011). Social outcomes associated with media viewing habits of low-income preschool children. *Early Education & Development 22,* 256–273.
6. Corporation for Public Broadcasting. (2011). *Findings From Ready to Learn, 2005–2010.* Retrieved from http://www.cpb.org/rtl/FindingsFromReadyToLearn2005-2010.pdf
7. Linebarger, D. L., McMenamin, K., & Wainwright, D. K. (2009). *Summative evaluation of* Super WHY! *Outcomes, dose, and appeal.* Philadelphia: University of Pennsylvania, Children's Media Lab. Retrieved from http://pbskids.org/read/files/SuperWHY_Research_View.pdf
8. Linebarger et al. (2009).
9. Metz, C. (1974). *Film language: A semiotics of the cinema* (Trans. M. Taylor). New York, NY: Oxford University Press.
10. National Association for the Education of Young Children & Fred Rogers Center for Early Learning (2012).
11. Cain, K., & Oakhill, J. V. (1999). Inference making ability and its relation to comprehension failure in young children. *Reading and Writing, 11,* 489–503.
12. Vandewater, E., Rideout, V., Wartella, E., Huang, X., Lee, J., & Shim, M. (2007). Digital childhood: Electronic media and technology use among infants, toddlers, and preschoolers. *Pediatrics, 119,* 1006–1015.
13. Guernsey, L. (2007). *Into the minds of babes: How screen time affects children from birth to age five.* New York, NY: Basic Books.

8 Authors and Audiences

In this chapter, you'll learn about

Becoming Authors

- How do students come to see themselves as authors who make important choices about their own work?

Understanding Target Audiences

- How do authors imagine target audiences as part of the composition process?

Direct and Embedded Instruction

- How do both analysis and creative composition activities help young students think abstractly about authors and audiences?

Making Inferences

- How does inference-making support literacy and academic achievement?
- Why does the use of a variety of message forms (print, visual, audio, digital) help children go beyond the information given to comprehend both the purpose and the content of messages?

In the world of elementary education, when people think of the concept of authorship, names like Jon Scieszka, Maurice Sendak, Tomie DiPaola, Roald Dahl, Ezra Jack Keats, A. A. Milne, Jerry Spinelli, Lois Lowry, and Avi may come to mind. Perhaps you have a favorite children's author whose work has inspired you.

By the time they enter school, children are already making sense of the variety of media they encounter on a daily basis—stories are stories. Whether talking about their favorite books, TV shows, games, or movies, children build from the imaginary situations they experience through print and mass media in their play.

But soon children also begin to become aware of their roles as audience members for their favorite stories and as themselves as authors of their own original stories. The relationship between *author and audience* is the most fundamental relationship in any form of media and communication.

Authors make creative and intentional choices when they create work and often have specific target audiences in mind. Audiences have expectations based on their own values and prior experience with media, including their understanding of genres and purposes.

The concept of authorship should not be restricted to print media. Children should know that photographers are authors. Filmmakers are authors. Video game producers are authors. Website creators are authors. Musicians are authors. Computer programmers and app designers are authors. Creativity comes in many forms. That's why it's empowering to learn how to write and draw well—these are two basic competencies that help us become authors.

Many children don't understand how the concept of authorship applies to their favorite media. They have been taught to think of authorship only in relation to print media. And because the world of a young child is often magical and media indulges their sense of imagination (as in the *movie magic* of special effects–laden seasonal blockbusters), children may react in a corresponding way to the invisible processes through which TV shows, movies, video games, and websites are created.

And yet by age 8, kids are also far more likely than their 5-, 6-, and 7-year-old classmates to begin to identify the broad contours of types of authors (writers, directors, singers, animators, programmers) and types of target audiences (boys, girls, kids, adults). If we ask children in second and third grade about advertisements, they might note what products are being advertised ("That's the one for cereal" or "This one is a toy commercial") or who the ads are for ("My mom uses that" or "That's just for girls").

It turns out that most children we have worked with in elementary classrooms not only accept new knowledge about authors and audiences but also have considerable curiosity about how media gets made. After all, they spend hours with all kinds of their favorite media—watching films and TV shows, reading books, and playing video games.

We wonder: How does learning to analyze media affect children's interpretations? Does knowing who the authors of films are and how films are made increase or decrease the pleasure of watching them? Does knowing that ads target specific audience members make young students feel empowered, cynical, or inspired to be young marketers themselves? Does it develop or dampen their materialism?

Researchers are starting to explore these questions. Some children have an "aha" moment when abstract concepts of authorship and audiences are discussed in relation to media they are familiar with. Their intuitive and emerging sense of the constructedness of media ("How did they make that?") now has the power of reasoning behind it. And when children have *vocabulary* to talk about the constructed nature of media texts, tools, and technologies,

---

The Signmaker's Assistant, by Tedd Arnold

This illustrated story for children ages 4 and older is simply the best media literacy picture book ever (see Figure 8.1). When the signmaker's assistant discovers the power of authorship, he gets carried away with his power. By discovering how his work affects real audiences in the community, we learn about our responsibilities as both authors and audiences.

Figure 8.1   Still From *The Signmaker's Assistant*

Then the real trouble started. Without store signs, shoppers became confused. Without stop signs, drivers didn't know when to stop. Without street signs, firemen became lost.

Source: Arnold (1992).[1]

their ideas can flourish, which is why we've included a list of media literacy vocabulary words for children at the back of this book (see Resource B). It's important to expand our discussion of texts to include other media producers and the audiences they actively imagine and connect to through their work.

TEACHING ABOUT TARGET AUDIENCES

In the media industry, audiences are conceptualized in very specific ways. A *target audience* is a specific group of people at which a particular media message is aimed. For example, food products may be marketed to women who do most of the grocery shopping to feed the whole family, and video games may be marketed to teen boys and young adult men who purchase them independently. Usually, we think of a target audience in terms of demographic characteristics, like age, race, social class, and ethnic background. It's a truism in the media industry that the biggest mistake you can make as a communicator is to try to make a message reach everybody and appeal to everyone. The more you know about your target audience, the more you can tailor a message to meet them where they live.

Can Grade 1 children learn to identify a target audience? Powerful Voices for Kids (PVK) instructors Kate and Mona thought the answer might be "yes." But they used two different strategies to explore the concept with the 6- and 7-year-old children they worked with.

As a Watchdog with interests in health and gender issues, Kate wanted to help her students distinguish between different kinds of gender role messages that target boys and girls in advertisements for children. She planned a creative production activity in which students would create an advertisement for the "wrong" target audience. That is, they would discuss whom a particular product in a magazine was for, and then reverse those assumptions through a drawing activity.

Prior to creating a print ad using crayons and markers, students first identified "who might like" to play with or use Barbie dolls, toy trucks, and perfume. The majority of the class decided on "girls," "boys," and "older women," respectively, and Kate wrote these answers on the whiteboard. Then Kate asked students to draw a new ad for the same product, but target "someone else"—a group different from the one they had chosen. She wrote other groups on the board: "older men" and "teenagers."

Students then worked in pairs to create these ads. One team drew a perfume advertisement for older men. Another group decided to draw a girl's truck advertisement. But when children actually began to draw, Kate realized that they were still replicating advertisements they had just viewed—the truck drawing included a picture of a boy, and the perfume advertisement included a picture of a woman. Kate believed that her students had not fully understood the assignment for a variety of reasons. She believed that her own expectations as the teacher were too ambiguous and that the concepts were still too unfamiliar to students.

Kate knew that there were no wrong answers, strictly speaking, when it came to inferring target audience from a text. After all, authors' immediate intentions can only be guessed at, though literary scholar Robert Scholes tells us that some guesses may be more useful than others.[2] She knew, for instance, that most of the children in her class identified Barbie dolls as girls' toys and action figures as boys' toys.

What she wanted to see was her students moving away from the simple answers that she had seen in informal conversations about audiences for television shows, advertisements, and movies. Her students frequently said that shows, ads, and films were for "everybody," even though follow-up questions revealed that often only "me and my sister" or "my older brother and my dad" were likely to be interested.

Kate noticed that her students frequently drew directly from concrete family experience but had trouble generalizing that experience into a broader category. For instance, students might say, "My mom loves this show, but my dad watches it, too," but had trouble saying, "Women love this show, but men watch it, too." Could children this young make use of an abstract concept like *audience*?

Kate reflected on this experience:

> I realized that you have to be more explicit in what you want. I feel like I had heard from other teachers, about the older kids [in the program], that it was easier to embed the ideas [in an activity]. Maybe to make it less like "school." But at this age that didn't seem to work, so I was more explicit.

Kate developed a new activity that would more clearly demonstrate the concept of targeting an audience. First, she simplified the range of potential answers. From conversations with her students, she knew that they were aware of gender differences, often debating whether a particular show, movie, or product was "really" just for girls or boys. For instance, one girl in Kate's class argued, "But I play football, too, so football isn't just for boys." Kate's students were not as clearly able to distinguish between different types of adults, often confusing teenagers and older adults. They seemed better able to think in terms of family relations—grandpa and grandma were "older men and women," mom and dad were "adult women and adult men," older brothers or sisters were "older boys and girls," and little brothers or sisters were "younger boys and girls."

PLAYING THE PART: ROLE-PLAYING TO EXPLORE THE CONCEPT OF TARGET AUDIENCE

To make it into a dramatic play activity, Kate created name tags with these categories on them. Each student in the class would wear a different name tag and act the part. A girl playing an "older man" might affect a speech pattern like a grandfather, and a boy playing a "young girl" might teasingly mimic a little sister. Next came the introduction of the "target" tool, a red bull's-eye made of construction paper. Kate showed her students a print or television advertisement and then asked them to put the bull's-eye on the audience being targeted.

Students enjoyed role-playing different audiences. She would ask one student to hold the bull's-eye tool. Then she would show a print advertisement or televised commercial. The student would then have to place the target on the appropriate target audience label. Afterward the class discussed the student's choice to check for consensus. Kate explained, "It was designed to really get them to understand that a target audience for an ad is not just anybody who watches that ad."

By using these types of learning games, Kate was able to reinforce the practice of targeting an audience. When she developed mnemonics and charts for these ideas, she found that her rising second graders could more easily participate in discussions of abstract concepts. Kate struggled with the same concerns about introducing ambiguity into her classroom that affect many elementary educators, particularly those working with younger children, but she was encouraged by the outcomes that resulted when the lessons were modified to meet the needs of her students.

Like Kate, Mona found that her students had a difficult time understanding the concept of target audience. Mona tried to explain it to her third-grade students, but as she recalls, they seemed only to answer with personal examples of audience members like "my dad" or "my friends."

Mona tried to explain the target audience concept during the first 2 days of the Powerful Voices for Kids program. But she quickly found that her students better understood the concept when it was revealed to them some time at the end of the week through an activity. She recalled the students' "aha" moment:

> It wasn't until we saw the Justin Bieber video for "Baby"—and I asked them, "Who do you think they're targeting?" The class response to my question was "What do you mean?" I said, "Well, who do you think they're trying to get to watch this video?" Then we talked about it and they were saying, "Yes, little girls or boys." I said, "And *that's* your target audience." And it was just like, [snaps her fingers] Ahhh!

As a Spirit Guide, Mona found that her most successful activities were the ones that unlocked her students' potential as authors of original works, including songs, commercials, public service announcements, and poetry. When students developed a coherent message and could then find a form through which to convey it, they not only created inventive work but also got it intellectually.

When Mona asked her students to tell her what a purpose is ("the reason something was created," e.g., to entertain you, to inform you, to persuade you), they had trouble articulating their answers. But when they created short advertisements for toys they invented in class, they had a clear understanding of their purpose—to get other kids to want to buy their toys.

Talking about a target audience for a given media text was not as successful for Mona's students as it was for Kate's students. Mona's students were able to discuss the target audience for a Justin Bieber video that they were familiar with but found it more difficult to discuss target audiences of products they were unfamiliar with, like cars or clothing. But when they created their own poetry about littering, they identified whom they wanted to reach with their work—other kids their age, the Philadelphia community, or parents of kids their age.

What's the Right Answer?

When thinking about authors and audiences, we always make *inferences* about what we read, hear, or see. There is no one right answer. But there are many questions we might ask of students that require them to make generalizations about media based on evidence, such as these:

- What do you think the authors' purpose was for making this?
- Who do you think the target audience was?
- What might someone else say about this text?
- What did the authors leave out?

DIRECT AND EMBEDDED INSTRUCTION TECHNIQUES

There are countless debates in the education world about the role of *direct or explicit instruction* (the explicit modeling of specific strategies) and *embedded instruction* (the learning of concepts through hands-on activities). Progressive educators have long derided direct instruction as a transmission model, in which teachers merely impart knowledge to their students without offering a way for students to take ownership of the knowledge for themselves. Direct instruction does not assume that students will develop insights on their own. Instead, direct instruction takes learners through the steps of learning systematically.

This is sometimes called the *gradual release of responsibility*.[3] When teachers explain exactly what students are expected to learn and demonstrate the steps needed to accomplish a particular academic task, students are likely to use their time more effectively and to learn more. Teachers who value direct instruction set clear goals for students, making sure they understand the goals. They present a sequence of well-organized assignments and ask frequent questions to see if the students understand the work. Finally, teachers give students opportunities to practice what they have learned. For elementary children, direct instruction designed to help them recognize and construct a main idea from a paragraph or a short passage has been found to be highly effective in supporting reading comprehension skills.[4]

Any teacher who has felt the pressures of high-stakes testing knows that not all concepts teach themselves, no matter how carefully designed the learning environment is. Some teachers are distrustful of long, drawn-out composition and production activities, believing they may distract from focusing on more specific learning targets. Education scholar Lisa Delpit has noted the ways in which composition activities that allow students to express their fluency without explicitly developing basic skills often leave them vulnerable in contexts in which those skills matter most, like high-stakes tests, college applications, or job interviews.[5]

Both direct instruction and embedded instruction through production activities have benefits for students when it comes to digital and media literacy. There are developmental considerations: In second grade, many students are just emerging from a period of development in which reality and fantasy are difficult to separate. Abstract reasoning is a cognitive challenge, and one that might benefit from a variety of approaches.

What's more, we found that both Kate's and Mona's classes did well in a TV card sort task that asked children to group images from television into categories to demonstrate their understanding of target audience and purpose. Both direct and embedded instruction on the concept of target audience helped Kate's and Mona's 8- and 9-year-olds—most of them students who had been selected for academic remediation—outperform a control group students who were several years older than they were.[6]

We know that there are no right answers when we talk about the inferences we make from media. And yet we continue to make inferences, some that are useful (understanding the ways in which some commercials are marketed to boys and some to girls at very young ages) and some that are less useful (gossip and speculation about the personal shortcomings of celebrities).

We found that offering an explicit vocabulary, modeling a reasoning process, and reading and writing with a variety of media genres and forms in a respectful environment that valued multiple interpretations really made a difference. This process actually strengthened students' abilities to create new and exciting work of their own and to take their first steps as authors themselves.

MEETING AUTHORS FACE TO FACE AND VIRTUALLY

Author visits can connect students to the real world of all forms of media production, from the process of writing children's literature to filmmaking, journalism, and web design. Steven Krasner, a former sports writer for the *Providence Journal*, has written several children's books and does writing workshops in schools. His school program, Nudging the Imagination, helps kids become independent and confident writers. Working collaboratively with children in Grades 4 and up, he cooks up a story with them by assembling a set of special ingredients: a catchy title, characters, settings, problems, situations, and dialogue. They write mystery dinner plays that children stage as fundraisers for their school. And kids always ooh and ahh when they learn that, as a sports writer, he got paid to watch baseball games.

Not only did students at Wayne Elementary School meet children's author and illustrator James Agee when librarian Sue Dahlstrom arranged for him to visit the school, but Grade 2 children also produced their own remix responses to his book *The Retired Kid* to present to him when he visited. Using the pages of his book as a model, children created their own pages by drawing and writing about the disadvantages and the advantages of being a kid. One child wrote that it's hard work being a kid "because you have to do homework." But guess what? "I will get smarter!" Another child wrote that it's hard work being a kid "because of siblings." But guess what? "They keep you company."

After children created their drawings, Mrs. Dahlstrom set up a mini-recording studio in her library and taped each child reading aloud from his or her writing. She then created a PowerPoint presentation using scans of each child's drawing and a hyperlink to the voice recording. Mr. Agee viewed the presentation with delight, and children learned that words, drawings, and even voices are all part of the author's toolkit.

Students also benefit from meeting real authors in the classroom through video pen pal exchanges and Skype chats. For example, children in Rapid City, South Dakota, got to meet children's author and illustrator Joe Cepeda when he visited the classroom via Skype. And Karla Duff, a sixth-grade teacher at a middle school of about 300 students in Oelwein, Iowa, never had an author visit the school until "Skype brought authors to us—free."

After trying out a Skype author visit for World Read Aloud Day in 2011, Karla arranged Skype author visits regularly for her students. Children have assigned roles on the day of the chat and run the whole event themselves, greeting the author as they welcome him or her to the classroom, asking questions they've formulated ahead of time, and even live-tweeting the Skype chat to share the experience beyond their classroom.[7] When students are able to ask questions of real authors and know that their own work is being seen by real audiences, it transforms their learning from something that just happens at school to the kind of learning that has an impact on the world around them.

PVK instructor Kate wanted her Grade 1 children to meet African American filmmaker and independent producer/director Barry Jenkins, director of *Medicine for Melancholy* (2008), a film that stars Wyatt Cenac of *The Daily Show with Jon Stewart*. But Barry Jenkins lived in California, and Kate's students were in Philadelphia. They decided to communicate using a form of video pen pal activity. First, Kate showed children Mr. Jenkins's film trailer from the Internet to introduce the them to the filmmaker's work. Then she and the children generated a list of questions they wanted to ask him, writing down their questions and recording them on video. Kate sent the video to the filmmaker by uploading it to an online video-sharing website, Vimeo. Mr. Jenkins took time out of his busy schedule to answer questions they had about his work. In fact, he created a short film with a musical soundtrack in which he answered each child's question—including "Who is your target audience?"

In responding to the question "Did you make your movie alone or with friends?" Mr. Jenkins explained that he made films with several of his friends from film school and that children can collaborate with their peers to work on creative projects, including stories, plays, and films. See the children's questions and the filmmaker's answers at www.powerfulvoicesforkids.com.

Your Phone Is an Audio Recording Device

Audio recording is a powerful tool for media literacy education. When you download the free app iTalk (http://italksync.com), you can capture high-quality sound from your cell phone with a single touch. You can play the recordings back instantly, and you can email them to your computer and use them in other applications.

MEASURING DIGITAL AND MEDIA LITERACY COMPETENCIES

Researchers are just beginning to understand how digital and media literacy interventions may affect the print literacy competencies of young children. In researching children's inference-making about television programs, we focused on the kinds of inferences that people make when they identify the purpose of media or why someone made it (e.g., "A commercial persuades you to buy products") and the target audience of media (e.g., "This was made for teenagers"). Teacher-librarians in the elementary grades identify these concepts as basic skills for information and media literacy. We wondered if there was any relationship between children's reading comprehension abilities as measured on widely recognized standardized reading tests and their ability to identify the purpose and target audience of a media message.[8]

We saw some observational evidence of meaningful learning experiences, the development of media production skills, and greater comfort among students to connect their in-school learning to their home media contexts, as you have seen in previous chapters. But we still wondered about how, in a test-driven educational environment, we might better be able to speak to the immediate concerns of principals, administrators, community and government stakeholders, and teachers by connecting some of our own successes to mandated summative assessment that they are required to administer and value.

When it comes to digital media and learning, we must begin with the end in mind. Sonia Livingstone asked this question of the digital and media literacy community: "What are digital learning projects designed to enable the learning of?"[9] This question inspired us to create the comprehensive list of learning targets that you'll find at the back of the book (Resource A). One thing that seems clear from our research is that younger students who had exposure to digital and media literacy enrichment (which, as you have noticed in our previous chapters, come in a variety of forms depending on classroom context) are successful in *making inferences* that are associated with comprehension and meaning-making.

No doubt about it: Inference-making is an essential component of reading comprehension and critical thinking. Some researchers have explored the ways in which children make inferences about narrative stories that are presented on television, finding that children who are exposed to adult commentary about TV shows are better able to make inferences that support narrative comprehension as compared with children who do not have access to adult commentary.[10]

But researchers have not yet addressed children's ability to make inferences about message purpose and target audience of a variety of types of television content. That's why we created a test, called the TV Sort Task, to explore children's inferences about television programs.

In the task, children were given a pile of images from a variety of familiar TV shows and asked to sort the cards. We first asked children if they could categorize television shows according to their target audience. For instance, an image from a commercial for children's cereal Fruity Pebbles might plausibly be identified as being "for children," while an image of a local news show might be seen as targeting adults. Then we asked children to sort the cards based on the purpose of the message, categorizing differences in why the show was made. A child might recognize that the Fruity Pebbles image may be recognized as "to get you to buy cereal" (to persuade), while the local news show was designed "to tell you what's happening in the city" (to inform). See Figure 8.2.

We found that rising second-, third-, and fourth-grade students who participated in the media literacy program outperformed their peers who

Figure 8.2 Image of Child at Work on TV Sort Task

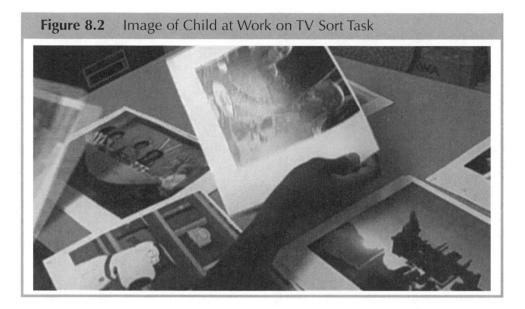

were not enrolled in the program. This was especially important because 75% of the students enrolled in the Powerful Voices for Kids program at Russell Byers Charter School were children who required academic remediation; that is, they were in the bottom quintile of their class. It appears that these children were able to learn to make inferences about the purpose and target audience of media messages, and they were better at this task than their more academically competent peers who had not enrolled in the PVK media literacy program.

However, for the Grades 5 and 6 children who participated in our study, performance on the TV Sort Task did not reveal statistically significant differences as compared with a control group of children from the same school who were not enrolled in the PVK program.

We have a lot of questions about our research. For instance, is the simple card-sort activity not complex enough for older students, whose observations were often extensive but unrelated to the specific questions about target audience and message purpose being asked? Is there value in finding other forms of assessment for older students to distinguish them from younger students who are still developing lots of foundational literacy skills?

When we looked at the performance of all students, we found that inference-making about purpose and target audience is highly correlated with students' reading comprehension as measured on standardized reading (but not math) scores. Our study is aligned with the work of other researchers who believe that making inferences and predictions about stories may actually precede new readers' development of basic reading comprehension.[11]

We wonder: To what extent does engaging students' inference-making abilities about multiple media forms have a beneficial impact on their print literacy skills over time? We wonder whether our very preliminary exploration of these ideas might offer a glimpse of some of the potential of introducing digital and media literacy concepts and activities with young children.

Student Learning Behaviors

By asking teachers to make a check mark next to the names of children who regularly displayed the following behaviors, we wondered how the Powerful Voices for Kids program may have affected children's behaviors in school.

1. The student asks meaningful questions.
2. The student is confident in expressing ideas verbally.
3. The student is eager to use media and technology.
4. The student makes connections to his or her life outside the classroom.

For Reflection and Discussion: Are these behaviors valued in your school? Should they be? Why or why not? What are some expected and unanticipated consequences of creating a learning environment where these behaviors are valued?

WHY IT MATTERS

Exploring the worlds of mass media, popular culture, and digital media may motivate some—but not all—children to apply the effort and practice required to master the skills of reading and writing print texts.

Kate shared a powerful story with us about one young student, whom we will call Bonnie, who showed particular difficulty with print literacy. When asked to write any words with a pencil, even her own name, she would set the pencil aside and claim that it was lost. When Kate challenged her, she took the pencil and broke it in half. Bonnie was given another pencil. She immediately snapped that one in half, too. Kate explained, "I don't understand what I can do to help her. She has so much to say in class; she's so smart—*so* smart—but she just can't write it down."

Educators strive to help children like Bonnie overcome anxieties about the demands and challenges of print literacy. We believe that there are a variety of forms of writing and communication that will add to Bonnie's toolkit. Some of these will help Bonnie use her mind well. As we have shown in this chapter, digital and media literacy education supports the development of abstract reasoning and inference-making that ties children's creativity directly to the many competencies involved in acquiring print literacy.

Lesson | Collaborative Storytelling

Lesson Description

Children work in teams of four to tell a story on four quadrants of a piece of paper using a sequence of images and language.

Objectives

Students will

- Pay attention and look at a message carefully to understand it
- Draw images and use written or spoken language to create
- Work with a partner to get something done
- Share their reaction to the work of others and get feedback on their own work from others
- Believe that their creative ideas have value to others

Vocabulary

Purpose

Sequential

Target audience

Collaborative

Messages

Character

Plot

Conflict

Resources and Materials

✓ Paper
✓ Pencils

Activity

Access

✓ Name some examples of media where you think you would need a team to create the product.

✓ Play a 4-sentence storytelling game. Students sit in a circle, and the first person says one sentence, the next person adds his or her sentence, and so on. The teacher writes down all four of the sentences on the board.

Analysis

✓ Review the story. Use the concepts, including sequence, collaboration, purpose, and target audience, to evaluate each collaborative story. Continue to practice until children are able to work together to create a coherent, unified narrative. What messages are being told in the story? How did the story change?

Composition

✓ Four children work on four sheets of paper, folded into four quarters, to draw the story. The first student draws the first sentence of the group story in the first panel. When each child completes his or her first panel, the paper is passed to the student on the right, who will draw the second sentence in the second panel, and so on. After all four panels are complete, the original artists should present their four different visual stories to the class.

Reflection

✓ See examples of collaborative stories at www.power fulvoicesforkids.com.

✓ Discuss how the stories changed among the groups, and review the benefits and challenges of working collaboratively on media messages.

Source: Created by Rachel Hobbs.

NOTES

1. Arnold, T. (1992). *The signmaker's assistant.* New York, NY: Dial.
2. Scholes, R. (2011). *English after the fall: From literature to textuality.* Iowa City: University of Iowa Press.
3. Pearson, P. D., & Gallagher, M. C. (1983). The instruction of reading comprehension. *Contemporary Educational Psychology, 8,* 317–344.
4. Baumann, J. (1984). Effectiveness of a direct instruction paradigm for teaching main idea comprehension. *Reading Research Quarterly, 20*(1), 93–116.
5. Delpit, L. (1995). *Other people's children: Cultural conflict in the classroom.* New York, NY: New Press.
6. Moore, D. C., Schlesinger, M., & Hobbs, R. (2012). *Understanding the authors and audiences of TV programs: A preliminary examination of the development of children's media literacy competencies.* Manuscript submitted for publication.
7. Messner, K. (2012, February 17). Author visits? A remote possibility: Using Skype to connect is fun and affordable. *The Digital Shift/School Library Journal.* Retrieved from http://www.thedigitalshift.com
8. Moore, Schlesinger, & Hobbs (2012).
9. Livingstone, S. (2011). Digital learning and participation among youth: Critical reflections on future research priorities. *International Journal of Learning and Media, 2*(2–3), 9.
10. Collins, W., Sobol, B., & Westby, S. (1981). Effects of adult commentary on children's comprehension and inferences about TV aggressive portrayals. *Child Development, 52*(1), 158–163.
11. Cain, K., & Oakhill, J. V. (1999). Inference making and its relation to comprehension failure in young children. *Reading and Writing, 11,* 489–503.

Part IV

Approaches to Teacher Education

9 Transforming Practice

In this chapter, you'll learn about

The Digital and Media Literacy Learning Curve

- How do teachers deal with their wide variety of skill and comfort levels with mass media, popular culture, digital media, and new technology?

Professional Development for Digital and Media Literacy

- How can various professional development models help inspire educators to try out new approaches to teaching and learning?
- What concepts from this book can I use to improve my practice?

Teacher Creativity

- How does the creative energy of teachers get activated and harnessed toward the use of instructional practices that improve student learning?

When Henry explained to friends, family, and other professionals that he would be working at Powerful Voices for Kids (PVK) during the summer of 2009 as a media literacy teacher, they responded by saying, "Oh, like teaching computers and stuff." Henry tried to explain that it was a bit more complicated, involving not just training in computers and emerging technologies but helping children make sense of the full range of mass media and popular culture in their lives, using media and technology as a resource to teach traditional literacy skills, and gaining information about social issues and other topics unrelated to media and technology.

Henry was about to get a deep-end dive into the media literacy education pool. On the first day of the Powerful Voices for Kids program in 2009, there he stood, along with eight other nervous-looking young teachers (most of them graduate students) all in their 20s or early 30s, in their bright blue t-shirts with the Powerful Voices for Kids logo, standing in the lobby of the school, waiting for 77 children to arrive. Few had worked with children younger than 12, although most had at least some experience as an instructor in summer camps, afterschool programs, religious education, or other informal learning situations. It was a time of great expectations.

The first day of class was exhilarating and exhausting. Here's how David reflected on his first day of teaching:

> Wasn't sure what to expect, but I thought that the kids were a lot smarter in ways I wasn't expecting; for one thing, they know technology like crazy, and I'm guessing they won't need very much time with technical instruction.

When he asked children about their media preferences that first day, there was a lot of talk about Michael Jackson, *Transformers*, and *Teen Vogue* magazine. Children talked about musical artists, including Lil Wayne and Cold Flamez.

David could see right away that children weren't sure about what was appropriate or inappropriate to share when it came to talking about TV shows, movies, and especially music. He recognized that many classroom teachers at the school "probably think that even the *Teen Vogue* stuff is risqué." That first week, he learned that while some kids are devoted to the Disney Channel, others are listening to gangster rap and heavy metal. As David wrote in his journal, "In other words, they're 12!"

With the help of energetic teachers, children created a wide range of communication artifacts while participating in the Powerful Voices for Kids program. They videotaped each other giving speeches, reenacting historical events, reading aloud, and reciting poetry. They interviewed other students and adults. They created music videos, public service announcements, digital stories, and mini-documentaries. They wrote scripts, built simple web pages, drew pictures, created comics, and programmed video game interactives.

But just looking at this work, you can't tell much about the process that was used to create it. This is one of the reasons why both students and teachers may develop unrealistic attitudes about what kind of media productions are possible. At our website, www.powerfulvoicesforkids.com, you can see examples of behind-the-scenes footage that shows the creative process from start to finish—because that's where the learning takes place.

TEACHING TEACHERS

By now, you're probably wondering how the educators we profiled in this book acquired the knowledge and skills they needed to integrate digital and media literacy into the elementary curriculum. How do teachers learn to use the many improvisational instructional practices described in this book and depicted in the PVK videos?

Some teachers, as we have seen, just naturally seem to adopt the habits of mind and instructional practices that support inquiry about children's experiences with mass media, popular culture, and digital media. Some benefit from the opportunity to observe the work of other teachers. *Guided conversations about practice* enable teachers to recognize how theoretical concepts get articulated through classroom practice. Still others need time to engage with children directly, encountering individual learners and probing to identify their needs, then experimenting with a variety of instructional approaches.

In recognition of this diversity and to better understand those factors that shape learning progression among teachers, we used a variety of models of professional development with instructors and elementary teachers over the course of several years. In this chapter, we share some of the practices we developed to meet the needs of teachers and share what we learned. We also consider the implications of our experience as it relates to the larger agenda of educational reform and technology integration in urban elementary education.

OVERVIEW OF OUR PROFESSIONAL DEVELOPMENT APPROACHES IN DIGITAL AND MEDIA LITERACY

We wanted to learn more about the strengths and limitations of various professional development models to support teachers' growth and learning.

Of course, there's no one right way to offer teachers a professional development experience. Since we were trying to reach teachers in both urban and suburban schools, we explored the use of five different models for delivering staff development over the course of 3 years:

1. A weeklong *summer institute* where a larger group of teachers experienced a graduate-level seminar style learning experience

2. A summer *open-doors program* where educators could participate for one or more days in a professional development program and observe classrooms and see media literacy in action during the summer learning program for children

3. An *in-school mentor program* where a graduate student mentor would offer an individual teacher (or small group) instructional support and coaching for a predetermined number of hours in their own classroom on a weekly basis

4. A *small learning community* where a small group of teachers met with us monthly over the course of one academic year; together we helped them integrate media literacy into their curriculum

5. A free online *website* for educators (www.powerfulvoicesforkids .com) with lesson plans and videos designed for use as part of an online learning staff development program for educators

Each of the approaches had some affordances and some limitations, as you will see from the descriptions that follow. They reflect the complex realities of working within the boundaries of time, budget, and circumstances involved in coordinating this work with teachers and school leaders. At the back of the book (Resource C), you'll see a list of the key ideas, concepts, and principles that are embedded in the Powerful Voices for Kids program. As readers like you bring this program into more school districts, we hope to more fully understand the impact of these approaches on the knowledge, attitudes, and skills of the teachers we reach.

Summer Institute

A weeklong summer institute for teachers enabled us to create an intensive professional development experience taught by a diverse faculty, including college professors, classroom teachers, media professionals, and educational technology specialists. We designed it in coordination with the Powerful Voices for Kids summer program for children so that participants would have the chance to observe and interact with children and instructors who were participating in the program.

After completing the program, we wanted teachers to (1) appreciate the role of media and technology in the lives of children and youth; (2) understand and apply the key theoretical concepts of media literacy in the context of 21st century literacies; (3) appreciate how mass media, popular culture, and digital media can be connected to K–8 subject areas; (4) explore how student multimedia composition can support print literacy development; and (5) examine issues of media and technology in the context of larger school reform and social justice agendas.

In the mornings, participants learned about the theory of media literacy, engaged in model lessons to deepen their understanding of the use of critical media analysis and media composition in the K–8 classroom, strengthened digital and media literacy competencies, and used discussion and dialogue to explore the complex role of mass media and popular culture in the lives of children and young people.

Each day of the program, teachers engaged in a media composition or production activity. Teachers created a basic web page to compose and to share their writing. They made simple videos using FlipCams. These practical skills prepared teachers to reenter their classrooms in the fall with a repertoire of exciting new ideas with which to connect with their students. In the afternoon, we offered structured opportunities to observe classrooms where PVK instructors were teaching children in Grades 1–6. We used viewing and discussion experiences and simple media composition activities with media and technology to provoke *pair-share interaction* as well as small- and large-group discussion.

The program was thematically structured over the course of 5 days to explore these questions:

- **Introduction to Media Literacy.** What competencies are essential to becoming a powerful communicator in contemporary society?
- **Understanding Today's Learners.** How can learning about children's interaction with media texts and technology tools help educators become more effective in the classroom?
- **Authors and Audiences, Messages and Meanings, Representations and Realities.** How can we best help children become critical thinkers in responding to media messages that shape their personal and social identity and their understanding of the world?
- **Who's Telling the Stories? Understanding News and Advertising.** How can children's engagement with storytelling, news, and advertising support reading comprehension, text analysis, and composition practices?
- **The Future of Literacy.** What role do teachers and parents play in developing a learning environment that meets the needs of 21st century learners?

Most educators who participated in our professional development programs were unfamiliar with web and video production, and all valued the opportunity to gain experience with media composition activities using video and online writing collaboration tools. Because the program was grant-funded, we were delighted to offer participants a Flip video camera to use for activities during the professional development program and then take home to use with their own students.

We held our summer staff development programs during the month of July, when our summer program for children was in full swing. This enabled us to experiment with discovering how to integrate learning experiences between participating educators in the professional development program with children and their graduate student teachers.

Open Doors and Model Lessons

Teachers, like everyone, learn by doing. That's why Renee has put the demonstration of media literacy model lessons at the heart of her professional development work with teachers ever since she first began teaching teachers in the Billerica Public Schools in Massachusetts and at the Harvard Institute on Media Education, beginning in 1992. What does this look like? A demonstration of a lesson plan or activity is followed by theoretical framing, debriefing, analysis, and reflection. This process enables the building of connections between theory and practice. Of course, there's rarely time to demonstrate the lesson in its entirety, but it's quite effective to *model incomplete practice*. Even a truncated mini-lesson of some sort can give teachers a feel for how the lesson will go when they experience it themselves as learners. At the conclusion of the lesson, we make some observations about how the lesson addressed or embodied a particular theoretical idea in media studies or education. Then, using a combination of pair-share, small-group, and large-group discussion activities, we invite observation, commentary, and extension in building off the lesson.

As part of this process, participants are encouraged to identify the assumptions, tacit goals, and embedded values of the lesson. Often these conversations open up some rich dialogue, as teachers debate the merits and limitations of specific curricular choices and imagine how students of different ages might respond to similar learning activities.

Whenever possible, we also took advantage of the opportunity to bring informal educators from the summer program together with both classroom teachers and children. Nearly every day of the summer institute, for example, we provided opportunities for classroom teachers to interact with elementary children through activities that encouraged dialogue about mass media and popular culture and made use of digital technologies like the Flip cameras.

The high level of transparency and trust sometimes made teachers feel as if they were teaching in a fishbowl. As PVK instructor Nuala Cabral described it,

> At first I was nervous having them in the room because it's like an added pressure: You feel like you're on stage, of course. But the classroom teachers were really there to learn about what we're doing, and they have a lot more experience than we do as teachers, and they were able to offer really supportive and encouraging feedback.

In-School Mentoring

The concept is simple: An in-school mentor works elbow to elbow with a classroom teacher for 3–6 hours per week in developing and implementing a lesson or project that involves digital and media literacy. Over a few years, Renee has experimented with placing graduate students and undergraduate students into K–12 schools to support teachers' work on a particular project. Often they are film, journalism, or communication students who have already acquired a conceptual understanding of media literacy, demonstrate competence with digital media, and have an interest in working with children and youth.

Most of the time, teachers were tremendously grateful for the support; when it comes to using technology in elementary schools, more hands, ears, and eyes can make a real difference in the success or failure of a project. Sometimes classroom teachers described their in-school mentors as "techies," a concept that both David and Renee both found problematic. In-school mentors were sometimes called in to address technology problems, when the school's wireless or SMART Board wiring wasn't functioning properly, for example.

To tell the truth, the jury's still out on how in-school mentors may help teachers integrate digital and media literacy into the classroom. In future research, we may be able to say more about the value of such individuals to support the teaching and learning of digital and media literacy in the classroom. But here, at the end of this book, we simply offer a glimpse of what it looks like—and feels like—to be an in-school mentor. As you'll see, one mentor, Maggie, developed some strong teaching skills through the experience, and children certainly benefitted from her work. But it's not as clear that the participating teacher learned much from Maggie's presence.

Maggie Ricco worked as an in-school mentor in collaboration with an urban elementary school where a group of Grade 5 and Grade 6 children were creating a "History of the 20th Century" website. The participating classroom teacher led the way in helping children write and research their short articles, but she was unfamiliar with the process of website production. She was unable to help her students with any aspect of the production project, including basic troubleshooting of the classroom wireless connection. For example, when one student, Walter, began the class by explaining that he had trouble logging in, Maggie brought him to the computer attached to the projector, and they walked through the log-in process together for everyone to see. She had hoped the collaborating teacher was paying attention, but, sadly, she was not.

One day, Maggie's lesson involved editing. In teaching children to construct web pages, Maggie put a lot of emphasis on certain formatting issues and sourcing images, for the sake of the audience wanting to read the completed work. She showed them the current state of their page about the life of Nelson Mandela, which was unfinished. The typeface was tiny and hard to read, and the image placement was disorienting. Many of the children picked out what was "wrong" about the web page right away. Children also discussed the process of finding appropriate images, as Maggie began to apply the image search process to the Mandela page. The collaborating teacher offered some informative commentary on why certain recognizable images are preferential in some cases.

When Maggie googled "Nelson Mandela," she found an image of him as a youth, wearing South African garb. Some of the children and the teacher said they would prefer the more familiar and well-known images of Mandela as an older man. However, Dolores, a student, argued that the image of him as a younger man showed his connections to Africa. According to Maggie, Dolores was one of the students who frequently pretended she didn't know what to do next, but occasionally came out with certain amazing responses and interpretations. Maggie took such pleasure in those small moments when Dolores showed herself to be the smart and thoughtful girl she was!

Maggie had been working with the kids long enough, after 8 weeks, to notice that it always seemed as though the students were initially competent and experienced enough to work independently on the website. But then, when she worked with children one on one, she saw behaviors that revealed their actual level of competence to be lower than she expected. She noticed differences between various children in their navigation skills on computers and the web. Many didn't seem to understand how search engines work. She wrote, "I wish I could put myself in their brains and figure out exactly what is challenging to them."

One day, Maggie struggled with two students, Devon and Cheryl, who continually insisted that they were "done" with a page and, without telling anyone, moved on to edit another page. Maggie caught them in the act and reminded them about the step-by-step process that students had agreed to use.

Maggie's major impact on that day was to offer students advice about how to get something done: Stick to seeing a single page through to completion before starting another one or working on a different page already in progress. "Finish what you started" was Maggie's mantra. Simply getting the project completed required a sustained focus for these Grade 5 and 6 students.

The in-school mentoring model is one of many models of professional development in education. When it's embedded in a university-school partnership model, as Powerful Voices for Kids is, it can be cost-effective even in the context of inevitable budget limitations. But the approach may be limited if in-school mentors intentionally or unintentionally replace the work of or compete with classroom teachers. Teachers who feel *supported* in their own ongoing learning and classroom practice are more committed and effective than those who do not.[1] As schools begin to integrate digital and media literacy into instructional practice, it is important to keep in mind key characteristics of the learning environment: Educators need to have a sense of themselves as agents of change, be able to deploy a set of models of action, and engage in team learning, where they "suspend assumptions and enter into genuine thinking together."[2]

Professional Learning Community

In designing and implementing a professional learning community at the Russell Byers Charter School, Renee wanted to support the development of elementary teachers while exposing new teacher educators to the practice of professional development. David Cooper Moore, Emily Bailin, and John Landis were apprentice teacher educators in a program that was designed to help elementary classroom teachers gain an understanding of media literacy while increasing their comfort in integrating multimedia production activities into existing curriculum.

Professional learning community (PLC) is a term used to describe a process by which teachers in a school, its administrators, and other partners continuously seek and share learning and then act on what they learn, enhancing their effectiveness as professionals so that students benefit.[3] Positive outcomes of professional learning communities include increased teacher efficacy, collective responsibility for student learning, reduced teacher isolation, as well as higher morale and job satisfaction.[4] Professional learning communities help support the process of school improvement by building productive relationships that support collaboration. They engage educators at all levels of experience in collective, context-specific learning, improving results in terms of school culture, teacher practice, and student learning. Going beyond the scope of study groups, such partnerships "require that group members reflect honestly and openly together about their own practice, intentionally seeking ways to do their work better and continually building their capacity to do so."[5]

In helping her own students learn to be teacher educators, Renee used the gradual release of responsibility model, where the responsibility for task completion shifts gradually over time from the teacher to the students. Over time, the teacher steps aside to function in a mentoring capacity, enabling the facilitators to lead the program. In this case, Renee designed and led the initial sessions, gradually turning over more responsibility for program design and implementation to David, Emily, and John.

Program Goals for the Professional Learning Community in Media Literacy

Participating teachers will

- Be more aware of the significant role of mass media, popular culture, and digital media in the lives of their students.
- Learn instructional strategies that connect digital and media literacy to student learning in the areas of language arts, science, social studies, health education, and the fine and performing arts.
- Increase confidence in using a variety of media and digital technology tools and online sharing tools with their students in ways that connect to existing curriculum.
- Promote expression and communication between faculty members in the building.
- Develop, implement, and assess a project that activates children's digital and media literacy competencies.

STRUCTURING PROFESSIONAL DEVELOPMENT

Over the course of the academic year, the professional learning community explored six themes: (1) What Is Media Literacy?, (2) Media Literacy Concepts and Visual Storytelling, (3) Using News and Current Events in the Classroom, (4) Mini-Lessons and Long-Term Projects, (5) Benefits and Challenges of Bringing Popular Culture Into the Classroom, and (6) Program Review and Next Steps. For each session, we also prepared learning objectives that outlined our own expectations for the discussion of the assigned reading, the production activity, and the theoretical and meta-cognitive understandings of the media literacy concepts being addressed.

Phase I consisted of formal learning—a series of six structured meetings (20 hours of total instruction) that included demonstrations of lessons, dialogue and discussion, an introduction to some literature from the field, the opportunity to develop media production skills using online media and technology tools, and considerations of how such instruction and practice might be implemented into existing curricula. Two components were particularly important: The professional development occurred during the academic year (including evenings and weekends) and on the school premises, and teachers received a modest stipend for participating in the program.

Phase II focused on individual mentoring that began in the last 2 months of the PLC and continued on through May, when final projects were completed. Each participant developed and implemented an original lesson plan integrating media literacy into the curriculum. To accomplish this, each facilitator was assigned three or four teachers to work with on a frequent basis to help brainstorm and design a lesson that would ultimately be implemented in the teachers' respective classes. You can see some of these lessons on the Powerful Voices for Kids website at www.powerfulvoicesforkids.com.

Each session included some form of media-production activity, during which teachers generally worked with a partner to compose or create some form of media as part of the learning experience. In the program, teachers created a series of PowerPoint slides, developed a digital comic panel using simple online software tools, wrote captions for a photo interpretation activity, and planned and implemented a screencasting project. Each production activity revealed teachers' level of comfort and familiarity with various types of digital technology and with the process of collaboration. After modeling and introducing the process, teachers worked with a partner to compose a message using a new media tool or text. Facilitators would circulate around the room observing and asking questions. Then we would gather as a large group to share the work that was created and reflect on the learning process.

THE ROLE OF PLANNING AND DEBRIEFING

Teaching people to be facilitators requires two layers of planning. With the facilitator team, our regular meeting cycle consisted of brainstorming, planning, meeting, and debriefing. Figure 9.1 shows the detailed structure of the preparation, implementation, and debriefing cycle. The facilitators met with Renee, the mentor, twice before each workshop. The first meeting was used to discuss the overarching theme and purpose of the next

Figure 9.1 Detailed Structure of the Professional Learning Community Program

1. Brainstorming Session	Mentor and facilitators meet to identify specific goals, develop ideas for lessons, and discuss the concepts for the next meeting.	
2. Planning Session	Mentor and facilitators meet again to cover meeting logistics, designate specific responsibilities of facilitators, review documents prepared for meeting, predict timetable, and anticipate range of participant behaviors for the upcoming meeting.	
3. PLC Meeting (3 hrs)	A. Ice Breaker	Facilitators and participants informally discuss recent experiences with media and popular culture during the past week.
	B. Model Lesson	The lesson is modeled and discussed.
	C. Discussion of Reading	Facilitators and participants discuss assigned reading, making connections to personal and professional experience.
	D. Production Activity	Participants explore media literacy concepts by collaborating to create media using technology tools.
	E. Group Critique and Reflection	Participants gather to view, reflect, and comment on what was produced.
	F. Recap and Plan for Next Session	Overall reflections of the evening are followed by a plan for next session; reading is assigned.
4. Facilitator Debrief	Facilitators meet to debrief, without the participants, and discuss highlights and lowlights of the meeting.	

session; the second meeting was used for logistics, designation of responsibilities, and prediction of how our instruction and discussion might play out with our participants.

It was not until the end of the six sessions that we realized how useful the process of *anticipating teacher response* proved to be. Having worked in the school on a variety of projects and programs in the past, the facilitators were familiar with the school culture and classroom teachers, allowing them to effectively predict possible directions and outcomes of discussions and activities. A familiarity with the school culture, including the administration, faculty, staff, children, and family members, turned out to be an important factor in the program's success.

Immediately following every session, we conducted a formal debriefing after participants had left, using the form of sharing "highlights" and "lowlights" from our perceptions, observations, and personal experience of the program. Although we all were tired, it was, in hindsight, one of the most important elements for new facilitators. The intensity of the debriefing sessions promoted reflective self-awareness and sometimes yielded an emotional authenticity that could only have occurred immediately after the sessions. In these debriefings, Renee, as the mentor, was frank about her perceptions of what was more or less effective with her own instructional practice, and she modeled the stance of a reflective practitioner. These meetings became an increasingly safe space for the group of new facilitators (and the faculty mentor) to be both confident and vulnerable and provide honest reflections and feedback about each other and ourselves.

This practice, called *collective debriefing*, is an instructional strategy that Renee has also used to intentionally build a learning community. Collective debriefing occurs at the end of each day of the program and consists of a structured sharing about highlights and lowlights of the day. This component of the program has proven to be a key element of the Powerful Voices for Kids program in supporting teacher professional development.

Collective debriefing also offers a safe space for sharing moments of celebration and honest self-reflection, increasing our sense of camaraderie with colleagues and empathy with students and their families.

But the practice has some limitations. On one occasion, Renee asked the PVK instructors to sit in the center of two concentric circles, as she had invited summer institute teacher participants to join the collective debriefing and sit in the outer circle. Two groups of teachers participated in the collective debriefing, reflecting on the learning that had occurred in the Powerful Voices for Kids program that day. However, it was the end of a long, hot summer day for the PVK instructors, and some of the more experienced classroom teachers who were summer institute participants asked complicated questions. They weren't familiar with the children who were participating in the program. Many of these teachers had not worked in urban schools. Others pointed out real limitations of the young instructors' classroom management styles and other challenges they faced as new and inexperienced teachers.

The session took an emotional turn as the PVK instructors revealed their sense of vulnerability and anxiety about the unpredictable elements and challenges of this work. There were choked-up voices, and anxiety levels were high. After all, these instructors were beginners at this work, in the process of discovering and learning for themselves. Their work didn't always turn out the way they expected it to. Fortunately, the more experienced educators rose to the occasion, remembering well their first years in the classroom and offering words of gracious support. We realized that the collective debriefing depends on an intense shared experience where people are willing to be vulnerable to each other and willing to listen openly *and* ask questions, while withholding direct criticism, judgment, and evaluation. When collective debriefing makes teachers feel that they are under a microscope, it can create feelings of discomfort that reduce its effectiveness.

CHOOSING AND USING MEDIA TEXTS FOR CRITICAL ANALYSIS AND PRODUCTION

Over and over again, we were faced with the challenge of teachers who had many conflicting, paradoxical, and curious opinions about whether (or not) and how (and how not to) choose media texts for classroom use. A kindergarten teacher told a story of children getting excited about SpongeBob when she even just mentions the character. Another teacher told us that children in elementary school shouldn't be listening to pop music at all because the content was targeting older teens and adults. Another worried that using popular culture in the classroom might go against parent and family values. Several teachers articulated the idea that teachers feel they have to compete with pop culture for children's attention.

One sixth-grade teacher mentioned a time when a student answered a question about American history by describing a scene from the animated show *Family Guy*. The teacher didn't know how to respond. The child's motives were sincere, that was certain. But he didn't feel comfortable acknowledging the student's information and ideas, given the source. Did children even understand the layers of irony and satire embedded in that often-profane show? However, when his students talked about TV wrestling shows, this same teacher felt more comfortable and would sometimes ask them questions about the characters or conflicts represented in the program.

In the eyes of children, parents and teachers can be clueless about popular culture sometimes. Elementary teachers often pointed out to us how difficult it can be to recognize when children were even making a verbal or nonverbal reference to a movie, TV show, celebrity, athlete, or other dimension of popular culture, since many teachers are unfamiliar with the media that children enjoy in the home. Even young children have acquired a sense of what is permissible to talk about in school. "You can't just ask them," one teacher said. "Children can be coy about explaining the connection," perhaps because even young children are aware which types of programs are considered "inappropriate" in the eyes of adults.

It's important for educators to reflect on our own attitudes about culture, in all its many forms. Whether we like it or not, most children in our schools get exposed to many adult-oriented forms of popular culture, so much so that wishing to protect them from it may be futile and misguided. One elementary teacher explained it this way: "Popular culture *is* culture. The parents at this school are young, involved, and have the opportunity to build relationships with their children through media in certain respects. Popular culture might help to make school more relevant." Another teacher recognized that her own preconceived notions about and uses of media complicated the question of bringing pop culture into her classroom. "It's important to know your kids," she said.

In order to provide an experience to open up metacognitive thinking about why teachers may choose to use popular culture texts, we gave a group of elementary school teachers 17 texts, including samples from traditional PBS children's television, Disney entertainment films, music videos, public service announcements, presidential speeches, and both professionally produced and amateur documentaries. We selected generically diverse texts in order to promote discussion among participants about what they consider to be appropriate choices for the classroom. Figure 9.2 shows the list of media excerpts we collected and placed on a wiki page for the teachers to review.

Teachers were invited to work with a partner to choose one of the texts, considering students' needs and abilities. Teachers were encouraged to predict the range of responses that might occur in classroom discussion, the texts' ability to challenge students and expand critical thinking abilities, and adherence to target lesson outcomes for a chosen text. Teachers offered various rationales for how and why some of the selected media texts could support student learning.

Figure 9.2 Exploring Popular Culture Texts in the Classroom

THEME: Community

- Unlitter Us public service announcement, music video
- *Sesame Street* "Places in our Neighborhood," music video
- Bruce Springsteen "Streets of Philadelphia," music video

THEME: Civil Rights

- "I Have a Dream" Remix music and speech
- *Eyes on the Prize* excerpt, documentary

THEME: Nutrition

- High-fructose corn syrup parody ad
- "High Fructose Corn Syrup: Get The Facts"
- CBC News "Corn Syrup Concern"

THEME: Heroes and Villains 1

- "Cyberchase" PBS children's animated narrative, excerpt
- "Sonic X" commercial children's animation, excerpt
- "Liberty's Kids: Benedict Arnold," PBS animated historical narrative, excerpt

THEME: Heroes and Villains 2

- "Word Girl: Re-Enter the Butcher," PBS children's animated narrative, excerpt
- "President Obama Addresses American Schoolchildren," speech excerpt
- "Spiderman 2 Lego," opening of Spiderman recreated with Lego figures

THEME: Heroes and Villains 3

- "Every Child a Hero: Help Save Lives," educational video featuring elementary students and teachers who plant trees and donate money to poor children
- "President Obama Addresses American Schoolchildren," speech excerpt
- "Hercules: From Zero to Hero," Disney film excerpt

During this process, teachers were asked to predict how their students might respond to the use of popular culture in the classroom. One said, "They might start dancing! Their excitement may be so big I can't contain it." Another talked about the value of using repeated viewing, recognizing that the giggle factor would be present at first, but then, at the second viewing, children would be more focused on commenting and responding appropriately to the online videos as a tool for learning.

Popular culture in the classroom adds a level of unpredictability because of the differences in taste and interpretation among different people. Paradoxically, it is precisely because popular culture media texts can cause unpredictable reactions that it motivates creative, critical, and divergent thinking. We discovered that making concrete decisions about the use of popular culture in the classroom reveals profound insights about differences in power, comfort, and differences in pedagogical approaches. This insight contributed to our interest in exploring teacher motivations, which you'll remember was a topic that we introduced in Chapter 2.

Media literacy education for teachers requires an environment in which different approaches to mass media and popular culture are embraced. It requires room for experimentation and failure. Collaboration between educators of different backgrounds, styles, and approaches is important. The diverse skills and knowledge that constitute sound media literacy pedagogy require an equally complex and adaptive approach to teacher education.

WHAT WE LEARNED

Because we were thinking about the needs of teachers as learners themselves, we made efforts to carefully document their experiences as learners. We encouraged instructors to document their experience through lesson planning and journal writing. We also made numerous classroom observations. To prepare the new instructors, we used a mix of whole-group learning, small-group activities, and individualized consultation. Here's a summary of what we learned about teaching teachers as the result of our adventures with Powerful Voices for Kids:

- **Deep Understanding.** Having a solid understanding of both the practice of critical analysis and the capacity to develop and implement a creative media-production process enables teachers to guide learners in developing both these skills.
- **Motivations Matter.** Teachers bring their own values and motives, their passions and intellectual curiosity, fully into the classroom as they shape their curriculum choices.
- **Emergent Curriculum.** Curriculum should emerge improvisationally from meaningful interactions between children and teacher but requires a solid base of careful planning and preparation by teachers. Recognizing and using teachable-moment opportunities takes practice in learning to manage unexpected or unpredictable moments.
- **The Learning Spiral: Ask Questions, Find and Use, Analyze, Reflect, Create, and Take Action.** Children ask questions, gather information, analyze it, and then compose messages using a variety of types of media forms and genres, guided by a teacher who coordinates children's collaborative participation.

- **Time for Sharing and Reflection.** Systematic written and small-group reflection among teachers builds confidence and promotes metacognitive thinking about student needs, learning goals, and curriculum choices.

Although you have encountered lesson plans at the end of each chapter of this book, we did not prepare lesson plans in advance for teachers to follow as part of our professional development practice. Actually, we were more than a little concerned that getting a fistful of lesson plans might deaden, instead of inspire, teacher creativity. We wanted to respect the expertise and knowledge that teachers bring into the classroom and didn't want to let our instructors off the hook as creative professionals. Instructors were invited to get to know their students and design learning experiences to meet their distinct needs.

By emphasizing creativity, curriculum innovation, and reflective thinking among the instructors, we aimed to create a rich learning experience for them and their students. This approach enabled us to examine how specific curriculum choices made by new teachers reflect and embody both their emerging understanding of their students and their own passions, attitudes, motivations, and values.

TEACHER CREATIVITY EMPOWERS LEARNING

Much of the visibility and positive energy that are now devoted to celebrating Web 2.0 teaching and learning comes from the fact that teachers are highly creative people who enjoy explaining ideas and sharing information in engaging ways. Teachers have always been creative professionals and authors, of course. But for many teachers, new digital tools provide different types of opportunities for them to exercise that creative impulse. By creating PowerPoint slides, worksheets, and videos, some teachers activate their own talents and imagination. For example, the website Cool Tools for Schools (http://cooltoolsforschools.wikispaces.com) lists over 300 digital resources that teachers can use for presentations, media production, and collaboration. Thousands of teacher-created websites and blogs offer a revealing portrait of this kind of creative energy at work.

Once upon a time, the creation of educational multimedia was the province of a small group of media professionals, working under the influential historical orbit of the Public Broadcasting Service. The making of educational videos was expensive and time-consuming. But today, nearly anyone can be a producer of educational multimedia. Creative people from the field of medicine and health were among those who took up the challenge of blending play and learning. Clinical psychologist Naif Al-Mutawa created *The 99*, a set of comic characters based on Islamic archetypes. And then there's *BrainPOP* (and *BrainPOP Jr.* for K–3 students), a collection of animated short educational videos created by Dr. Avraham Kadar, a physician who wanted to teach his young patients about asthma. Or consider the work of Herb Mahelona and Amy Burvall, two high school history teachers in Hawaii who have created the History for Music Lovers YouTube channel, composing music video parodies, including "The French Revolution" (sung to the tune of "Bad Romance," by Lady Gaga) and "Renaissance Man" (sung to the tune of "Blister in the Sun," by the Violent Femmes). They were motivated to make history music videos as a way to capture the attention of their students by rekindling their own passions for history and tapping into to their mutual interest in pop music of the 1980s. Many educators have benefited from the work of these remarkable teachers and the many others who have been able to share their creativity using the Internet and social media. The popularity of TedEd and the Khan Academy point to the impact of harnessing teacher creativity by linking it to digital media and learning.

As we have seen in this book, instructors and teachers bring enormous reserves of creativity to their practice. Both Osei and Mona taught children how to understand the elements of a popular song, write lyrics, and perform them in front of a camera. It was easy for them to do this because they had experience as singer/songwriters and performers themselves. John taught students the basic concepts of interactive media by introducing them to computer programming, which was familiar to him. David's experience as a filmmaker made it easy for him to guide students through the process of making a number of short videos. And after Ms. Jared, an art teacher, had finished reading a scholarly article on digital and media literacy, she taught herself to use Comic Life, a simple software tool for creating comics by composing a multipanel spread, combining photographs and language to summarize and respond to what she had learned.

WHEN TEACHER CREATIVITY GETS OUT OF CONTROL

But there can be a bit of a downside to teachers' creativity, too. We hate to admit it, but some teachers may get wrapped up in themselves as creative producers, sometimes to the detriment of their students. Their own projects may end up taking center stage, and kids become performers, assistants, or merely audience members.

This has long been a paradigm in youth media production. Even back in the 1960s and 1970s, when teachers first began to use 8mm film cameras to make movies with children, the general formula was for the teacher to initiate a project, write the script, and then assign roles to children, who served as actors, costumers, camera operators, and makeup specialists. Children were part of the creative process, certainly, but they were helping support the teacher's creative initiative.[6] Renee once observed a young instructor who had used his students to make his own special film: a playful parody of the film *Planet of the Apes*. The instructor was intensely involved in all aspects of the production, writing the script, designing costumes, and filming. But the children in his program were clearly less engaged and interested in the project. Few children seemed to understand the concept of parody or registered even a basic understanding of the purpose of the teacher's film. While a couple of kids were engaged, it was clear that for most participants, the whole thing was a rather boring and uneventful experience.[7]

When experimenting with media production, some educators may become inspired to create media that helps them better deliver the content of their curriculum. When teachers take it upon themselves to make PowerPoint slides about famous American presidents, videos about math formulas, or podcasts about animal habitats, the content reflects teachers' curriculum choices about what children need to know. These creative educational materials may indeed lead to robust learning. But they may also encourage teachers to simply use digital media as another way to lecture or transmit content, contributing to a traditional pedagogy that positions students primarily as audience members receiving a dose of information or edutainment. We are concerned about the possible underlying assumption: that learners are so disengaged and alienated from learning that teachers must create elaborate productions simply in order to capture and hold attention. That's not the direction we intend for digital and media literacy education.

But because many forms of professional development in educational technology offer teachers how-to tutorials (to create a podcast, a blog, or a video), it's often a natural impulse for teachers to want to create their own educational content. Many will spend hours upon hours in the summer and on weekends to do so. Sometimes these productions are remarkable; in other cases, they are a poor substitute for professionaly created multimedia. Students may end up on the losing end if digital learning consists of merely activating teachers' own creativity, without a focus on creating learning environments where learners themselves can be creative and use digital tools for self-expression and communication.

CREATING POWERFUL LEARNING COMMUNITIES

Today, educators have an increasing number of options for advancing their knowledge and skills through both face-to-face and online professional development programs, including seminars, workshops, conferences, and other gatherings. Online professional networks, where educators can share and learn from each other, are especially useful in helping inspire teachers to see themselves as lifelong learners. In recent years, there has been an explosion of interest in helping teachers use digital technology tools in supporting their professional development.

In many types of professional development programs, the power of the specialist with external expertise is emphasized. Teachers may watch an online interview of a well-known expert, for example, or attend a conference where that individual is speaking. Some of these professionals inevitably get raised to "guru" status as their efforts are perceived to make a valuable contribution to the continuing education of teachers.[8] But as everyone knows, access to an educational guru alone will not create transformative change. Some combination of external expertise and peer support networks is thought to be most effective in supporting teacher growth and development.[9] Our approach to professional development is rooted in the formation of a learning community, where through a combination of demonstration and modeling, experimentation, collaboration, and reflection, educators gain confidence in exploring new pedagogies that meet the needs of their students.

A number of processes are used to encourage, extend, and structure a professional dialogue about teaching and learning. Such dialogues begin by explicitly identifying core values. In this regard, our work is aligned with the approach developed by Ted Sizer and the Coalition of Essential Schools. As you have seen from the vignettes and examples described in this book, both in-school and out-of-school learning environments are places where all students learn to use their minds well, activating head, heart, and spirit through encountering people, places, events, and ideas in all their real-world complexity. In the Powerful Voices for Kids program, we use mass media, popular culture, and digital media to create an educational program designed to make connections between children's home cultures and their needs as learners. We want children's interests and developing understanding of the world to be recognized and valued as a driving center of the inquiry process, not the inert pots of knowledge specified by the subject matter.

To accomplish this, we aimed to personalize teaching and learning so that the choice of teaching materials and specific pedagogies could be placed in the hands of the educational staff.[10] By accessing, analyzing and evaluating, composing, reflecting, and taking action, students do the work of learning, with the teacher coaching and provoking students to "learn how to learn and thus to teach themselves."[11] We wanted students to be able both to display their knowledge and to use it in responding to culturally meaningful aspects of their life.

But when we step back a little, we must inevitably be humbled, because as educational historians have revealed, there's a pattern to the way in which media technologies get addressed in the context of public education. First, there is a great flourish of expectations and enthusiasm about the new avenues for educational innovation. Then, research fails to establish any appreciable differences between traditional classroom teaching and learning with new technologies. As one researcher puts it,

> Gradually, it becomes clear that the technologies go along with some practical inconveniences and complications that hinder teaching rather than support it. Sometimes the learners or their parents express their objections. After a while it turns out that application of the new technology in educational practice remains quite limited. In the end everything remains unchanged, while the opponents (mostly teachers) and supporters (innovators and governing bodies who made the investments) end up in mutual accusations.[12]

Regardless of how, why, or even *if* new technologies are integrated into elementary classroom environments, we believe that many essential skills can be developed as early as kindergarten to empower students to see themselves as communicators in a complicated 21st century media landscape. Understanding how to best connect kids' often messy "home" culture to their school environments is necessarily complex work. It requires teachers' deep and empathetic understanding of their students' needs, competences, and interests. It requires teacher educators' respect for the many motivations that drive teachers to use—or choose not to use—media and technology in their classrooms.

And it requires researchers like us not to lose sight of *why* we think digital and media literacy is so important, as a way to strengthen all of students' many literacy practices, from pencil and paper to speaking and listening to reading and writing to video production and computer programming and more. It's a way to invigorate teachers and administrators to change their school cultures with an eye toward the critical thinking and creative skills that students need in their future academic life and careers.

REVIEW

We've shared what we have learned from the many different kinds of teachers and learners who have participated in the Powerful Voices for Kids initiative. We've learned that teachers' approach to digital and media literacy depends on their existing attitudes and beliefs about media, popular culture, technology, and their big-picture goals of teaching and learning. In ways we still only partially understand, we've learned that our own values and priorities as educators shape the choices we make in bringing digital and media literacy to young learners.

We shared our experiences working with children ages 9–11 by learning about the ways that young children can become powerful communicators by using their creativity and collaboration skills to address real issues in an urban community, including issues like homelessness and littering. We're confident that children can use their powerful voices to make a difference in the world, in ways large and small.

Children also experience the power of authorship when they write and draw and tell stories. Technology tools can support the discovery of this power. And when students ask questions about celebrity culture and mass media and social media, it turns out that managing the unpredictability of classroom conversation is a key factor in creating a robust learning environment. Activating children's critical thinking skills about popular culture and advertising enables them to get the best from popular media like television, music, and video games while minimizing its problematic features.

When we explored how to engage the youngest children in the primary grades with digital and media literacy, we took a close look at teachers who are working to develop children's understanding of language and other symbol systems, like photographs, animation, and drama. Learning about concepts like author, audience, and purpose in conjunction with familiar texts like TV shows and advertising can support children's comprehension skills and academic achievement by activating inference-making skills that support comprehension skills across print, visual, sound, and digital media formats and genres.

Finally, we shared a little about the staff development models we used from field-testing the PVK program. We're closer to developing a comprehensive approach to digital and media literacy education for K–6 learners, but we are aware that this work will take many forms as teachers determine what's best for the young learners in their particular communities. By reading about our experiences in helping young children develop the key competencies they need to make sense of their increasingly digital and media-saturated world, we hope you have been inspired to bring some of these ideas and practices to the children and educators in your community. We look forward to continuing the learning with you at our online community at www.powerfulvoicesforkids.com.

NOTES

1. Rosenholtz, S. (1989). *Teacher's workplace: The social organization of schools.* New York, NY: Longman.
2. Senge, P. (1990). *The fifth discipline: The art and practice of the learning organization.* New York, NY: Doubleday (p. 10).
3. Hord, S. M. (1997). *Professional learning communities: Communities of continuous inquiry and improvement.* Retrieved from http://www.sedl.org/pubs/change34/welcome.html
4. Jalongo, M. R. (1991). *Creating learning communities: The role of the teacher in the twenty-first century.* Bloomington, IN: National Educational Service.
5. Mediratta, K. (2004). *Constituents of change: Community organizations and public education reform.* New York, NY: New York University, Institute for Education and Social Policy (p. 2). Retrieved from http://annenberginstitute.org/sites/default/files/product/217/files/Constituents_of_Change.pdf
6. Moore, D. C., & Hobbs, R. (2012, July). *Cine-kids: The origins of youth media production.* Paper presented at the Northeast Film Symposium, Bucksport, ME.
7. Hobbs, R. (2010). *Digital and media literacy: Connecting culture and classroom.* Thousand Oaks, CA: Corwin.
8. Avalos, B. (2011). Teacher professional development in *Teaching and Teacher Education* over ten years. *Teaching and Teacher Education, 27,* 10–20.
9. Avalos (2011).
10. Coalition of Essential Schools. (2013). *The CES common principles.* Retrieved from http://www.essentialschools.org/items/4
11. Coalition of Essential Schools (2013).
12. Westera, W. (2010). Technology-enhanced learning: Review and prospects. *Serdica Journal of Computing, 4,* 159–182. See also Cuban, L. (1986). *Teachers and machines: The classroom use of technology since 1920.* New York, NY: Teachers College Press.

Part V
Extras

Resource A

Learning Targets for Digital and Media Literacy With Young Learners

Use these competencies and learning targets to design your lessons and help students self-assess their learning.

Access	Primary (K–3)	Intermediate (4–6)
Listening skills	When I listen, I pay attention and look at the speaker.	I am aware that listening is important, and I use my body and my attitude to affect how well I listen.
Viewing skills	When I view, I pay attention and think about what I'm seeing.	I comprehend messages that I see on a screen.
Reading comprehension	I decode written symbols and sound out words.	I comprehend and make inferences from text to understand unstated meanings.
Identify information needs	I am confident in asking questions.	I generate questions when I learn new information.

(Continued)

(Continued)

Using effective search and find strategies	I recognize where information can be found.	I can use a variety of source materials to find what I need, using both a library and online media.
Learning how to learn	I am comfortable and confident that I can learn new things.	I explore, experiment, and use trial and error to figure things out.
Troubleshooting and problem solving	When I have a problem, I believe that I can find a solution.	When I have a problem, I try a variety of strategies to fix it.
Keyboard and mouse skills	I use a mouse or trackpad to navigate using a computer or other digital device.	I use proper keyboard techniques to type documents.
Familiarity with hardware, storage, and file management practices	I save documents that I create on a computer.	I know how to save documents to different parts of the computer.
Understanding hyperlinking and digital space	I understand that the things I see and do using a computer have been made by different people.	I recognize that a link takes me to another information source and can use links in my own creative work.
Gaining competence with software applications	I play and learn with computer games and apps.	I use computer apps for school-related projects.
Using social media, mobile, peripheral, and cloud computing tools	I can connect a computer to a printer, a cell phone, or a data projector.	I can upload and download files from a computer to the Internet.
Authorship, Collaborative, and Creative Competencies		
Self-expression	I believe that my creative ideas and opinions have value to others.	I am confident in creating ideas and information to share with others.
Identifying purpose, target audience, medium, and genre	I distinguish between messages designed to inform, persuade, and entertain, and between fiction and nonfiction.	I recognize the genre of a message and use clues from a text to determine a message purpose and target audience.
Brainstorming and generating ideas	I listen to others and contribute ideas that add value and relate to the topic.	I am comfortable working in a creative team.
Composing creatively	I draw images and use spoken and written language to create.	I take pride in my creative work and try to do my best.

Working collaboratively	I work with a partner to get something done.	I recognize that every member of a team has an important role to play.
Giving and receiving audience feedback	I share my reaction to the work of others and learn things when people share their reactions to my work.	I give warm and cool feedback that helps others improve their work.
Editing and revising	I make changes to my work based on feedback.	I am grateful for feedback that helps me improve my work.
Using appropriate distribution, promotion, and marketing channels	I take pride in sharing my work with others.	I can decide when I want my creative work to be shared online.
Playing and interacting appropriately in formal and informal situations	I play and learn in ways that are respectful of others.	I am responsible for my behavior in a variety of play and learning situations.
Curating: Selecting materials carefully to accomplish a purpose	I select various texts to inform, entertain, and persuade.	I make choices carefully to accomplish a specific goal as a communicator.
Remixing: Using bits of others' work to create something new	I use other people's creative work and make choices when I create.	I know the difference between remix and plagiarism, and I do not use cut-and-paste as a substitute for my own writing.
Issues of Representation		
Recognizing how symbols stand for the ideas and things they represent	I know that symbols represent real things.	I understand how signs and symbols relate to the things they stand for.
Identifying the author, genre, purpose, techniques, and point of view of a message	I can recognize that authors make messages and know how to find the author in different types of media.	I recognize how authors use various genres and techniques to communicate a point of view.
Comparing and contrasting sources	I can show how similar things go together.	I can compare and contrast messages in a variety of forms.
Evaluating credibility and quality	I know the difference between the truth and a lie.	I use strategies to distinguish between a good-quality source and a poor-quality one.

(Continued)

(Continued)

Understanding one's own biases and world-view	I feel respected when I express my opinions and preferences.	I am aware of how my attitudes shape my choices as a receiver and sender of messages.
Recognizing power relationships that shape how information and ideas circulate in culture	I know that some messages are more important than others.	I recognize how some messages get widely shared and others are ignored or not easy to find.
Understanding the economic context of information and entertainment production	I recognize the difference between ads and TV shows.	I recognize advertising in everyday life, including in my home, school, and neighborhood.
Examining the political and social ramifications of inequalities in information flows	I like feeling included when people are sharing information and entertainment.	I understand that people have different levels of interest in computers and the Internet and that this may affect their future.
Social Responsibilities of the Communicator		
Acknowledging the power of communication to maintain the status quo or change the world	I know that signs, symbols, and messages from people can make a difference in my life.	I believe that powerful communicators can make a difference in solving many real-world problems.
Understanding how differences in values and life experience shape people's media use and their interpretation of messages	I know that people in different parts of the world live differently than I do.	I am aware of how my personal interests and family background influence my media preferences and choices.
Appreciating benefits, risks, and potential harm of messages and media	I know that messages and media can influence my own feelings, thoughts, and ideas.	I can offer actual examples of how media and technology have benefits, risks, and potential harms.
Applying ethical judgment and social responsibility to all communication situations	I feel good when I am kind to others.	I treat people with kindness in real life and when I'm online.
Understanding how concepts of *private* and *public* are reshaped by digital media	I know that some messages are meant just for me, while others are designed for a large group of people.	I make good choices about how I share information about myself when I am online.

Appreciating and respecting legal rights and responsibilities (copyright, intellectual freedom, etc.)	I feel proud of the work I create.	When I use other people's work as part of my own creative work, I don't just copy it—I transform it into something new.
Taking action: Using the power of communication to make a difference in the world	I see how adults use communication to improve things.	I create messages that inspire people to make changes that improve my school and my neighborhood.

General Composition Skills

Communicating a personal reaction and point of view	I can use words to express my feelings and ideas.	I create book and movie reviews to share my opinion.
Speaking to an individual and demonstrating listening skills	I can share ideas with someone and listen to his or her ideas.	I am effective in getting and maintaining the attention of a listener and am respectful in sharing talk time fairly with him or her.
Speaking to a large group and responding to feedback	I can speak loudly and clearly so my message is understood by a group of people.	I can make a formal presentation using PowerPoint slides.
Using writing and images to inform, persuade, and entertain	I can use writing and images to inform, persuade, and entertain.	I make choices when I compose a message to accomplish a particular goal.
Composing in a variety of formats, including email, review, reports, film scripts, music lyrics, web page, nonfiction, fiction, and other genres	I can create a poem, compose a dialogue or a song, make a drawing, and take a photo to express my ideas.	I can send email, write a short script, and create a web page using the codes and conventions that are appropriate.
Composing for a variety of audiences, including peers, family, educators, special interest groups, government leaders, and members of the general public	I change my message depending on the audience I am trying to reach.	I can share ideas with older and younger people.

Medium-Specific Skills

Performance as Composition

Using heart, voice, and body to convey feelings and ideas	I use my voice and body to express feelings and ideas.	I perform expressively in a dramatic performance.

(Continued)

(Continued)

Demonstrating creativity and imagination	I believe that I am a confident and creative person.	I show my creativity and my confidence when I communicate.
Participating as a team member or leader in a performance	I can work with a group of people to put on a performance or show.	I can play different roles when working on a group project.
Using time well throughout the process of idea development, planning, rehearsal, and performance	I can stay on task when I'm creating.	I can help others stay on task while we're working in a team.
Image Composition		
Creating a photographic image	I can use a camera to compose a photograph.	I can be intentional in using camera angles, color, and framing when I create a photo.
Selecting, cropping, and sequencing images for a specific purpose and target audience	I can sequence a series of images to tell a story.	I can crop images and use headlines to shape their meaning.
Audio Composition		
Using technology to create an audio recording	I can make an audio recording.	I can be intentional in using language, music, and sound to create an audio recording.
Being highly aware of sound, noise, and tone while recording	I can use my voice appropriately when I am recording.	I recognize how sounds and background noise are recorded.
Selecting and assembling audio and musical excerpts	I can choose audio clips for a specific purpose.	I can make strategic choices in the use of multiple audio clips.
Video Composition		
Using a video camera to record images and sound	I can use a cell phone or video camera to enact a simple story.	I can be intentional in the use of camera position, backgrounds, and lighting when recording video.
Selecting and sequencing images, language, and sound to accomplish a specific purpose and reach a particular target audience	I can select and sequence images to tell a story.	I can make choices of various images to create a coherent narrative or informative sequence.

Social Media Composition		
Thinking about audience and purpose while composing	When I am online, I am aware of my purpose and my audience.	When I am online, I make purposeful and strategic choices as a communicator.
Respecting privacy	I know how to share appropriately when I am online.	I respect the rights of others when I share information.
Being socially responsible and sensitive to others	I demonstrate respect to others when I am online.	I can offer examples of problems that may occur when people are not socially responsible and sensitive to others when online.
Digital Media Composition		
Using software tools to create messages in a variety of forms (wiki, blog, podcast, interactive multimedia, etc.)	I can make a digital illustration.	I use many different digital tools to create messages using image, language, sound, and interactivity.
Using a process of iterative problem solving throughout the creative process	I can make changes to my work to improve it.	I revise and modify my work in order to make it the best it can be.

Resource B

Glossary for Kids

These are the fundamental vocabulary words of digital and media literacy for children in grades K–6.

Action adventure: A genre of storytelling that presents thrilling and exciting situations. Sometimes action and adventure films are realistic, but sometimes they are fantasy—a world of make-believe brought to life through imagination and special effects.

Actor: The real person who pretends to be a character. Robert Downey Jr. is the actor who pretends to be Iron Man in the *Iron Man* movies. We never see the actor Tom Kenny in an episode of *SpongeBob Squarepants*, but his voice is what they use to turn SpongeBob into a funny character.

Ad structure: Advertisements create problems that products can solve. A shoe commercial might claim that special shoes help you jump higher or run faster. A commercial for a cleaning product might claim that this product will help you clean your clothes.

Advergames: Advertisements that appear to be video games. When you play an advergame, you are having fun, but you may also be watching a commercial for a product. You might also be linked to a company's website.

Advertising: The business of selling things to people. An advertisement persuades someone to buy something. If an advertisement is on television, it is called a commercial. An advertisement for a new film is called a trailer. An advertisement that you can play like a game is called an advergame.

Animation: A series of drawings edited together to create the illusion of smooth movement. Animations can be 2-D so that they look "flat," or drawn by hand, like Bugs Bunny, Dora the Explorer, or Bart Simpson. They can also be 3-D so that they look "full," or created by a computer, like Buzz Lightyear, Kung Fu Panda, or the Transformers. You can make an animation yourself by creating a flipbook.

Antisocial: Antisocial media encourage negative and unhealthy actions and behaviors. Sometimes we enjoy things that we know are wrong, like cartoons that are violent or characters that use foul language. It's our job as audience members to figure out what's OK and not OK about all different kinds of media.

App: An application is a program created by computer authors— programmers—to do something specific on a computer, laptop, or cell phone. Some apps are games, like *Angry Birds* or *Temple Run*. Other apps run educational programs. Apps can be designed to play music, help you shop for products, or read news stories. It all depends on what the app is supposed to do and how the programmer created it.

Audience: Someone who experiences the work of an author. Audiences read, watch, listen to, play with, and use lots of different kinds of media.

Author: Someone who creates a media message. Authors might be writers, artists, photographers, musicians, directors, animators, producers, or programmers.

Browser: A program that helps you use the Internet by displaying computer code. Firefox is a browser, and so is Internet Explorer.

Character: A make-believe creation of an author. Characters are fictional, meaning they do not exist in the real world, but only in media. SpongeBob Squarepants, Clifford the Big Red Dog, and Iron Man are all examples of characters.

Comedy: A genre of storytelling that tries to make people laugh.

Content: All of the different choices you make about what your media is about, how your story will be told, and what people, places, or objects you might represent in your media. Is this a picture of firefighters? Is it a story with a moral, like Aesop's Fables? Is it a movie about the Revolutionary War?

Distribution: How media is spread to lots of people. You might sell people individual CDs, DVDs, or apps. You might provide the media on the Internet. Or you might put the media on television, in theaters, or on billboards.

Drama: A genre of storytelling that deals with serious subjects. Some dramas make us happy, and some can make us cry.

Fame: What happens when lots of people know who you are. Celebrities get famous for lots of reasons—because they have a song that lots of people listen to, because they're good at sports, because they're in movies or TV shows, or because they have important jobs, like the president of the United States.

Form: All of the different choices you make about what your media is, how it will look or sound, and how people will experience it. Is it a black-and-white movie? Is it a 3-D video game? Is it a realistic drawing?

Frame: What's included in a photograph. Make a rectangle with your fingers by making two Ls with your hands and connecting your thumbs on one hand to your index fingers on the other. Now look through the rectangle you've created—that's your frame.

Genre: Categories of media that lots of people recognize. When you watch TV, you know some categories right away: Some shows are reality shows, some are cartoons, some are crime shows, and still others are news, commercials, or sports.

Headlines and captions: Headlines are the words that newspapers use to get your attention to read an article. They are usually in a large font, meaning the letters are larger. Captions accompany photographs used in a news article. What can you tell from just from reading the headline and the caption of an article online or in the newspaper?

Illustration: A drawing that shows you what something looks like. An author who draws an illustration of a plant may want to show you all the different parts of the plant.

Links: Pieces of code that connect one website to another website. You will see links as different-colored text within a website. When you click on that text, you will open the link, which will bring you to a new website.

Live action: Shows and movies that star real actors. Some live action films still have lots of special effects, like superhero movies.

Logo: A picture or design that a company uses to get people to remember it without using words. Think about the McDonald's "golden arches," the Nike "swoosh," or the Facebook "f."

Meanings: Messages that you have to work to figure out. For instance, to understand the meaning of a word, you have to know how it was made (with different letters) and how it was used (context clues from the sentence). You need knowledge to make meaning. Knowledge comes from our learning, experiences, feelings, and culture. Lots of different people make meaning in different ways.

Media: What we use to communicate to other people. You can communicate to people through print, the things that you read, like a book or newspaper article. You can also communicate through visuals, things you can see, like photographs and movies. You can communicate through audio, things you can hear, like radio broadcasts and songs. And you can communicate through interactive media, things you can use or play with, like video games, cell phones, and websites.

Message: What a piece of media is telling you. Sometimes media tells you its message directly; an advertisement might tell you to buy a product. Sometimes media tells you its message indirectly; funny videos don't "tell" us to laugh, but they make us laugh when we watch them.

Montage: A collection of shots. When you watch TV shows and films, you are watching a montage of lots of different shots put together.

Movie magic: The authors who create movies, including producers, directors, camera operators, editors, and animators, create what is called movie magic. Movie magic might be created through camera tricks, animated special effects, special makeup, or other tricks in the production and postproduction of a movie.

Photograph: A camera's representation of reality. When you take a photograph, you are creating an image through the camera's "eye," which is called a lens.

Point of view: The person we are supposed follow along with in media. Books, shows, and movies are often told from the point of view of the main character, whom we follow through the story. News media like newspapers, TV news, and informational websites sometimes present the point of view of the author, including the writer, the speaker, or the news company. Different people have different points of view. For example, even if you and your friend have the same experience, you might tell a different story or have a different opinion. Sometimes people with different points of view disagree with each other.

Postproduction: Changing and editing your work. This is the part of the production cycle where you figure out "how things go together," whether you're making a collage from photographs, a video from lots of shots or recordings, or revising an essay.

Preproduction: The planning steps that you take before you create a media message. This includes developing your ideas and imagining what the audience will see, read, or hear; writing down your plan or your script; designing what your media will look or sound like; assigning roles and responsibilities; and getting together materials and information you'll need.

Private and public: Things that are private are not shared with people you do not know and trust. Things that are public are shared with everyone. Where you live is something that you usually keep private, because you wouldn't want just anybody coming to your house any time they wanted!

Production: The actual creation of new media. This might involve writing things down, making art, making music, taking pictures, recording videos, or programming on a computer.

Programs: Computer codes that tell a computer what to do. You can create video game programs that let you move characters through an imaginary world, or you can create programs that help you create music.

Promotion: All the ways that are used to attract people's attention. You might see a little commercial, a promotion for a new television show. You might join a contest to win tickets to a new movie. Or you might just see someone waving at you on the street with a sign about a new store or demonstrating a new product at a shopping mall.

Prosocial: Prosocial media encourage positive and healthy actions and behaviors. A prosocial theme might encourage you to be respectful to parents, help others in need, or go outside for some fresh air.

Public service announcement: A PSA provides information about an important issue. PSAs teach the public about something they need to know in a way that is easy to remember. Perhaps you've seen a PSA about how important it is to not litter and to recycle, or about how dangerous it is for adults to talk on the phone while they drive a car.

Purpose (inform, persuade, entertain): When authors communicate, they have their reasons or goals. This is their purpose in creating a message. When you inform, you provide information that people want or need. When you persuade, you try to convince someone to think, feel, or do something. When you entertain, you try to create an intense mood or feeling that attracts people's attention.

Reality TV: A genre of television that represents the lives of real people as a true story with a beginning, middle, and end or as a contest or competition between individuals. Real people who are not celebrities appear on television as part of a contest or story about their real lives.

Remix: What happens when you create new media out of a different piece of media. You might remix pictures from a magazine in a collage. You might remix scenes from a favorite TV show to create a new video. Or you might remix part of a favorite song with different singing, music, or beats.

Representation: How real things are presented in different kinds of media. When you draw a picture of a dog or a tree, you are creating a representation. When a book, film, song, or video game tells a story, it is representing real things.

Shot: What is recorded between the time you start recording a video and the time you "cut," or stop recording. Shots are edited together to make movies.

Story structure: Beginning, middle, end: The beginning of a story is where we are introduced to a problem that needs to be solved by learning about characters and setting. The middle of the story is where we figure out what the character will do to solve the problem. Usually, the story gets complicated in the middle by other characters and situations. The *end* of the story reveals how the character solves the problem.

Target audience: The group of people that media was created for. We never know exactly who will see or enjoy media, but authors make choices about whom they want to see or enjoy it.

Text: Any media that has a message and a meaning. Texts aren't only books, but also music, films, websites, video games, photographs, and all other forms of media.

URL: The address of a website. You type the URL—a series of words and letters—into your browser to get to the website you are trying to go to. For instance, the URL for Powerful Voices for Kids is http://www.powerfulvoicesforkids.com.

Resource C

Glossary of Concepts

These concepts reflect some of the fundamental ideas presented in this book.

Activist: A teacher whose use of digital media offers students opportunities to take action for civic engagement and social justice.

Appropriate and inappropriate: Agreed-upon but often unspoken rules for what kinds of content can be shared in a particular context or situation. Children usually discover what adults consider inappropriate through trial and error, but it can also be an open, thoughtful discussion topic in the classroom.

Celebrity culture: The persistent aspiration to become famous. Sometimes celebrity culture empowers students to express themselves creatively or work hard in school or afterschool activities. But sometimes celebrities send the wrong messages, and teachers may feel a desire to protect students from the aspects of celebrity culture that seem problematic.

Civic engagement: Promoting core values of democracy and critical autonomy in a media-rich environment.

Cool tools: A focus on the novelty of new technologies and classroom tools over their actual educative value.

Co-viewing and joint media engagement: Co-viewing is the act of watching, reading, or listening to alongside a child—seeing, hearing, and experiencing the same media as the child. Joint media engagement brings co-viewing into interactive media and includes exploring and playing with interactive media along with children.

Demystifier: A teacher who reveals how media and technology messages are constructed in order to activate students' awareness of authorship and critical thinking.

Do-it-yourself (DIY) media: Media constructed without the use of expensive professional tools. Teachers with knowledge of online resources, multiple forms of media production, computer programming, or other skills often create DIY solutions to media and technology integration issues in schools. Teachers figure out how to do everything from downloading YouTube videos before class to creating a custom PowerPoint presentation for a SMART Board.

Empowerment–protection spectrum: Educators who teach with and about media in the classroom have different attitudes about the role of media in children's lives. Media and technology can empower students to create and share new ideas and develop powerful voices in their families, communities, and the world. But educators also have a responsibility to protect students from potential risks and harm of media, particularly in matters of privacy, cultural awareness, and developmental ability.

Global village: A concept developed by media theorist Marshall McLuhan that imagines the electronically wired world as an interconnected "village." In the global village, "tribes" form based on shared interests, values, and perspectives.

Guided conversation: To help people become metacognitive learners and process information to reach their own conclusions, this method of focused conversation involves discussing a series of open-ended questions that include objective, reflective, interpretive, and evaluative questions.

Inference making: A part of the reading process that includes the ability to "go beyond the information given" in order to make informed judgments, evaluations, or predictions from evidence or clues in a media text. People also make inferences by using information about the context in which the message is presented.

Learning how to learn: A term used to describe the process of inquiry based on exploration, asking questions, and trial and error.

Mass media: Media distributed to large audiences through major media conglomerates. Television and major cable networks, Hollywood films, and other national or global broadcasts qualify as mass media.

Messy engagement: What happens when students access and create media and share their thoughts and feelings about the role of media in their lives. Messiness includes, but is not limited to, behavioral disruptions, asking questions that teachers can't or won't answer, making noise and getting physically excited, and going "off task" by exploring questions and ideas outside the parameter of the lesson. These elements can be redirected to intensify and deepen a learning experience. Managing messiness requires that teachers use improvisational skills and reflective practice.

Motivator: A teacher who uses media and technology as a springboard to students' creativity.

Nonoptimal uses of video in the classroom: Practices that weaken the instructional and educative power of screen media, including (1) lack of instructional motivation for using video; (2) no pausing, rewinding, or reviewing of content; (3) using screen media as a break from instruction; (4) using screen media as an opportunity for teachers to "tune out"; (5) using screen media as a reward for good behavior; (6) using popular culture media for superficial illustrative purposes or as a "hook"; (7) using screen media to control student behavior.

Open-ended and closed questions: Open-ended questions are divergent—there are many different answers to the same question. Closed questions are convergent—there is essentially one correct answer. Factual questions require students to recall specific information. Evaluative questions encourage students to explain their thoughts, feelings, and opinions. Interpretive questions require students to discuss messages and meanings in a work. Interpretive responses are based on shared evidence but may lead to different responses from different students.

Orchestrated improvisation: The art of thinking spontaneously on one's feet to change, revise, or reject part or all of a lesson based on unexpected situations. Orchestrated improvisation requires lots of tools, but may not stick to a rigid script.

Popular culture: Media touchstones shared by many people. Popular culture encompasses all forms of media, but often teachers view popular culture as "youth culture," ignoring the ways that adults' popular culture can always be reintroduced to younger generations (as in the popular *Guitar Hero* and *Rock Band* games). Similarly, adults can share in the pop culture of young people, watching the same television shows (from a PVK student: "My dad watches *Gossip Girl*!") or playing the same video games (e.g., group Wii sessions with the whole family).

Rappin' grandma: When teachers use attention-grabbing digital media popular culture in the classroom as a gimmick or to be perceived as "cool" or relevant.

Recitation script: A pattern of classroom talk where the teacher initiates with a question, students raise hands, the teacher selects student, the teacher generates topics and poses questions with known answers, student responses are short, and elaboration is not encouraged. When the recitation script is used, teachers discourage students' attempts to introduce other topics and carefully direct the scope of the dialogue in ways that may discourage intellectual curiosity.

Reflective practice: A term used to capture the process of thinking about the choices made before, during, and after teaching. When teachers reflect on action, they engage in a process of continuous learning, which is one of the defining characteristics of professional practice.

Screencasting: The simultaneous recording of any screen media and a voiceover. Often used for tutorials, screencasting can also be used for student analysis of media and critique of professional or student work.

Semiotics: The study of how symbols represent the world through language, images, sounds, interactive design, and technology.

Social media: Websites designed to create online communities between users. Popular examples include Facebook and Twitter.

Socialization: The process through which a child learns to behave and interact with others in a variety of contexts. Students learn how to control their behaviors (and "how to go to school"), how to collaborate and share, and how to express themselves in dialogue with others.

Spirit guide: A teacher whose use of media and technology is sensitive to students' social and emotional needs.

Spot the Shot: A game in which students clap their hands every time a new shot appears on the screen. For instance, at the beginning of a Metro Goldwyn Mayer (MGM) studio film, students would clap once when the lion mascot appears. Then they would clap again at the following title credit.

Style-over-substance problem: Valuing the aesthetic qualities of student media work without asking questions about the accuracy of information, the quality of content, or the originality of concept. New tools automate many stylish features of media production, making it difficult to differentiate "easy" style from "hard" substance. For instance, transitions and sound effects in multimedia presentations (e.g., PowerPoints) can be added with a single click, but they cannot cover up shoddy research or poor reasoning.

Teacher 2.0: A teacher who values participation in fan cultures at home and school and integrates a variety of digital media practices into the classroom.

Techie: A teacher who engages students with digital media and technology tools.

Text: Any media that can be read, analyzed, or interpreted. We often consider only books and other print media to be texts, but texts also include photos, videos, audio, and interactive or digital media.

Trendsetter: A teacher who uses digital media and technology to connect school subjects to students' interest in popular culture and mass media.

TV sort task: An activity designed to measure students' understanding of target audience and message purpose based on inferences they make from categorizing various TV shows.

Warm and cool feedback: A process of critique that helps authors develop their work. Warm feedback is the sharing of positive responses to a work. Cool feedback is a form of constructive criticism that offers authors ideas that help them imagine ways to strengthen or improve the work.

Watchdog: A teacher who teaches about media and technology because of concern about the economic and institutional systems of power in media.

Resource D

About the PVK Instructors

PROGRAM LEADERSHIP AND TRAINING STAFF

Renee Hobbs is the founding director of the Harrington School of Communication and Media at the University of Rhode Island, where she maintains the Media Education Lab.

Laurada Byers is the founder of the Russell Byers Charter School in Philadelphia.

David Cooper Moore is a filmmaker, blogger, and media literacy educator who served as program director of Powerful Voices for Kids, the university-school partnership initiative described in this book.

John Landis is the technology coordinator at Russell Byers Charter School in Philadelphia, where he teaches a digital and media literacy course at all grade levels.

Kristin Hokanson is a technology consultant for Discovery Education and a former classroom teacher.

Sherri Hope Culver is an assistant professor at Temple University's School of media and communication.

Kelly Mendoza is a senior manager of professional development at Common Sense Media, in San Francisco.

INSTRUCTORS IN THE POWERFUL VOICES FOR KIDS PROGRAM

Osei Allyne is a PhD student in anthropology at the University of Pennsylvania. He is also a hip-hop and spoken work artist who has worked under the stage name Manchilde as the lead vocalist of the hip-hop group Butta Babees.

Emily Bailin is a PhD student in the Education and Communication program at Columbia University Teachers College.

Aggie Ebrahimi Bazaz is a filmmaker who explores the diasporic Iranian experience to spark conversation about the Iranian American community as an emerging voice in American culture. She is currently the program and member services manager for the National Alliance for Media Arts and Culture (NAMAC).

Nuala Cabral is a filmmaker, activist, and media literacy educator. She is a co-founder of FAAN Mail, a media literacy and media activism project based in Philadelphia.

Angela Carter has worked in the music business and was responsible for developing artists and advancing their careers through touring, film and television, and endorsement opportunities.

Maria Cipollone is a doctoral student in the PhD program in mass media and communication at Temple University.

Henry Cohn-Geltner is a media instructor at WHYY, where he offers courses in media literacy and video production at the Dorrence Hamilton Learning Commons.

LaShon Fryer is a graduate of Temple University and a youth development specialist.

Rachel Hobbs is a fundraiser at Grassroots Campaigns, Inc.

Tanya Jackson is the co-director of the Youth Documentary Workshop at the Educational Video Center, in New York City.

Val Laranko is a graduate of Temple University's program in broadcasting, telecommunications, and mass media.

Deirdre Littlejohn is teaching video skills at Lea Elementary School in Philadelphia.

Maggie Ricco is a graduate of Temple University's School of Communication and Media.

Nicole Warncke is a digital media literacy educator in Seattle with YTech and Puget Sound Off. She presented with Colleen McDevitt at the National Association for Media Literacy Education conference in Los Angeles in July 2013.

Raphaele Saiah has interests in photography, art, and design and is a graduate of Temple University.

Kate Spiller is a web and multimedia production assistant and has worked as a teacher's assistant at a Philadelphia charter school.

Index

CORWIN

A SAGE Company

The Corwin logo—a raven striding across an open book—represents the union of courage and learning. Corwin is committed to improving education for all learners by publishing books and other professional development resources for those serving the field of PreK–12 education. By providing practical, hands-on materials, Corwin continues to carry out the promise of its motto: **"Helping Educators Do Their Work Better."**